Lecture Notes in Computer Science 6699

Commenced Publication in 1973
Founding and Former Series Editor
Gerhard Goos, Juris Hartmanis, an

Raffaella Bernardi   Sally Chambers
Björn Gottfried   Frédérique Segond
Ilya Zaihrayeu (Eds.)

Advanced Language Technologies for Digital Libraries

International Workshops on
NLP4DL 2009, Viareggio, Italy, June 15, 2009 and
AT4DL 2009, Trento, Italy, September 8, 2009

 Springer

Volume Editors

Raffaella Bernardi
Ilya Zaihrayeu
University of Trento, Povo, Italy
E-mail: {bernardi; ilya@disi.unitn.it}

Sally Chambers
The European Library, c/o De Koninklijke Bibliotheek
The National Library of the Netherlands
The Hague, The Netherlands
E-mail: sally.chambers@KB.nl

Björn Gottfried
University of Bremen, Germany
E-mail: bg@tzi.de

Frédérique Segond
Xerox Research Centre Europe, Meylan, France
E-mail: frederique.segond@xrce.xerox.com

The image on the cover is by Björn Gottfried and Lothar-Meyer Lerbs.
It shows how characters get extracted out of a document image.

ISSN 0302-9743   e-ISSN 1611-3349
ISBN 978-3-642-23159-9   e-ISBN 978-3-642-23160-5
DOI 10.1007/978-3-642-23160-5
Springer Heidelberg Dordrecht London New York

Library of Congress Control Number: 2011935867

CR Subject Classification (1998): H.3.7, H.2, H.3, H.4, I.2.7, F.4.2

LNCS Sublibrary: SL 1 – Theoretical Computer Science and General Issues

Typesetting: Camera-ready by author, data conversion by Scientific Publishing Services, Chennai, India

Printed on acid-free paper

Springer is part of Springer Science+Business Media (www.springer.com)

Preface

Digital libraries have been a hot topic since the 1990s. Companies such as Google, Yahoo and Microsoft have set up partnerships with digital libraries in order to make billions of digitized pages available. European and national digital library projects, such as Gallica, Quaero or Europeana, MultiMatch or CACAO are flourishing. The recent market penetration of the eBook and its accessibility through different types of devices, such as PDAs and mobile phones, make digital libraries of any kind, as well as the associated technologies, even more important.

Libraries have always been the source of innovative ideas in the area of information management. The very idea of a database, in a sense, is derived from library card catalogues. Even recently, the introduction of the "faceted search" paradigm is directly and explicitly derived from the work of the Indian librarian Ranganathan. In addition, the very first systems to allow a kind of "free text search" were library systems, where it was possible to type in a word and to retrieve all books with a title containing that word.

Today, despite the increasing number of libraries present on the Web, there remains a gap between the digital library world and the Internet world. The paradigm of information access in libraries has remained quite separate from that of information access on other textual databases, such as the Web. In the former case, the tendency has been toward standardization and extensive use of metadata, whereas in the latter, the paradigm of free text search has become predominant. However, thanks to the Semantic Web, there is some "reunification" of the two worlds, through initiatives such as Linked Open Data.

The transition from paper to digital libraries transforms the way library collections are used. Physical collections are described in a structured way, using metadata. Increasing digital collections are unstructured in the form of full text. This volume concentrates on both the technologies that are used to analyze and enrich metadata and those needed to process full-text content.

The different chapters cover the many facets of the digital library technologies, ranging from the different aspects of search, including multi-formats, personalized, multilingual and semantic, to new ways of using digital libraries that have been made possible thanks to advanced technologies.

The first part of this volume concentrates on innovative advanced search capabilities, which is probably the most crucial for users of digital libraries, enabling them to find what they are looking for in an easy, precise and fast manner. Users have changed, and while some years ago the typical user of a library system was someone who had almost no experience with searching in databases, today's library users have high expectations from digital libraries as they became familiar with search engines from the Web.

Although library collections are being increasingly digitized, there is still a good number of documents where the textual content is inaccessible, as they are only available in the form of an image, e.g., from scanned books.

In the first chapter, "Efficient Search in Hidden Text of Large DjVu Documents," Bien presents a system that makes use of regular expressions and advanced linguistic technologies to search scanned texts with poor OCR. However, OCR technologies are not good enough to be able to take into account different fonts from ancient digital documents that represent a large segment of books present in digital libraries.

Chapter 2, "Towards Processing of Historic Documents" by Gottfried and Meyer-Lerbs, presents an innovative approach in image processing to analyze documents containing Gothic print.

In the third chapter, "Hierarchical Classification of OAI Metadata Using the DDC Taxonomy," Waltinger et al. address the issue of providing subject access to scientific documents. They propose a method to automatically classify documents according to the Dewey Decimal Classification (DDC), relying only on metadata records that have been harvested via the Open Archives Initiative Protocol for Metadata Harvesting (OAI-PMH).

In the fourth chapter, "Moving Towards Adaptative Search in Digital Libraries," Kruschwitz et al. focus on search personalization for improving search capability. They propose to support users' query modification and navigation through the building of domain knowledge that automatically adapts to users' specific interests.

The following four chapters focus on the use of linguistic resources to perform query processing in order to enhance a search.

As digital library content is increasingly multilingual, innovative search should address the problem of multilingual access. While national classification systems describe the world in different ways, establishing links between these subject heading systems is likely to be lengthy, costly work, requiring significant ongoing maintenance. On the contrary, in the information retrieval domain, there are already solutions that provide a high degree of user satisfaction in the free text search world. Chapters 5 and 6 propose using Wikipedia to improve cross-lingual search.

In chap. 5, "Automatic Gazetteer Generation from Wikipedia," Bosca and Dini use Wikipedia as a parallel structured corpus to automatically extract translations and spelling variations of named entities.

In the same vein, in chap. 6, "Hybrid and Interactive Domain-Specific Translation for Multilingual Access to Digital Libraries," Jones et al. propose using Wikipedia to extract domain-specific multilingual dictionaries and use hybrid methods to perform automatic translation of short queries.

Precision in search also depends on the ability of the system to precisely "understand" the user's query. In other words, it depends on the system's ability to perform query disambiguation. Semantic disambiguation of the query is the focus of chaps. 7 and 8.

In chap. 7, "Metadata Enrichment via Topic Models for Author Name Disambiguation," Bernardi and Le propose using classification numbers and subject headings of digital collections to perform semantic disambiguation of author names. In addition, they propose extracting topic models from Wikipedia to enrich metadata when classification numbers and subject headings are not available.

In chap. 8, "Semantic Disambiguation in Folksonomy: A Case Study," Andrews et al. focus on the use of folksonomies to perform semantic disambiguation of queries. They propose a method that automatically transforms free text tags into a formalized annotation model based on concepts that can then be used to support semantic disambiguation.

The final two chapters of this volume describe how advanced linguistic analysis can be used to make different uses of digital library content, when the whole content of documents is available, as is often the case for scholarly and scientific literature.

In chap. 9, "Advances in Deep Parsing of Scholarly Paper Content," Schafer and Kiefer report on how natural language processing annotations generated by the automatic deep parsing of 8,200 scientific papers can support semantic search, citation classification, question answering and definition exploration.

Along the same lines, the last chapter, "Robust Argumentative Zoning for Sense-Making in Scholarly Documents" by Teufel and Yen, presents a method to perform robust rhetoric classification of sentences contained in scientific articles in order to propose new ways of reading to scholars.

As you will see, advanced technologies for digital libraries is a hot topic both in the domains of librarianship and computer science. The aim of this volume is to facilitate the closer cooperation of these two disciplines in order to foster ongoing digital library innovation.

The volume originates from two workshops, NLP4DL and AT4DL, held in Viareggio and in Trento, respectively, in 2009. We would like to thank the participants of the workshops, the reviewers and Program Committee members. Our thanks also goes to the volume's Program Committee members who helped us select the contributions. Their help made it possible for us to achieve our goal and present how state-of-the art language technologies are applied to the challenges faced by digital libraries.

April 2011   The Editors

Organization

Editors

Raffaella Bernardi	University of Trento, Italy
Sally Chambers	European Library, The Netherlands
Bjoern Gottfried	University of Bremen, Germany
Frédérique Segond	Xerox, France
Ilya Zaihrayeu	University of Trento, Italy

Editorial Committee

Pierre Andrews	University of Trento, Italy
Galja Angelova	Bulgarian Academy of Sciences, Bulgaria
Aliaksandr Autayeu	University of Trento, Italy
Pushpak Bhattacharyya	Indian Institute of Technology, India
Biswanath Dutta	University of Trento, Italy
Nicola Ferro	University of Padova, Italy
Abdelhakim Fraihat	University of Trento, Italy
Fausto Giunchiglia	University of Trento, Italy
Stefan Gradmann	Europeana, Humboldt-Universität zu Berlin, Germany
Manuel Kirschner	KRDB, Free University of Bozen-Bolzano, Italy
Udo Kruschwitz	Essex University, UK
Andreas Lattner	University of Frankfurt, Germany
Thu-Dieu Le	University of Trento, Italy
Mikolaj Leszczuk	AGH Krakow, Poland
Vincenzo Maltese	University of Trento, Italy
Elena Pavan	University of Trento, Italy
Stefan Pletschacher	University of Salford, UK
Viliam Simko	CIANT, Prague, Czech Republic
Junichi Tsujii	University of Tokyo, Japan

Table of Contents

Efficient Search in Hidden Text
of Large DjVu Documents

Janusz S. Bień

Formal Linguistics Department, University of Warsaw,
Browarna 8/10, 00-927 Warszawa, Poland
jsbien@uw.edu.pl
http://www.klf.uw.edu.pl

Abstract. The paper describes an open-source tool which allows to
present end-users with results of advanced language technologies. It relies on the DjVu format, which for some applications is still superior to
other modern formats including PDF/A. The DjVu GPLed tools are not
limited just to the DjVuLibre library, but are being supplemented by various new programs, such as pdf2djvu developed by Jakub Wilk. It allows
in particular to convert to DjVu the PDF output of popular OCR programs like FineReader preserving the hidden text layer and some other
features.

The tool in question has been conceived by the present author and
consist of a modification of the Poliqarp corpus query tool, used for National Corpus of Polish; his ideas have been very succesfully implemented
by Jakub Wilk. The new system, called here simply Poliqarp for DjVu,
inherits from its origin not only the powerfull search facilities based two-
level regular expressions, but also the ability to represent low-level ambiguities and other linguistic phenomena. Although at present the tool
is used mainly to facilitate access to the results of dirty OCR, it is ready
to handle also more sophisticated output of linguistic technologies.

1   DjVu Technology and DjVuLibre

The DjVu technology, described by its authors as *an image compression technique, a document format, and a software platform for delivering documents images over the Internet* [4, p. 2] was originally developed by Yann Le Cun, Léon
Bottou, Patrick Haffner, and Paul G. Howard at AT&T Laboratories in 1996.
AT&T Laboratories acquired several patents for some aspects of the technology,
but didn't offer any product using or supporting DjVu[1]. The broad rights to the
patents have been purchased by LizardTech (it later became a part of Celartem
Technology Inc., which in 2009 appointed Caminova Inc. "to develop, distribute
and manage its DjVu document imaging technology", cf. http://www.caminova.

---

[1] Although the patents in question are valid only in USA, they definitely delayed the
practical applications of the format (fortunately software patents are not allowed at
all in European Union and a lot of other countries).

R. Bernardi et al. (Eds.): NLP4DL/AT4DL 2009, LNCS 6699, pp. 1–14, 2011.

jp/en/), which in 2001 allowed to use patented techniques in the software distributed under the GNU General Public License; as the wording of the statement was considered unprecise, in 2002 it was supplemented by an additional clarification. The implementation of the DjVu technology available on the GNU GPL licence is called DjVuLibre. It is worth reminding that GNU GPL provides the user with 4 freedoms (http://www.gnu.org/philosophy/free-sw.html):

1. The freedom to run the program, for any purpose.
2. The freedom to study how the program works, and adapt it to your needs.
3. The freedom to redistribute copies so you can help your neighbor.
4. The freedom to improve the program, and release your improvements to the public, so that the whole community benefits.

In consequence, it is most appropriate for academic research.

DjVu has several features. First of all, it provides very efficient algorithms for image compression; the best of them are still available only in the form of commercial and quite expensive products. Secondly, it provides an efficient way to transfer the compressed images over the Internet, even on relatively slow lines. Moreover, it provides also an efficient way to display the image on the end-user's computer, using such tricks as progressive decoding (which decompresses only this part of the image which is to be displayed), downloading the next page in the background etc.

DjVu allows to store every page in a separate file and download only the pages which are really needed, which is of crucial importance especially for large dictionaries, which are not read in a sequential way. Another feature of crucial importance is the possibility to accompany the scans by the hidden text layer, which can be searched, copied etc.

From a user's point of view it is the DjVu viewer which is important. There exist several of them, both commercial and free, for various platforms, palmtops and cellular phones included. All the viewers profit from the DjVu design features allowing the viewer to simulate the operations on a paper document in comparable time, as illustrated by the table 4 in [4, p. 6]:

Action	Real-word equivalent	Acceptable delay
Zooming/Panning	Moving the eyes	Immediate
Next/Previous Page	Turning a page	< 1 second
Random Page access	Finding a page	< 3 seconds

From the very beginning, DjVu viewers allowed to highlight specified fragments of a remote text. For example, the address

```
http://www.leoyan.com/century-dictionary.com/04/index04.djvu?djvuopts=
&page=p2719.djvu&zoom=100&showposition=0.48,0.34&highlight=1084,3451,
1004,344
```

points to the entry *hardware* in the online edition of the famous *The Century Dictionary and Cyclopedia* (published from 1888 to 1891), referenced also later in the paper. The main part of the address describes the primary document file, which in this case is just an index to the files containing individual pages of the 4th volume of the dictionary. The parameter `page` describes the page using its name which happens to coincide with the name of the file containing it. The `highlight` parameter specifies pixel coordinates of the rectangle to be highlighted, and the `showposition` part guarantees that the visible area of the page will contain the highlight.

This very useful feature was however very little used because there was no easy way to identify the coordinates of the area to be highlighted. Therefore in 2008 I asked Jakub Wilk (then a student of mine) to extend djview4 allowing to create such URLs conveniently after marking a region with a mouse. The patch has been submitted to the Sourceforge tracking system on 9th February and by 29th February it has been reimplemented more efficiently by Léon Bottou, the author of the program, who included it in the official distribution. I think this feature is extremely important for academic research, as it allows to quote a specific fragment of a digitalized work when including its image is technically difficult or not desirable.

When accessing a document with a highlighted fragment, the page is displayed in the default resolution and in the default position, so it could happen that the highlighted fragment is not immediately visible. The free but closed source LizardTech viewer for MS Windows had a solution to the problem in the form of the `ShowPosition` parameter. In May 2008 I asked for an identical feature in djview4 and just several months later (in June 2008) Léon Battou implemented it. So if you send an URL referring to a highlighted fragment of text, the receipient will see it exactly as the sender (with some minor exceptions).

2 DjVu and Portable Document Format

Portable Document Format (PDF) is an open standard (formally since July 1, 2008) for document exchange introduced by Adobe Systems in 1993. A subset of the specification is known as PDF/A and described in the international standard ISO 19005-1:2005 *Document management – Electronic document file format for long-term preservation – Part 1: Use of PDF 1.4 (PDF/A-1)*.

Reportedly already version 1.0 of the specification allowed to create "sandwich PDF" containing both the scans and hidden text layers, predating in this respect DjVu, which however for years provided better compression (at present the compression ratio is comparable) and is still in many aspects more convenient.

Thanks to the open character of the PDF standard it became very popular, both as the output of scanning programs and stand-alone scanners, and as an input for printing, ranging from personal printers to professional devices. Moreover "sandwich PDF" is used also as the output format of many OCR programs, including the widely-used Abby FinerReader.

To have the best of both worlds, in 2008 Jakub Wilk created the first version of the pdf2djvu program, which he has since then actively maintained and developed; the software is hosted at http://code.google.com/p/pdf2djvu/. It is released under the terms of the GNU General Public Licenses and available in the package form in major free operating system (GNU/Linux and FreeBSD) distributions, such as Debian, Ubuntu and OpenSuse; it can be compiled also for MS Windows. The current version of the program is 0.7.5 (released on 20th January 2011) and supports such features as

- compressing the scans the DjVu way, trying to split them into front and background;
- optionally preserving hidden text;
- optionally preserving the document outline;
- optionally preserving hyperlinks (with some limitation intrinsic for the DjVu format);
- optionally preserving and updating the document metadata.

The program is able in particular to preserve and update the metadata in the XMP format; XMP stands for Extensible Metadata Platform (http://www.adobe.com/products/xmp/) which is becoming more and more popular.

The expensive commercial DjVu document creators provide better compression than pdf2djvu, but are available only for MS Windows and include built-in OCR programs which cannot be controlled by the user. In consequence, *pdf2djvu* used alone or with an OCR program of choice is a viable competitor in many circumstances.

3   Searching the Hidden Text Layer

Every DjVu viewer allows for searching the hidden text layer, but for large remote documents it is inefficient as it defeats the purpose of splitting the document into separate pages: to access the hidden text, all the pages have to be loaded, and if the search is repeated, they are reloaded multiple times. On the other hand, if the document is available locally, djview4 offers very efficient and convenient incremental search which seems to be absent in other viewers.

Hence, the optimal solution is to use some kind of index and a search engine. Yann LeCun, one of the creators of the DjVu format, implemented JSSindex (JavaScript Search Engine, http://sourceforge.net/projects/jssindex/), an interesting search tool for collections of documents in HTML, PS, PDF, and DjVu, but unfortunately oriented only at English language texts and very difficult to modify and extend. A simple search engine has been provided for *Century Dictionary Online* (http://www.global-language.com/CENTURY/) mentioned earlier. Although it looks like this is a special purpose software written for the specific task, this electronic edition created by Jeffery A. Triggs sets standards for an efficient and convenient access to DjVu documents. Another electronic edition prepared by Triggs is *Jamieson's Etymological Dictionary of the Scottish Language Online* (http://www.scotsdictionary.com/); it allows to choose between two search engines: Hunter and Amberfish. Hunter is commercial software developed by Alternative Output Inc. (`http://www.alternativeoutput.com/`), used by a few customers, one of them being Oxford University Press, which reportedly uses it for the online version of *Oxford English Dictionary*. Amberfish is an open source text retrieval system developed by Etymon Systems; the company seems to no longer exist, but the software is still available at `http://sourceforge.net/projects/amberfish/` and `https://github.com/nassar/amberfish`.

Although general purpose search engines are quite useful, there is a whole family of interesting software which treats texts as linguistic objects, namely corpus management software. One of the most sophisticated systems of this type is Poliqarp (*Polyinterpretation Indexing Query and Retrieval Procesor*), an open source tool developed in the Institute of Computer Science of Polish Academy of Sciences (`http://poliqarp.sourceforge.net/`). It has been in use for several years, now also for the National Corpus of Polish (`http://nkjp.pl/`); this should guarantee its continuous maintenance. An important factor is also a user community familiar with its query language. The current maintainer of Poliqarp and implementor of the recent extensions designed primarily by Adam Przepiórkowski (cf. [8]) is Jakub Wilk.

The Poliqarp query language has been inspired by Corpus Query Processor, a component of Corpus Workbench developed at the University of Stuttgart (now an open source system, cf. `http://cwb.sourceforge.net/`, but it was not so when the development of Poliqarp started). The basic principle is to use two levels of regular expressions. One level is applied to strings representing the values of linguistic features of a word, the actual spelling of the word being one of them. The second level of regular expressions is applied to words or their sets defined with the first level expressions. In consequence the query language is very powerful (it seems that practically all queries available in e.g. Hunter and Amberfish mentioned above can be expressed in Poliqarp), but less user-friendly than in simpler systems.

The idea to use Poliqarp for searching hidden text of DjVu documents has been conceived by the present author in 2008 and formulated first as a term project for Computer Science students. The background and the results of this preliminary attempt were presented in [2]. A research grant allowed to implement later a more efficient and elegant solution described below, and to support the development of some other tools mentioned in the paper.

The results of the search in the hidden text layer may be successful only if the text really represents the content of the scan. Usually it is not the case as the hidden text layer is created by 'dirty OCR', i.e. an unattended OCR process. Hence it is important to estimate easily the quality of the hidden text. Upon my request of May 2008 Léon Bottou in a few days included in djview4 the possibility to display hidden text for the scan fragment under the cursor; another added feature is the possibility to display the whole hidden layer at once. It allows e.g. to spot the OCR errors which are to blame if the search misses a target (such errors can be now corrected with the help of Jakub Wilk's program djvusmooth available in several Linux distribution including Debian Squeeze; the program is still under development, so it should become more convenient to use in the near future). On the other hand the same purpose can be served by graphical concordances mentioned below.

4   Poliqarp for DjVu

Poliqarp for DjVu, also known under the code name marasca, is an extension of Poliqarp allowing, at least in principle, to use the full power of the program to search hidden text in DjVu documents. Its development is one of the tasks supported by the Polish Ministry of Science and Higher Education's grant entitled *Text digitalization tools for philological research*. By the end of the project, i.e. late 2011, the stable version of the system will be released under the terms of the GNU GPL license. It is worth noting that although at first the system was just a modification of Poliqarp, we contribute in return to the original project. Since March 2010 the National Corpus of Polish has used the marasca version of the WWW Poliqarp client.

Poliqarp for DjVu was implemented by Jakub Wilk according to the design of the present author. It has been available for testing since December 2009 at http://poliqarp.wbl.klf.uw.edu.pl. It operates by augmenting a standard Poliqarp corpus with information about the bounding box coordinates of the text tokens. The text and the coordinates are provided in hOCR format [3] generated with the djvu2hocr program bundled with Jakub Wilk's ocrodjvu software (http://jwilk.net/software/ocrodjvu). Thanks to pdf2djvu it allows to apply Poliqarp for DjVu to the results produced by practically all important OCR programs. Moreover, recently a converter from the PAGE (Page Analysis and Ground-truth Elements) format [6] to hOCR has been developed, which allows Poliqarp to handle, at least in principle, numerous texts prepared in the very format by the so called library partners in the framework of the IMPACT project (*IMProving ACcess to Text*, www.impact-project.eu).

As of February 2011, four important Polish dictionaries are available for testing Poliqarp for DjVU:

- "Warsaw dictionary", more precisely *Słownik języka polskiego* (Dictionary of the Polish Language) by J. Karłowicz, A. Kryński and W. Niedźwiecki published in Warsaw in 8 volumes in 1900–1927. It has been scanned by the library of the University of Warsaw, which used Abby FineReader 8 for OCR; the resuls contain many mistakes but seem to be usable.
- *Słownik polszczyzny XVI wieku* (Dictionary of the 16th century Polish). The work started in 1949 and is still in progress. Its digitalization has complex history, which has been described elsewhere (cf. [5] and [1]). Since December 2010 all the 34 already published volumes have been available. Most of them are scanned and the OCR is, unfortunately, of rather low quality. Thanks to the sponsor of the dictionary, Foundation for Polish Science, which recently made publication on the Internet a formal requirement for further funding, the last two volumes are digitally born; the same files that were used for printing were converted by Jakub Wilk with his pdf2djvu program, so the

physical and electronic versions have the same appearance and content. Two earlier volumes were preserved in the internal format of the typesetting system used; when typeset again, the resulting PDF files have slightly different appearance due to some minor changes in the system and fonts. As the content remained identical, these volumes are also available as digitally-born.

– Second edition of Linde's dictionary. *Słownik języka polskiego* (Dictionary of the Polish language) by Samuel Bogumił Linde were published in 4 volumes (two of them are split into two parts, so it makes actually 6 volumes) in 1807-1814, the second edition has been published in 1854-1861. This is one of the most important historical dictionaries not only from the Polish point of view, as all definitions are also given in German and there is a lot of quotations from other languages (including Old Slavonic, Greek and even Hebrew) and dialects, some of them already extinct. The mixture of languages and scripts makes OCR extremely difficult; at present the hidden text layer has been prepared with Abby FineReader 10 set to Polish language. In consequence the fragments in Polish are of quite good quality, while the remaining parts are completely unusable; this is however already a sufficient help for readers trying e.g. to locate an entry, which are ordered according to rules which are different from contemporary ones. We have some plans to improve the quality of the hidden text, but this is outside the scope of the present paper.

– *Słownik geograficzny Królestwa Polskiego i innych krajów słowiańskich* (The Geographical Dictionary of the Polish Kingdom and other Slavic Countries), a gazetteer in 15 volumes of almost 1000 pages each, published in 1880-1914, extremely useful for genealogical research. The gazetteer covers Poland in its borders before the partitions between Russia, Germany and Austria, but due to the censorship it was impossible to state this explicitly in the title.

From a user's point of view, Poliqarp for DjVu enhances Poliqarp proper with functionalities present already in *The Century Dictionary Online* and *Jamieson's Etymological Dictionary of the Scottish Language Online*, namely with linking hits (keywords in the KWIC index) to the scans with highlighted hits. To quickly sort out false positives caused by the low quality of "dirty OCR", Poliqarp for DjVu additionally provides so called graphical concordances, i.e a KWIC index with the scan snippets created on the fly. Figure 1 shows a graphical concordance for a non-trivial query in Linde's dictionary. The purpose of the query is to find the occurences of the abbreviation *Syr.* meaning *Syryjski* (i.e. Syriac [language]). The problem is that the same abbreviation refers also to *Syreniusza zielnik* (i.e. Syreniusz' herbarium), but in such a case it is followed by a page reference in the form of a number. Hence regular expression

```
Syr "\." "[^[:digit:]].*"
```

specifies 3 tokens:

1. the character string `Syr`,
2. a full stop,
3. a token that does not start with a digit.

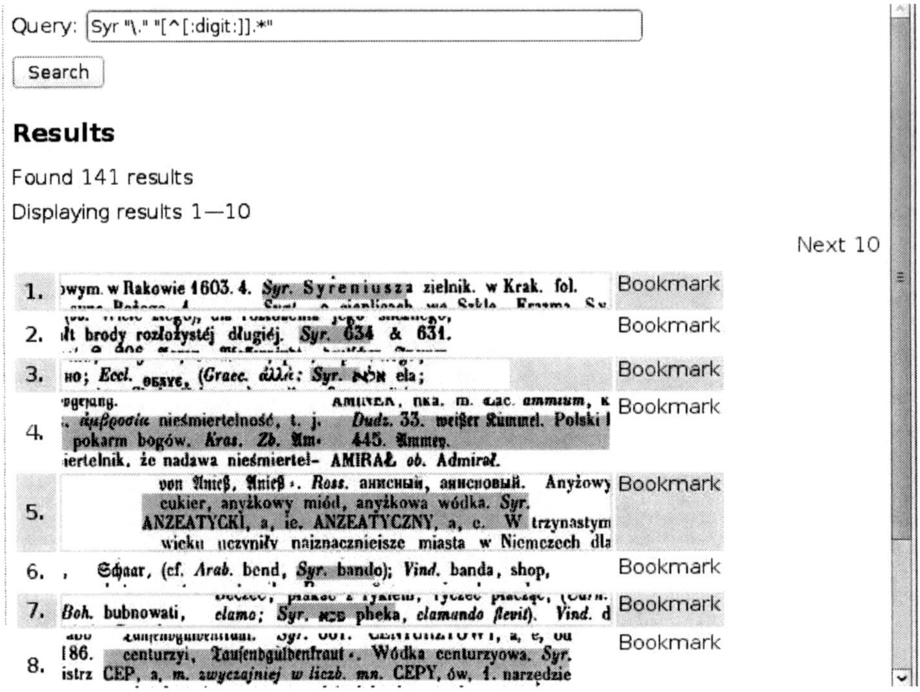

Query: `Syr "\." "[^[:digit:]].*"`

Search

Results

Found 141 results

Displaying results 1—10

Next 10

Fig. 1. Graphical concordances in Poliqarp for DjVu

Before going into the details of the regular expression syntax let us note that most of the hits are obviously correct. Hit number 2 is a false positive due to an OCR error, the digit has been misinterpreted as a letter. Hit number 4 may seem incorrect, but actually this is a result of size limitation of the displayed snippet.

Let us have a look now at an example illustrating how the power of regular expressions can be used to circumvent the OCR errors. The following expression

```
("[CĆOGU]ze[sś]" | "[CO][z/]o[sa]") "\."
```

seems to match all the occurences of the abbreviation *Czes.* (meaning Czech language) in the Warsaw dictionary, which has been recognized as Cześ, Gzes, Czos, Ozos etc., as illustrated in figures 2 and 3.

Let us analyze the structure of the query. The top level of the query consists of three second level regular expressions and has the structure

```
(RE1 | RE2) RE3
```

which means that we are searching for RE3 immediately preceded either by RE1 or by RE2.

Expression `"\."` denotes simply a full stop ending the abbreviation. Because the full stop in regular expressions means "any character except new line" (in this meaning it occurs close to the end in the first example), it has to be escaped

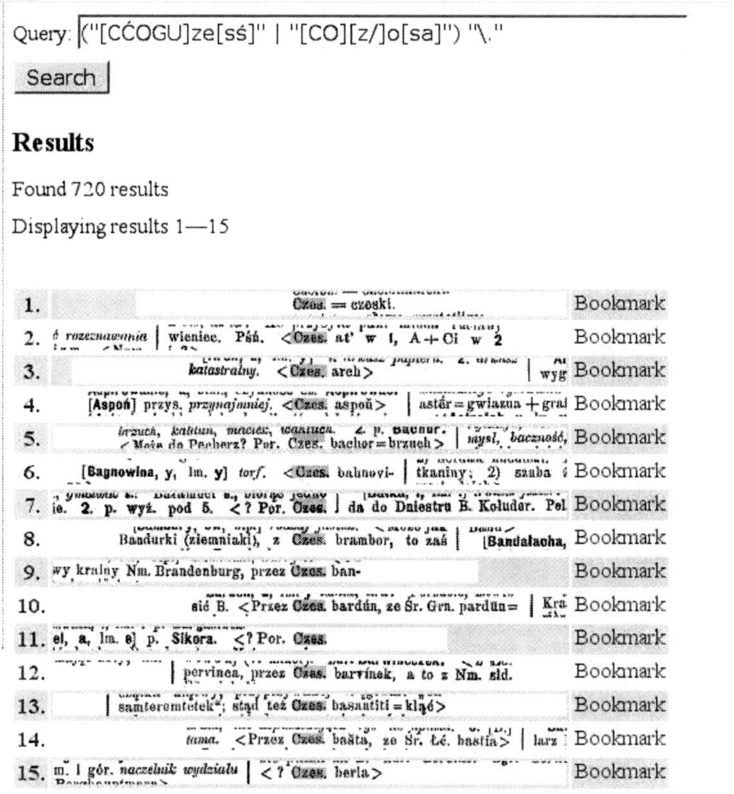

Fig. 2. Graphical concordances for dirty OCR

with backlash to recover its standard meaning. Quotes are needed to distinguish the levels of regular expressions.

Expression `"[CĆOGU]ze[sś]"` matches words consisting of 4 characters. The second and third one must be respectively z and e, the first and last may be any character from the respective bracketed list. If such a list starts with ^, it means the the list specifies characters which are not allowed, as in our first example.

The bracketed list may contain also predefined names of character classes, as exemplified by `[:digit:]` in the first example. Another use of this construct is demonstrated by a query usefully applicable to the dictionary of the 16th century Polish:

`"[[:upper:]]{3,}" within body meta orig=pdf`

It allows to search for headwords, always spelled in capitals. The query matches also the Roman numbers referring to centuries, but it doesn't do much harm and avoiding this makes the query much more complex. The results are presented in figure 4.

The top level regular expression is simple and consists of only one component, it is however supplemented by two clauses. The first clause limits the search to

Query: ("[CĆOGU]ze[sś]" | "[CO][z/]o[sa]") "\."

[Search]

Results

Found 720 results

Displaying results 1—15

1.	s=> czcionkarski. **Cześ.** = czeski. częstot.	Bookmark
2.	wieniec. Pśń. < **Czes.** at' w I,	Bookmark
3.	. arkusz hatastralny, < **Gzes.** arch> fArcha, y	Bookmark
4.	przys. przynajmniej. < **Czes.** aspoń> IAstenja, i	Bookmark
5.	do Pęcherz? Por. **Ozes.** bachor = brzuch > [	Bookmark
6.	y] torf. < **Ozes.** balmoyi- na> Bagnowisko	Bookmark
7.	. < ? Por. **Ozes.** balamutiti = pleść, gadać	Bookmark
8.	(ziemniaki), z **Cześ.** brambor, to zaś z	Bookmark
9.	Nm. Brandenburg, przez **Cześ.** ban- dora, bandurka	Bookmark
10.	zawiesić B. < Przez **Ozes.** bardiin, ze Śr.	Bookmark
11.	<?Por. **Ozes.** brhel, Słń. brglez	Bookmark
12.	Łć. peiTinea, przez **Ozes.** baiTinek, a to z	Bookmark
13.	samteremtetek", stąd też **Ozes.** basantiti = kląć> [	Bookmark
14.	B.j tama. <Przez **Cześ.** basta, ze Sr.	Bookmark
15.	Berlisko. < ? **Ozes.** berła> XBerłowładca, y	Bookmark

Fig. 3. Standard concordances for dirty OCR

the section named **body**; sections are defined during the corpus building, in our case this sections refers to the part of dictionary containing the entries. The second clause refers to metadata assigned to the publications included in the corpus. In our case this is non-standard metadata which allows to limit our search to digitally-born volumes.

The second level expression consists of two parts: the character specification [[:upper:]] and the quantifier {3,}. The character specification is just a single element bracketed list, and the element is the name of a character class (also written in brackets); the class [:upper:] denotes, as expected, all upper case characters; the meaning of "all" depends on an operating system property called locale, but can be safely assumed to mean at least all characters present in the Basic Multilingual Plane of the Unicode standard (www.unicode.org).

The quantifier {3,} means that the preceding element has to occur in a word at least three times; in the case of our dictionary it means that we skip the initials of authors (in the dictionary every entry is signed by its author) but match the head of entries longer than two letters. Other popular quantifiers are: * (the preceding element occurs any number of times or does not occur at all; the construct was used in the first of our examples), + (the preceding element occurs at least once), ? (the preceding element occurs at most once).

Query: |"[[:upper:]]{3,}" within body meta orig=pdf

Search

Results

Found 10000 results

Displaying results 1—15

1.	SIĘ] [PRZEMIEŚĆ] **PRZA**	(67) sb f	Bookmark
2.	, Cn brak, Linde **XVI**	– XVII w. 1	Bookmark
3.	brak, Linde **XVI – XVII**	w. 1. Konflikt	Bookmark
4.	CzechEp 137. P 2 **PRZA**	PRZA b. Sprawa sądowa	Bookmark
5.	137. P 2 PRZA **PRZA**	b. Sprawa sądowa,	Bookmark
6.	3. sprawa. LWil **PRZACIEL**	PRZASNY 3 PRZACIEL cf PRZYJACIEL	Bookmark
7.	. sprawa. LWil PRZACIEL **PRZASNY**	3 PRZACIEL cf PRZYJACIEL PRZADZIAD	Bookmark
8.	. LWil PRZACIEL PRZASNY 3 **PRZACIEL**	cf PRZYJACIEL PRZADZIAD cf PRADZIAD	Bookmark
9.	PRZACIEL PRZASNY 3 PRZACIEL cf **PRZYJACIEL**	PRZADZIAD cf PRADZIAD PRZANKI Sł	Bookmark
10.	PRZASNY 3 PRZACIEL cf PRZYJACIEL **PRZADZIAD**	cf PRADZIAD PRZANKI Sł stp	Bookmark
11.	PRZACIEL cf PRZYJACIEL PRZADZIAD cf **PRADZIAD**	PRZANKI Sł stp, Cn	Bookmark
12.	cf PRZYJACIEL PRZADZIAD cf PRADZIAD **PRZANKI**	Sł stp; Cn,	Bookmark
13.	Cn, Linde brak. **PRZASNEK**	(7) sb m	Bookmark
14.	Linde).] Cf **PRZAŚNICA**	, PRZAŚNIK, [PRZAŚNYSZ	Bookmark
15.	] Cf PRZAŚNICA, **PRZAŚNIK**	, [PRZAŚNYSZ] LWil	Bookmark

Fig. 4. Standard concordances for digitally born texts

The regular expressions are far from being user-friendly, they may be confusing even for an experienced programmer. Their use is however so ubiquitous that learning them is a good investment. On the other hand, there exist already various tools for editing and debugging regular expressions and we hope to adapt one of them in the future to Poliqarp. For the time being the best approach is to start with a simple general query and to refine the search by adding additional restrictions.

5   Lemmatization, Morphosyntactic Tagging and Polyinterpretations

The standard linguistic corpus workflow includes two important steps: morphosyntactic analysis and disambiguation (cf. eg. [7, p. 14]). Morphosyntactic analysis assigns all possible interpretations to a word, in particular all possible canonical forms of the word. For example, the Polish word *mam* can be a form of MIEĆ (*to have*), MAMA (deminutive of *mother*) or MAMIĆ (*to deceive*); moreover even for a fixed canonical form there are often different values of morphological categories possible. Disambiguation is usually performed by a program using stochastic rules to select the interpretation suitable for the given context; of course the results are sometimes wrong. Therefore Poliqarp allows to store and access all the interpretations and to compare them; for example, the user can search for words which where unambiguous already at the level of morphosyntactic analysis etc. (cf. section 3.5 of [9]). This unique feature of Poliqarp is called polyinterpretation.

All this features related to language technology are present also in Poliqarp for DjVu. Moreover, some of them can be used on a lower level then originally intended.

When working with historical texts, e.g. with the quotations in the dictionary of 16th century Polish, we have different but analogical problems on the spelling level: letter y may mean contemporary y or j, letter i may mean contemporary i or j (so e.g. *przyymuiemy* is now spelled *przyjmujemy*) etc. Listing all possible interpretation of a letter can be considered an analogue of the morphological analysis, while reconstructing the contemporary spelling according to some inferred rules is an analogue of the morphological disambiguation by a stochastic tagger. The main difference is purely technical and consists in the fact that the latter interpretation processes do not operate on linguistic features, but on the canonical form field (in Poliqarp the features are represented differently than the textual and canonical forms). This possibility has not been yet used in practice, but we hope that it will be in due time.

For many purposes a simplified form of morphological analysis is quite useful. So called lemmatization consists in assigning the canonical form, i.e. the lemma, to the given word form; the process is sometimes also called stemming. It is relatively easy for English, so it is often built into some search engines like JSSIndex mentioned earlier, but quite difficult and costly for inflectional languages like Polish. The tools used for the National Corpus of Polish do not seem to be directly applicable to historical texts, so it is still an open problem. One of the possible solutions is to organize collaborative work of volunteers who would enter the requested information by hand.

6   Towards Collaborative Proofreading and Lemmatization

The important innovation of Poliqarp for DjVu is the ability to bookmark the hits with Firefox and other browsers based on the Gecko engine. The bookmark refers to the appropriate page of the DjVu document with the hit highlighted. The name of the bookmark is created by JavaScript code and contains the following elements:

– the abbreviated name of the dictionary,
– the text of the query,
– the timestamp (to distinguish different hits of the same query).

Additional information can be added by the user either by editing the name or by using, in Firefox and some other browsers, the tags field. Hence the user can not only bookmark hits easily for his own use, but also mark and correct OCR mistakes. The problem is how to organize sharing of this information.

From purely technical point of view, the tools are already available in the form of the Firefox Sync plug-in, which is to become a standard feature of the browser, and the Sync server (formerly called Weave) which collects information from the plug-ins. There is however a serious problem of privacy, because it is not possible to grant access only to the Poliqarp error-correcting bookmarks. The simplest solution seems to export the relevant bookmarks locally and submit them to the dedicated server by a special program.

We are of course aware of various specialised tools for collaborated proofreading, but our general philosophy is make OCR error report extremely easy for a casual user, and to move the burden to the receiving side. One of possible scenario is to convert the collected reports into annotations in a special copy of the document to be used later with Jakub Wilk's DjVu editor djvusmooth (`http://jwilk.net/software/djvusmooth`) mentioned earlier.

7   Concluding Remarks

Poliqarp for DjVu is a powerful tool for searching the hidden text layer of DjVu documents, which can be created in particular by converting PDF files used for printing or output of OCR programs. Although the Computer Science principle *garbage in, garbage out* is generally valid, the sophisticated queries allowed in *Poliqarp* may partially alleviate the problem of bad quality OCR. For digitally born or thoroughly proof-read texts the program is even more useful.

Acknowledgment

The work described in the present paper is supported by the Polish Ministry of Science and Higher Education's grant no. N N519 384036.

References

1. Bień, J.S.: Digitalizing dictionaries of polish. In: Bogacki, K., Cholewa, J., Rozumko, A. (eds.) Methods of Lexical Analysis: Theoretical Assumption and Practical Applications, Wydawnictwo Uniwersytetu w Białymstoku, Białystok, pp. 37–45 (2009), `http://bc.klf.uw.edu.pl/71/`
2. Bień, J.S.: Facilitating access to digitalized dictionaries in djvu format. Studia Kognitywne - Études Cognitives 9, 161–170 (2009), `http://bc.klf.uw.edu.pl/160/`
3. Breuel, T.: The hOCR microformat for OCR workflow and results. In: Proceedings of the Ninth International Conference on Document Analysis and Recognition, pp. 1063–1067. IEEE Computer Society, Los Alamitos (2007), `http://madm.dfki.de/publication&pubid=4373`
4. Le Cun, Y., Bottou, L., Erofeev, A., Haffner, P., Riemers, B.W.: DjVu document browsing with on-demand loading and rendering of image components. In: Internet Imaging, San Jose (January 2001), `http://leon.bottou.org/papers/lecun-2001`
5. Piotrowski, T.: Digitization of Polish historic(al) dictionaries. Review of the National Center for Digitization 6, 95–102 (2005), `http://elib.mi.sanu.ac.rs/files/journals/ncd/6/d009download.pdf`
6. Pletschacher, S., Antonacopoulos, A.: The PAGE (Page Analysis and Ground-Truth Elements) format framework. In: International Conference on Pattern Recognition, pp. 257–260. IEEE Computer Society, Los Alamitos (2010), `http://www.cse.salford.ac.uk/prima/papers/ICPR2010_Pletschacher_PAGE.pdf`

7. Przepiórkowski, A.: The IPI PAN Corpus: Preliminary version. Institute of Computer Science, Polish Academy of Sciences, Warsaw (2004), `http://nlp.ipipan.waw.pl/~adamp/Papers/2004-corpus/`
8. Przepiórkowski, A.: TEI P5 as an XML standard for treebank encoding. In: Proceedings of the Eighth International Workshop on Treebanks and Linguistic Theories (TLT 8), pp. 149–160 (2009), `http://nlp.ipipan.waw.pl/~adamp/Papers/2009-tlt-tei/`
9. Przepiórkowski, A., Buczyński, A., Wilk, J.: The National Corpus of Polish Cheatsheet (2006), `http://nkjp.pl/poliqarp/help/en.html` (accessed 2011-02-08)

Towards the Processing of Historic Documents

Björn Gottfried and Lothar Meyer-Lerbs

Centre for Computing and Communication Technologies
University of Bremen, Germany

Abstract. This chapter describes methods required for transforming complex document images into texts. The goal is to make the contents of those documents available for search engines, which are not born-digital but converted from a physical medium to a digital format. Established optical character recognition methods fail for documents for which no assumptions can be made regarding the, probably unknown, symbols contained in the document, historic documents being the example domain par excellence. This paper, however, has a much broader goal: it outlines fundamental problems as well as a methodology in the dealing with documents containing unknown and arbitrary symbols in order to provide a basis for discussions and future work within the digital library community. In particular, future advances will more closely require the interaction of researchers concerned with such diverse topics as document digitisation, reproduction, and preservation as well as search engines, cross-language processing, mobile libraries, and many further areas. Adopting a general view on the presented issues, researchers of the aforementioned areas should be sensitised for the problems met in processing complex, especially historic documents.

1 Introduction

In the last decade several digitisation projects have been carried out. Whole books and even entire collections of libraries have been transformed into a digital format in order to provide them by what has been introduced several years ago as digital libraries. Apart from digitised content, digital libraries also include content referred to as born-digital, that is content which was created in a digital format. While the latter offers the user a sophisticated functionality to search through the content, this is impossible for printed material that just has been converted into a digital format.

In particular, in the last decade many projects have been established to digitise and archive the cultural heritage. The idea is to save the material from a loss and to distribute it through the web in order to make it available everywhere. Some of the most prominent projects include

- the project Gutenberg (`www.gutenberg.org/wiki/Main_Page`),
- the Google Books Library Project (`books.google.com/`), and
- the Million Book Project (`www.ulib.org/`).

A digitised book, however, is nothing else than a collection of images which result from scanning the according book. Therefore, most digitised collections just make available more or less large images of the contents of the books. In order to access that content,

R. Bernardi et al. (Eds.): NLP4DL/AT4DL 2009, LNCS 6699, pp. 15–28, 2011.

equally like for born-digital content, it is necessary to extract the text contained in these images. The field of document image processing is concerned with this analysis. This scientific area has been established many years ago, even before the mass digitisation projects started. The problems that arise when applying document image processing methods to document images are manifold, which is the reason for why only a small segment of scanned documents is available for search engines. Most document images are too complex regarding their layouts, fonts, and components; sometimes, even different languages are intermixed and different symbol systems are used within single documents. Established optical character recognition software is unable to successfully process such documents.

In particular, there is a large segment of books that has been published before the twentieth century. Those publications are especially difficult to access by means of search engines since they contain complex fonts, many special characters, and even symbols unknown today. Additionally, they suffer from several other problems, such as pages being yellowed, blotted, and distorted. In order to make the contents of such books available new means are required which enable the processing of historic fonts. While sophisticated image processing methods are required for this purpose, the basic idea is rather simple: for each document, which might be a single certificate, a letter, or a whole book, a document specific font is generated out of that document. This specific font derives from visual features which can be extracted out of document images. These features enable the classification of characters and of every kinds of symbols, since at this stage no assumptions are made concerning the underlying language. Referring to such visual features, which can be arbitrarily complex shape features, the font of a historic document can be arbitrarily complex itself. While the recognition of the underlying characters is not included in this process, a subsequent mapping process has just to follow for the extracted characters to be recognised with respect to a particular alphabet. In this sense, this paper describes the very first step necessary to apply other advanced technologies to such documents, for instance, to search through these documents, to deal with cross language processing issues, or to even evaluate the content at the semantic level.

This chapter is about the processing of difficult, especially historic documents. The results include methods which are about the extraction of texts from images, in particular, for those documents for which standard optical character recognition methods fail. Secondly, for each such document a document specific font is extracted, that defines for each character class a visually optimal exemplar; taking those exemplars for all characters a document can be reproduced on different media, e.g. on smart phones to access contents from everywhere, by referring to the new document specific scalable font. Thirdly, methods are investigated that are fast regarding the whole analysis process; this is important inasmuch a library would have to analyse large collections in a reasonable time. Eventually, a large compression rate is achieved since fonts are represented by means of vectors which are much more compact than the according images, which do frequently have a particular high resolution in order to make the original document persistent as precise as possible. It is shown how this approach works by analysing documents of a Fraktur type.

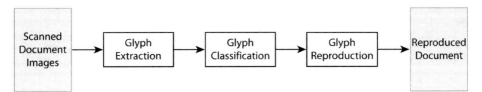

Fig. 1. The process chain

The body of this chapter is structured as follows. In Sect. 2 the methodology as a whole is outlined. It divides into three main stages: font extraction, glyph classification, and document reproduction, which are described in turn in Sects. 3 to 5. Conclusions are drawn from this work in Sect. 6, links of the presented work to different topics within the digital library community are given in Sect. 7, and a summary in Sect. 8 closes this chapter.

2   The Approach

The methodology for extracting texts out of documents containing unknown symbol sets is outlined in this section. Each document is processed as indicated in the flowchart shown in Fig. 1. Whole repositories of scanned document images are to be analysed and enter this process chain.

2.1   Glyph Extraction

In the first step, the symbols which are found on the document pages are extracted out of these document images, more precisely, out of all document images pertaining to one document, a book, a certificate or something else. From now on we use the notion of a glyph which represents the visual appearance of a symbol. A symbol, like an 'a', might be represented by different glyphs within different fonts; or, in different languages, glyphs might even represent different symbols. Furthermore, for the time being we neglect that a symbol might be represented by either exactly one or by more glyphs, which are either single or multi-piece regions in the image.

The assumption is that each document contains a font which might be quite specific to this document, because glyphs could be part of such a document which are not in use anymore today (e.g. a font of a Fraktur type). Accordingly, two different documents might contain very different glyph sets which is the reason for why those different documents should be processed separately.

The extraction of the symbols of a document requires image processing methods that are able to determine regions in images which represent exactly one glyph. Such regions are to be determined as precisely as possible, because similar glyphs are to be distinguished and the glyphs are to be reproduced in a later step in order to reproduce documents with a high quality.

2.2   Glyph Classification

The second step is about putting those glyphs into equivalence classes which represent the same symbol within the present document specific font. Those regions that represent exactly one glyph can be characterised by means of shape descriptions. Each glyph in a document needs to be represented uniquely by such a shape description; ideally, each occurrence of the same glyph would have the same shape description. In this way, the glyph extraction process takes into account the specific glyphs of the given document, namely the shapes of those glyphs. As a consequence, from each document a document specific font containing a particular glyph set can be extracted. This glyph set corresponds to an arbitrary symbol set which has been employed in the according document.

While accuracy is a fundamental requirement of the first step, efficiency is important for glyph classification. This is because taking a single document page there might be already a few thousands of glyphs on a page, the number varying with the size of the given font. That is, a huge number of glyphs is to be classified when taking a whole book. In order to process a book in a reasonable time, shape descriptions are to be investigated which allow a fast glyph classification.

2.3 Glyph Reproduction

Having extracted and described the glyphs' shapes in the previous steps, their reproduction can be based on these shapes. For this purpose, it is sufficient to reproduce their outlines and inner holes which can be represented in a SVG[1] vector format. Since the classification step results in equivalence classes for glyphs, each class can be represented by exactly one glyph in its vector format. This has the consequence that glyphs which are correctly classified but which suffer from deficits concerning how they are depicted in the original document, can be reproduced as if all visual defects have been automatically corrected. Each glyph class can be represented by a particular good exemplar.

The two main requirements for glyph reproduction are a good compression rate and a scalable glyph representation. The first requirement enables the compressed representation of large books. In this way, less memory is required for the encoded documents than for their original document images. This enables also the transfer of large documents among devices as well as to display them on devices with restricted memory resources, such as on smart phones. The latter also requires to change the scale of the font so as to make it optimally visible on a small device. This will be possible through the second requirement.

3   Extraction of Glyphs

The extraction of glyphs requires sophisticated methods which are, unfortunately, to a large degree dependent on the given image material. The latter might suffer from several different problems, such as yellowed, blotted, or distorted pages. A number of different methods have been investigated; the most important results are found in [7]. In the following we show how a specific set of image processing filters enable the extraction of glyphs from a journal series of the nineteens century containing Fraktur glyphs[2].

---

[1] Scalable Vector Graphics.

[2] Die Grenzboten, 28. Jahrgang, 2. Semester 1. Band, Leipzig 1869.

In order to extract glyphs from the document images (top left of Fig. 2), first of all colour images are converted to grey tone images (top right of Fig. 2). A Sigma-filter is applied in order to suppress artefacts [6]; such filters maintain edges, while the background is smoothed (bottom left of Fig. 2). Connected components which represent single glyphs are determined by applying binarisation filters, such as Sauvola [9] or Shafait et al. [11] (bottom right of Fig. 2).

Starting from the connected components a Euklidean distance map is computed (EDM) (top left of Fig. 3). The connected components are extended by two points into each direction in order to grasp the grey values from the surroundings of each connected component. This is required for later reproducing the glyphs appropriately (top right of Fig. 3). The connected components are then cut off the denoised image and the gaps are filled with grey tone values with a bilinear approximation method; the resulting image shows the background (bottom left of Fig. 3). The extended connected components are subtracted from this background image and the result is inverted in order to get black glyphs on the white background (bottom right of Fig. 3). Deskewing algorithms can be applied to this image in order to correct the orientation of glyphs with respect to the document page, without being exposed to blurrings and other artefacts of the background. The connected components of this final image can be forwarded to the glyph classification methods.

4   Classification of Glyphs

As argued above, a fundamental constraint in the present application is efficiency. Suitable features for classifying binarised glyphs should enable fast comparisons. This is hardly possible when employing complex templates that describe shapes in a sophisticated and detailed way. By contrast, the most compact features characterise shapes by means of single numeric values. Textbook examples include the compactness of a glyph, its radius ratio, aspect ratio, convexity, and Hu moments [5]. Comparisons based on such features stick to a constant runtime complexity, since they describe glyphs independently of the number of components, which might either be contour points or all points contained within a glyph. It is therefore worthwhile to investigate whether such features are sufficiently precise.

While those single numeric features mentioned in the previous paragraph are not precise enough, it has been shown how qualitative features complement those established features while sticking to the same runtime complexity [7]. These features are based on a system of shape properties introduced in [3]. Instead of computing those features on all contour points, glyphs are first of all approximated by straight segments which frequently represent a glyph much more compact, since many glyphs contain a number of straight segments.

It is then the idea to describe a glyph shape with respect to single glyph segments. That is, the shape of a glyph extends over a specific range defined by each single segment. This latter is referred to as a segment's scope that can be succinctly described as to be left-of a segment, right-of it, on top, below and by some further directions which

Die Mecklenburgischen Domainenbauern u
Verfassung.

Co

Mittelst eines an das Finanzministerium
Rescripts vom 16. November 1867 wurde die Ve
im Großherzoglich Mecklenburg-Schwerinschen D

Die Mecklenburgischen Domainenbauern u
Verfassung.

Co

Mittelst eines an das Finanzministerium
Rescripts vom 16. November 1867 wurde die Ve
im Großherzoglich Mecklenburg-Schwerinschen D

Die Mecklenburgischen Domainenbauern u
Verfassung.

Co

Mittelst eines an das Finanzministerium
Rescripts vom 16. November 1867 wurde die Ve
im Großherzoglich Mecklenburg-Schwerinschen D

Die Mecklenburgischen Domainenbauern u
Verfassung.

Co

Mittelst eines an das Finanzministerium
Rescripts vom 16. November 1867 wurde die Ve
im Großherzoglich Mecklenburg-Schwerinschen D

Fig. 2. Preprocessing steps: original, greyvalue image, noise reduction, and binarisation

Die Mecklenburgischen Domainenbauern u
Verfassung.

Co

Mittelst eines an das Finanzministerium
Rescripts vom 16. November 1867 wurde die Be
im Großherzoglich Mecklenburg-Schwerinschen D

Die Mecklenburgischen Domainenbauern u
Verfassung.

Co

Mittelst eines an das Finanzministerium
Rescripts vom 16. November 1867 wurde die Be
im Großherzoglich Mecklenburg-Schwerinschen D

Fig. 3. Next preprocessing steps: Euklidean distance map (EDM), connected components extended by two points according to EDM, bilinear averaged background, and enhanced image to be used for describing the glyphs

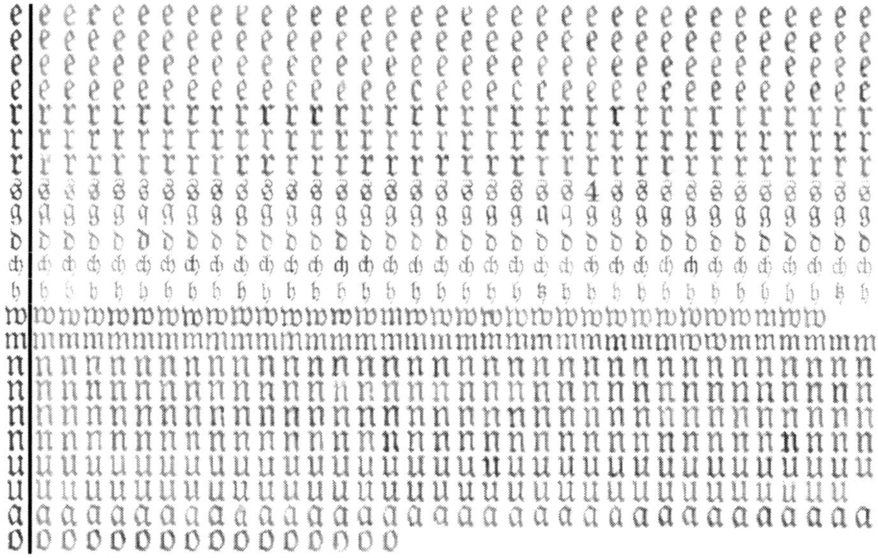

Fig. 4. Even similar glyphs could be told apart, as can be seen for the two glyph classes in the last two rows. But the compression is not optimal: among others, there are four classes for the glyph 'e', three 'r'-classes, four 'n'-classes, and two 'u'-classes.

can be combined to assemble to many different scopes. Counting their frequencies for each segment of a glyph, the scope histogram [10] is obtained. It describes the shape of a glyph in a significantly different way than other shape descriptions, why it in fact improves classification results when adding scope histograms to Hu moments and the other numeric features. Further improvements of this technique are expected by considering the orientation variance of glyphs which is neglected by all of the features used. Additionally, we aim at looking at interior contours of holes, entailing the consideration of more distinctive glyph properties which are, in our evaluation, solely taken into account by Hu's approach.

Current methods employed are computationally more expensive but result into better classification results. The horizontal and vertical profiles of single glyphs as well as a pixel correlation approach is employed [4]. The latter relates all image points to their neighbourhood with regard to their differences in grey tone values. By this means classification results are obtained with errors less than one per cent. A trade-off between this error rate and the compression rate of the obtained font representation is observed: the lower the compression rate the more precise the classification result and vice versa. Fig. 4 shows the classification results obtained for some similar glyph classes. The first column indicates the prototype glyph of a class, while all other objects in the same row pertain to the same class.

5   Reproduction of Glyphs

We aim at extracting document-specific fonts from historic document images. For their high-quality reproduction size, style and kerning information as well as subtle character

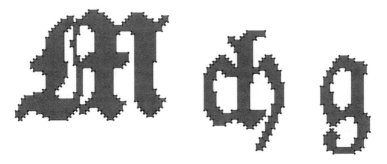

Fig. 5. Three examples for Fraktur letters: M, ch and g, generated by the described approach

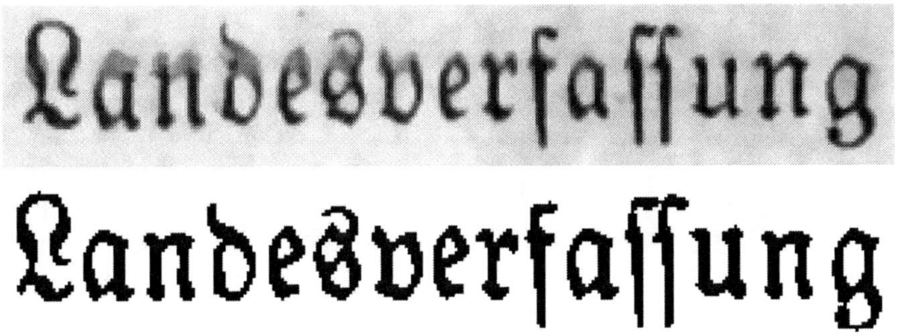

Fig. 6. Section from a document page including blurred glyphs which can be neatly reproduced

details are needed. Established optical character recognition methods are confined to correctly classifying glyphs. Here, however the idea is to assign unicode codepoints to prototype glyphs from the unicode 'private use area' and encode the generated fonts with unidentified glyphs. This allows reflowing of text and high speed text searches from examples – in essence a fast form of word spotting.

In detail, in order to generate a font, an edge following algorithm is applied on the binarised glyphs as well as on their holes, see Fig. 5. The obtained paths can directly be translated to SVG. In this way, it is possible to reproduce thousands of glyphs in a couple of seconds, meaning for a typical document page a processing of about ten seconds on a standard office laptop, on which no particular optimisation algorithms have been used.

Some of the advantages of the whole approach are illustrated in Fig. 6. A couple of the glyphs in this document are blurred. After the glyphs have been extracted and classified, each correctly classified glyph can be represented by a neat prototype glyph. Its SVG representation can eventually be scaled up and down arbitrarily, so that it fits the device where the document page is to be displayed. Figs. 7 and 8 in the appendix show two different examples with very different fonts and their final reproduction.

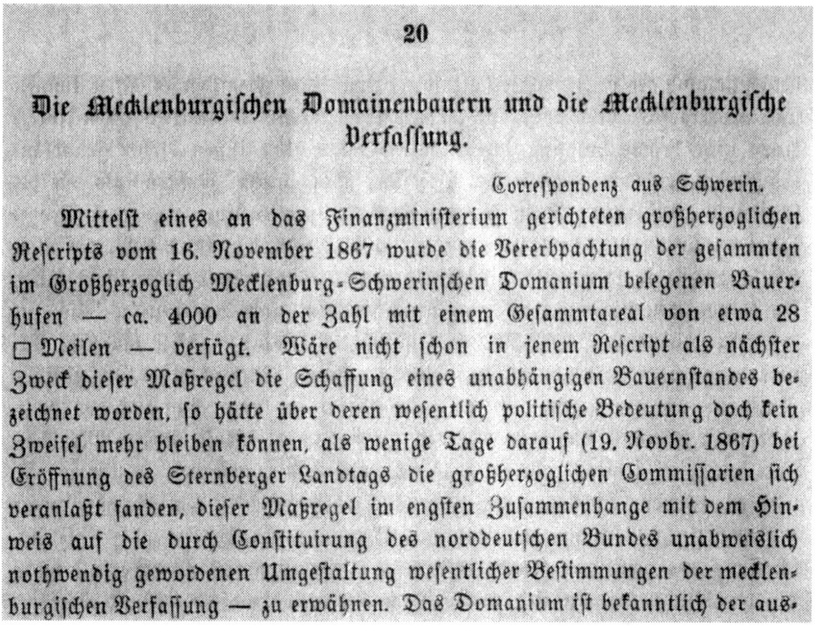

20

Die Mecklenburgischen Domainenbauern und die Mecklenburgische Verfassung.

Correspondenz aus Schwerin.

Mittelst eines an das Finanzministerium gerichteten großherzoglichen Rescripts vom 16. November 1867 wurde die Vererbpachtung der gesammten im Großherzoglich Mecklenburg-Schwerinschen Domanium belegenen Bauer-hufen — ca. 4000 an der Zahl mit einem Gesammtareal von etwa 28 ☐ Meilen — verfügt. Wäre nicht schon in jenem Rescript als nächster Zweck dieser Maßregel die Schaffung eines unabhängigen Bauernstandes be-zeichnet worden, so hätte über deren wesentlich politische Bedeutung doch kein Zweifel mehr bleiben können, als wenige Tage darauf (19. Novbr. 1867) bei Eröffnung des Sternberger Landtags die großherzoglichen Commissarien sich veranlaßt fanden, dieser Maßregel im engsten Zusammenhange mit dem Hin-weis auf die durch Constituirung des norddeutschen Bundes unabweislich nothwendig gewordenen Umgestaltung wesentlicher Bestimmungen der mecklen-burgischen Verfassung — zu erwähnen. Das Domanium ist bekanntlich der aus-

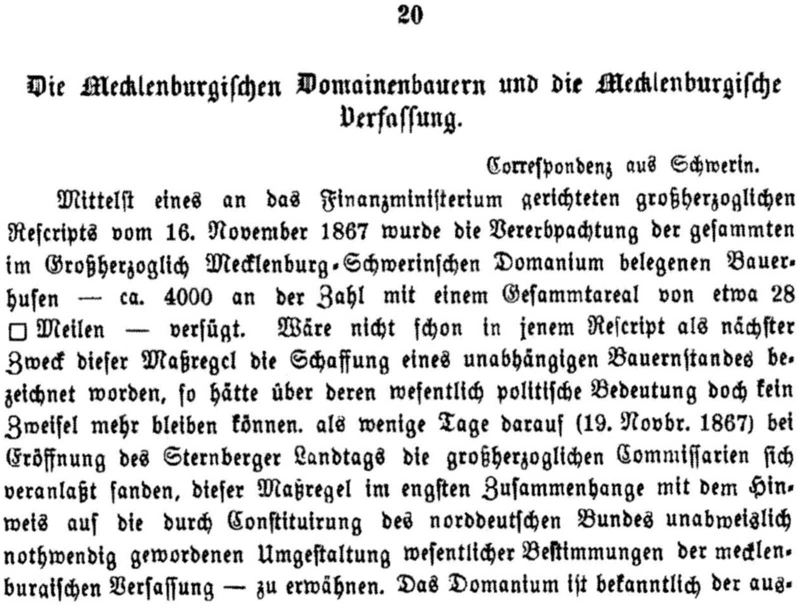

20

Die Mecklenburgischen Domainenbauern und die Mecklenburgische Verfassung.

Correspondenz aus Schwerin.

Mittelst eines an das Finanzministerium gerichteten großherzoglichen Rescripts vom 16. November 1867 wurde die Vererbpachtung der gesammten im Großherzoglich Mecklenburg-Schwerinschen Domanium belegenen Bauer-hufen — ca. 4000 an der Zahl mit einem Gesammtareal von etwa 28 ☐ Meilen — verfügt. Wäre nicht schon in jenem Rescript als nächster Zweck dieser Maßregel die Schaffung eines unabhängigen Bauernstandes be-zeichnet worden, so hätte über deren wesentlich politische Bedeutung doch kein Zweifel mehr bleiben können. als wenige Tage darauf (19. Novbr. 1867) bei Eröffnung des Sternberger Landtags die großherzoglichen Commissarien sich veranlaßt fanden, dieser Maßregel im engsten Zusammenhange mit dem Hin-weis auf die durch Constituirung des norddeutschen Bundes unabweislich nothwendig gewordenen Umgestaltung wesentlicher Bestimmungen der mecklen-buraischen Verfassung — zu erwähnen. Das Domanium ist bekanntlich der aus-

Fig. 7. Die Grenzboten, 28. Jahrgang, 2. Semester 1. Band, Leipzig 1869; SuUB, Bremen

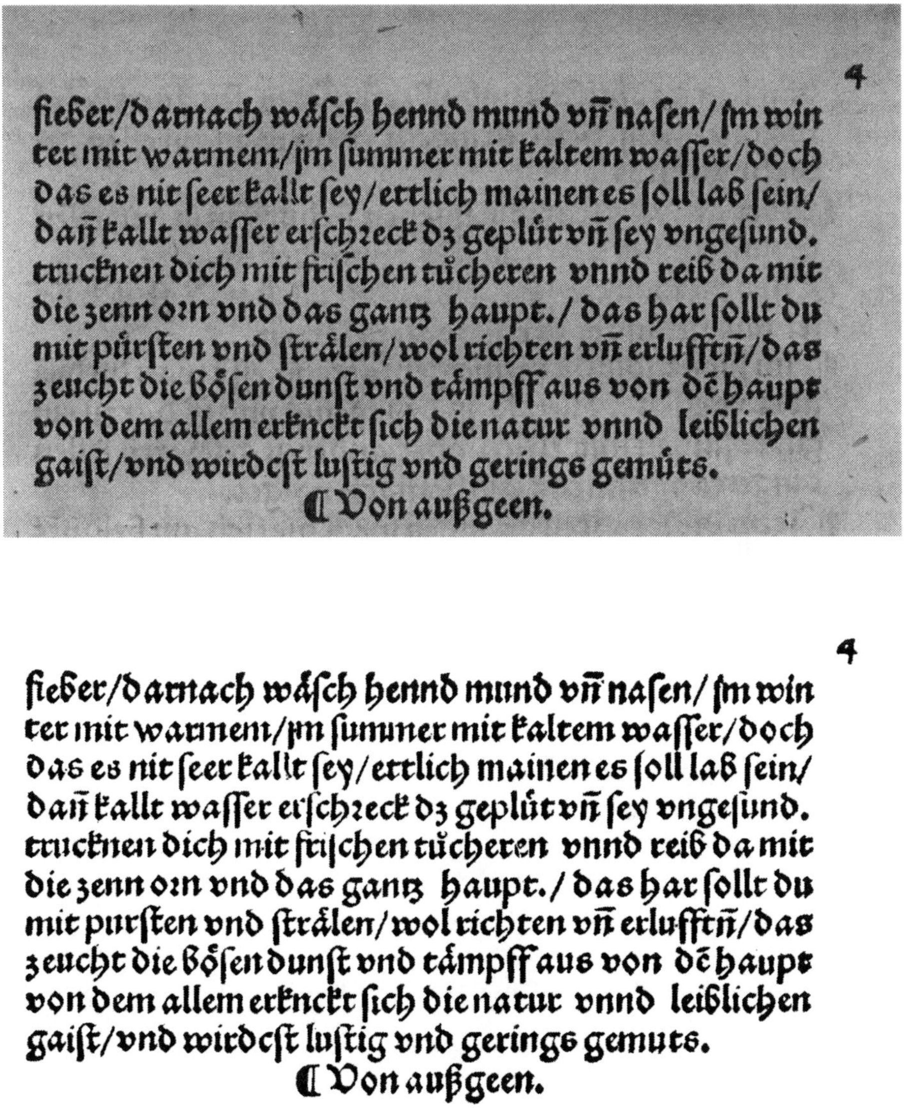

fieber/darnach wäsch hennd munnd vñ nasen/ym win
ter mit warmem/ym summer mit kaltem waffer/doch
das es nit feer kallt fey/ettlich mainen es foll laß fein/
dañ kallt waffer erfchzeck dz geplüt vñ fey vngefund.
trucknen dich mit frifchen tücheren vnnd reiß da mit
die zenn ozn vnd das gantz haupt./ das har follt du
mit pürften vnd fträlen/wol richten vñ erlufftñ/das
zeucht die böfen dunft vnd tämpff aus von dẽ haupt
von dem allem erknckt fich die natur vnnd leißlichen
gaift/vnd wirdeft luftig vnd gerings gemüts.
            ℂ Von außgeen.

fieber/darnach wäsch hennd munnd vñ nasen/ym win
ter mit warmem/ym summer mit kaltem waffer/doch
das es nit feer kallt fey/ettlich mainen es foll laß fein/
dañ kallt waffer erfchzeck dz geplüt vñ fey vngefund.
trucknen dich mit frifchen tücheren vnnd reiß da mit
die zenn ozn vnd das gantz haupt./ das har follt du
mit purften vnd fträlen/wol richten vñ erlufftñ/das
zeucht die böfen dunft vnd tämpff aus von dẽ haupt
von dem allem erknckt fich die natur vnnd leißlichen
gaift/vnd wirdeft luftig vnd gerings gemuts.
            ℂ Von außgeen.

Fig. 8. Ellenbog, Ulrich: Ain wunderbaere jnstruction und underwysung wider die pestilentz, Memmingen, Albrecht Kunne, 1494; Bayerische Staatsbibliothek

6   Discussion

Evaluations of the presented method already show promising results. However, much progress is expected regarding further investigations into how to improve the presented methods. For example, qualitative shape descriptions can be improved wit respect to many aspects. When they reach the same classification performance than the methods currently employed, they would significantly reduce the computational complexity.

A fundamental observation, however, is that it is hardly possible to obtain the same classification results as those described in this work for arbitrary documents. Historic documents, in particular, but also other complex documents which cannot be processed by optical character recognition methods available today, would benefit from the described approach. But the difficulties met with document images concern arbitrary kinds of noise, and also, every kind of complexity concerning the document layout. What we have left out in our current evaluations are diagrams, illustrations and images which can all occur on document images and which are to be separated from the text. Furthermore, the latter sometimes runs along more columns, posing yet other challenges. This list of difficulties can be extended ever more, making it impossible to process arbitrary documents automatically.

Because of the aforementioned difficulties, we aim at developing a kind of assistance system for document processing which makes use of automatic processing methods, which, however, can be adjusted by the user within every step. As a consequence, documents with an arbitrary complex contents and layout will be successfully dealt with, although not fully automatically. This is what our approach distinguishes from others who argue in favor of a fully automatic processing approach [8].

7   Future Challenges

Apart from the discussed document processing issues, new challenges will require a tighter and interlinked cooperation among researchers coming from different areas within the digital library community. Some of these challenges are as follows, showing the place of the presented work within the digital library community:

- There might be complex documents from all sorts of areas containing every kinds of sophisticated symbols which are to be transformed into a digital format; the methodology described in this paper will be of use in these cases.

- Complex documents to be analysed could benefit from other successful document processing projects that are well accessible through library catalogues which provide features about their source of origin. The latter might give great indications about the success of specific document processing parameters. Catalogues could be enriched with meta-data about such features.

- While the parsing of content takes place at a much more abstract level of document representation, failures in document processing might have been kept undetected. Dealing with known languages during grammatical parsing, such failures could be detected when the parsing fails itself. A link back to the document processing level would inform the latter about misspellings.

- Multilingual documents are faced with the problem of special characters that are specific to a given language, such as in German or Swedish. The document specific font of a document would include all available symbols since no restrictions are made regarding the presence of more than one alphabet.

- The organisation of repositories should take into account limitations met at the document image processing level. The resulting transformations might suffer from different problems and could be assigned with a particular grade of quality. This is of importance if the documents enter further anlysis tools.

- The context of the document image with all its characteristics could give hints about when, where, or under which circumstances the document has been written, printed, or published. This knowledge in turn can be of great value when evaluating the content itself.

- Specific problems at the level of language analysis, such as disambiguation, could benefit from background knowledge obtained with the aid of the underlying document. That is, it might be impossible to resolve ambiguities at the linguistic level, but when deriving the age of some given document, background knowledge can inform us about the possibility that specific meanings of a word or a phrase would make sense for a given period.

- Data integration at a rather basic level can benefit from and make use of the same knowledge as in the previous examples, namely concerning whatever can be derived from the document images about the period when the document has been published or from which location it is.

- Document retrieval can take place at different levels of abstraction. Digital content can be easily accessed at the symbolic level, employing all currently available means of search engines. But document images which could not be translated into a text format with a sufficient grade of quality can instead be searched by query-by-example [1] or even with the aid of query-by-sketch approaches [2].

This list is presumably not complete. But it shows the diversity of future challenges and indicates the broad spectrum of methods necessary from different areas. Scientists from those areas have to collaborate closely to manage these challenges.

8 Summary

This paper presents a method for extracting texts from images. As opposed to optical character recognition methods, no assumptions are made regarding the underlying language. Instead documents can be processed which are made of an arbitrary large and complex symbol set.

The overall goal is not confined to present that method. Rather, links to other areas within the scientific community of digital libraries are established in order to provide an agenda for future research that will deal with ever more complex challenges for dealing with and managing documents at all conceivable levels.

Acknowledgements

This work was partially funded by the DFG (Deutsche Forschungsgemeinschaft), project Venod (HE 989/10-1). The 'Staats- und Universitätsbibliothek' Bremen and the 'Bayerische Staatsbibliothek', Munich, provided many fine examples of historic printed document images.

References

1. Flickner, M., Sawhney, W., Niblack, H., Ashley, J., Huang, Q., Dom, B., Gorkani, M., Hafner, J., Lee, D., Petkovic, D., Steele, D., Yanker, P.: Query by Image and Video Content: The QBIC System. Computer 28, 23–32 (1995)
2. Gottfried, B.: Shape from Positional-Contrast — Characterising Sketches with Qualitative Line Arrangements. DUV - Deutscher Universitätsverlag, Springer Science+Business Media, Wiesbaden (2007)
3. Gottfried, B.: Qualitative Similarity Measures - The Case of Two-Dimensional Outlines. Computer Vision and Image Understanding 110(1), 117–133 (2008)
4. Ho, T.K.: Random decision forests. In: ICDAR 1995: Proceedings of the Third International Conference on Document Analysis and Recognition, p. 278. IEEE Computer Society Press, Washington, DC, USA (1995)
5. Hu, M.-K.: Visual pattern recognition by moment invariants. IRE Transactions on Information Theory 8(2), 179–187 (1962)
6. Lee, J.-S.: Digital image smoothing and the sigma filter. Computer Vision, Graphics, and Image Processing 24(2), 255–269 (1983)
7. Meyer-Lerbs, L., Schuldt, A., Gottfried, B.: Glyph extraction from historic document images. In: Proceedings of the 2010 ACM Symposium on Document Engineering. ACM, New York (2010)
8. Pletschacher, S.: A self-adaptive method for extraction of document-specific alphabets. In: ICDAR 2009: Proceedings of the 10th International Conference on Document Analysis and Recognition, pp. 656–660. IEEE Computer Society, Los Alamitos (2009)
9. Sauvola, J., Pietikäinen, M.: Adaptive document image binarization. Pattern Recognition 33(2), 225–236 (2000)
10. Schuldt, A., Gottfried, B., Herzog, O.: Towards the visualisation of shape features the scope histogram. In: Freksa, C., Kohlhase, M., Schill, K. (eds.) KI 2006. LNCS (LNAI), vol. 4314, pp. 289–301. Springer, Heidelberg (2007)
11. Shafait, F., Keysers, D., Breuel, T.M.: Efficient implementation of local adaptive thresholding techniques using integral images. In: Document Recognition and Retrieval XV, San Jose, CA, p. 6 (January 2008)

Hierarchical Classification of OAI Metadata Using the DDC Taxonomy

Ulli Waltinger[1], Alexander Mehler[2], Mathias Lösch, and Wolfram Horstmann

[1] Bielefeld University - Artificial Intelligence Group, Germany
[2] Goethe University Frankfurt, Institute of Computer Science
Bielefeld University Library, Germany
uwalting@techfak.uni-bielefeld.de
mehler@em.uni-frankfurt.de
{mathias.loesch,wolfram.horstmann}@uni-bielefeld.de

Abstract. In the area of digital library services, the access to subject-specific metadata of scholarly publications is of utmost interest. One of the most prevalent approaches for metadata exchange is the XML-based *Open Archive Initiative* (OAI) *Protocol for Metadata Harvesting* (OAI-PMH). However, due to its loose requirements regarding metadata content there is no strict standard for consistent subject indexing specified, which is furthermore needed in the digital library domain. This contribution addresses the problem of automatic enhancement of OAI metadata by means of the most widely used universal classification schemes in libraries—the *Dewey Decimal Classification* (DDC). To be more specific, we automatically classify scientific documents according to the DDC taxonomy within three levels using a machine learning-based classifier that relies solely on OAI metadata records as the document representation. The results show an asymmetric distribution of documents across the hierarchical structure of the DDC taxonomy and issues of data sparseness. However, the performance of the classifier shows promising results on all three levels of the DDC.

Keywords: Digital Library, Dewey Decimal Classification, OAI-PMH, SVM, Hierarchical Classification.

1   Introduction

Over the past years, an enormous amount of academic work has been published electronically on the Web, posing new challenges to the domain of digital library services. Enabling users to access this mass of scholarly information in a structured manner is thereby of utmost interest to the community. In this context, document servers storing scientific documents and their metadata (so-called *repositories*) became a major backbone of scholarly communication. Currently, the most prevalent approach for metadata exchange is the *Open Archive Initiative* (OAI) *Protocol for Metadata Harvesting* (OAI-PMH)[1]. The protocol defines

---

[1] http://www.openarchives.org/OAI/openarchivesprotocol.html

R. Bernardi et al. (Eds.): NLP4DL/AT4DL 2009, LNCS 6699, pp. 29–40, 2011.

an XML-based data format and a simple communication framework that serve as a basis for building value-added services (e.g. federated search) on top of aggregated metadata [1]. An explicit design goal of OAI-PMH was to keep the barriers for its implementation as low as possible. This is also reflected in the structure of the OAI metadata format, where the minimal requirements for expressing a valid record are fairly loose—the common baseline is defined by the *Dublin Core Metadata Element Set* [2], whereas all fields are optional. Because of this simplicity, OAI-PMH quickly became widely adopted by digital libraries around the globe. However, the practices of metadata management wildly differ across repositories [3,4,5], which holds especially true for subject indexing. Hence, aside from subject headings and free keywords, a wide range of classification schemes both universal and subject-specific are in use [5]. In terms of building value-added services for digital libraries, this is a severe problem, as many potential services would require consistent subject indexing—think, for example, of federated topic-based browsing the contents of several different repositories. That is, normalizing the heterogenous subject indexing of OAI records from different repositories is central to the debate of an enhanced search experience within the digital library domain.

This contribution addresses the problem of automatic enhancement and normalization of OAI metadata records in terms of subject indexing according to the *Dewey Decimal Classification* (DDC) [6]. The DDC is a hierarchical library taxonomy (see Table 1 for an excerpt) and one of the most widely used universal classification schemes worldwide. Our general aim is to automatically assign Dewey numbers to OAI metadata records in order to introduce a consistent subject indexing. More specifically, we explore the hierarchical structure of the DDC taxonomy within three levels using a machine learning-based text classifier. We argue that through the categorization of documents (represented through OAI records) according to their (DDC-oriented) topic, whereas topics are organized in a hierarchy of increasing specificity [7], a better perception of the provided information by the user may be fulfilled. For the actual classification task, we make use of *Support Vector Machines* (SVM), which have been shown to be efficient and effective for text classification.

The rest of the paper is structured as follows. In Section 2 we discuss the related work with regards to hierarchical text categorization and OAI metadata enhancement. Section 3 presents the experimental methodology of the hierarchical classification of OAI metadata. In Section 4 we provide the results with regards to corpus characteristics and classifier performance. We conclude in Section 5 with some discussion and directions for future work.

Table 1. Outline of the top three levels of the DDC

No.	Label
600	Technology
630	– Agriculture and related technologies
636	– – Animal husbandry

2 Related Work

Currently, the user's need for information on the web is primarily served by search engines and their linear list of resultant website snippets. Just like OAI metadata-based document representations, web search snippets can be regarded as short content summaries of the underlying (web) documents. In this regard, several approaches have been proposed on result-list classification in order to identify different categories or genres, focusing on different levels of granularity [8,9], or using variations of the suffix tree clustering [10,11,12,13]. Although these approaches also use a minimized document representation, by means of search result snippets only, they primarily aim to identify meaningful keywords which subsequently serve as representative topic labels for the resultant document clusters. With reference to the use of hierarchies for text classification, several approaches have been proposed. Most studies in this area have focused on a flat classification, where predefined categories are treated individually and separately [14]. Others introduced hierarchical document classification approaches by using automatically generated hierarchies inter alia using linear discriminant projection to generate more meaningful intermediate levels of hierarchies [15,16]. In the context of a two-level-based hierarchical classification, Dumais and Chen (2000) [17] have proposed a method for classifying web documents into a two-level hierarchy web directory using a supervised text classifier. Our approach differs in terms of that not only an universal classification taxonomy (the DDC) as target scheme is used but also OAI metadata information only as a reference point for the classification task.

With regards to an subject metadata enhancement the project *CrissCross* [18], a cooperation between German National Library and Cologne University of Applied Sciences aims to produce a mapping between the *German Subject Headings Authority File* (SWD) and the DDC. The proposed *Degree of Determinacy* technique is based on a string matching / overlap algorithm between SWD and DDC keyword cluster. More precisely, significant terms of the SWD are interrelated to DDC categories and subsequently summarized into subject heading cluster. With reference to the application of machine learning techniques to the domain of digital libraries, Krowne and Halbert (2005) [19] presented a comparative evaluation of four automatically generated browsing interfaces based on different classification schemes. The authors used between 21 and 25 different categories as their classification schemes and represented each record by concatenating the Dublin Core fields *title*, *description*, and *subject fields*. Subsequently, different classification and clustering techniques (*SVM, Naïve Bayes, Rochio*, and *kNN*) on the article set of the *Encyclopedia of Southern Culture* were applied. The evaluation was based on user feedback of 144 participants (e.g. comment, event, and click-through-rate). The results showed that the *Rochio* classifier outperformed all other models by a significant margin.

In Hagedorn et al. (2007) [20] the authors present a two-fold strategy for automatically enhancing OAI metadata records. At first, they applied an automated clustering technique (*Latent Dirichlet Allocation*) to create 500 different topic clusters of OAI metadata records. Once more, the contents of the Dublin Core *title*, *subject* and *description* fields served as input for document representation. Subsequently, the cluster labels were mapped onto an in-house classification system. More precisely, volunteers mapped each generated cluster label onto one or more sub-level categories of the classification scheme.

Wang (2009) [21] presents a semi-automatic DDC classifier operating on a corpus of records in the *Machine-Readable Cataloging* (MARC) format. In particular, the author proposes a method for restructuring the DDC category tree by merging categories, and flattening or chopping sub-trees. By this means, the author forms a more balanced data set to overcome problems of data sparseness resulting from a skewed distribution of documents across categories. SVM classifiers trained on this restructured data set outperformed a Naïve Bayes baseline model, and achieved a classification accuracy of nearly 90% in the best case. However, the described approach requires human interaction during the prediction phase to achieve acceptable performance values.

In Mehler and Waltinger (2009) [22] a topic classification model using the DDC as the target scheme is presented. The authors present two different DDC-related classifier (*Search Engine Quotient* and *Wikipedia*-based *Open Topic Model*) and evaluated several content-related classifiers (e.g. *Latent Semantic Analysis*) used in digital libraries. The results show that SVM-based classifier in combination with the content fields of the Dublin Core scheme performs best. In this context, we continue this approach in combining a machine learning-based text classifier with the exploration of OAI metadata records as a source of document representation, while focusing on the *hierarchical structure* of the DDC as the target classification scheme.

Table 2. Outline of the OAI metadata record of Dimitrov et al. (2009) [23]. Dots indicated omitted content.

```
 1   ...
 2      <record>
 3         <metadata>
 4           <oai_dc:dc xmlns:oai_dc="http://www.openarchives.org/OAI/2.0/oai_dc/" ... >
 5             <dc:title>Computing Principal Components Dynamically</dc:title>
 6             <dc:creator>Dimitrov, Darko</dc:creator>
 7             <dc:creator>Holst, Mathias</dc:creator>
 8             <dc:creator>Knauer, Christian</dc:creator>
 9             <dc:creator>Kriegel, Klaus</dc:creator>
10             <dc:subject>Computer Science - Graphics</dc:subject>
11             <dc:subject>Computer Science - Computational Geometry</dc:subject>
12             <dc:description>
13                 In this paper we present closed-form ...
14             </dc:description>
15             <dc:description>
16                 Comment: 32 pages, 4 figures
17             </dc:description>
18             <dc:date>2009-12-30</dc:date>
19             <dc:type>text</dc:type>
20             <dc:identifier>http://arxiv.org/abs/0912.5380</dc:identifier>
21           </oai_dc:dc>
22         </metadata>
23      </record>
24   ...
```

3   Hierarchical Classification of OAI Metadata

In this section, we describe the method used for the hierarchical classification of OAI metadata records. The basic idea behind our approach is to use SVM-based text classifier to automatically assign Dewey numbers to an existing set of unlabeled OAI metadata records in order to introduce a consistent subject indexing. This approach implies two contraints, which are important within this kind of classification scenario. First, our general goal is to automatically classify scientific documents, journals and presentations with up to 100 pages, though using a reduced document representation for the actual classification task (Section 3.1). Second, we focus on the hierachical structure of the DDC taxonomy within three levels using the numerical notation as the target categories. Though, documents may be classified into multiple categories within the DDC hierarchy (Section 3.2).

3.1   OAI Metadata Representation

We approach the task of classifying documents by relying solely on their metadata records. That is, we do not take into account the actual full texts. Instead, we represent each document by the contents of the *title*, *subject* and *description* fields [19,20] of its OAI record (see Table 2). Previous work [22] has already shown that promising classification results can be achieved this way — at least when using the top level of the DDC. Consequently, we are interested in the classification performance when applying this methodology to the *hierarchical structure* of the DDC, as a start restricted to its top three levels. With regards to training and evaluation corpus construction, we used the OAI data set aggregated by *Bielefeld Academic Search Engine* (BASE) [5], since BASE is currently one of the largest OAI service providers with more than 25 million OAI records aggregated. For each available OAI record, we determined whether a reference Dewey number was present. Next, we performed the preprocessing [24] with regards to language identification and lemmatization of the used *Dublin Core* fields. At last, we constructed two separate data sets for English and German data containing the preprocessed records that were labeled with their reference Dewey numbers. Note that we selected only those records for corpus construction whose *Dublin Core description* fields (that usually hold the abstract of the document) contained more than 100 bytes of text to avoid problems of data sparseness ($5,868$ English and $7,473$ German records). With respect to the second and third level categorization of the DDC, we had to reduce the minimum size to 30 bytes in order to have sufficient training data ($20,813$ English and $37,769$ German metadata records).

3.2   SVM-Based Classification

For the classification of the OAI records, we used the kernel-based classification method of *Support Vector Machines* (SVMs)[2]. SVMs have already shown their

---

[2] SVM^{light} [25].

Fig. 1. Results of SVM classification on the second level ordered by F1-Measure (y-axis) and SVM-Index (x-axis) using German OAI-Data

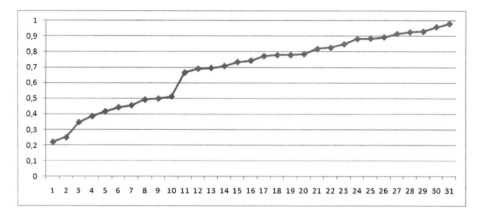

Fig. 2. Results of SVM classification on the third level ordered by F1-Measure (y-axis) and SVM-Index (x-axis) using German OAI-Data

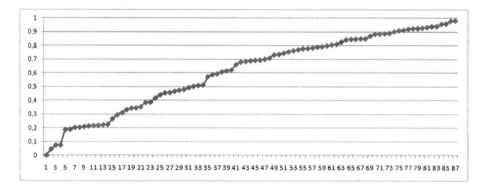

capacities for the task of text but also metadata categorization [22,25]. In general, an SVM is formalized to determine a hyperplane between the positive and negative training examples by predicting the best parameter that maximizes the distance (margin of the hyperplane) between both sets. With regards to the hierarchical structure of the DDC, we applied a three-level strategy for the classification task. That is, a separate binary classifier is learned to distinguish each class from all other classes within the same level of the target scheme. Note that any input record can be categorized into none, one, or even more than one categories within each level. More precisely, while having on the top level 10 categories given, the second level of the DDC includes 100 divisions, while the third level comprises 1,000 possible classes. Finally, we applied TF-IDF [26] as feature weighting function to build the OAI-based real-valued feature vectors used for the training of the SVMs. For each DDC-class within the same level of specificity, a separate SVM was trained in a *one-against-all* setting using a linear kernel. The results were evaluated using the *leave-one-out cross-validation* estimation reporting *F1*-Measure as the harmonic mean between *precision* and *recall*.

4   Results

With regards to the results of the OAI-classification experiments using the first-level of the DDC as the target scheme (see Tables 3–4), we can identify a reasonable classification accuracy. Using a minimized document representation by means of OAI records for the classification task, we were able to achieve an *F1*-Measure of 0.81 for the English language and an *F1*-Measure of 0.79 for the

Table 3. Results of SVM classification on the first level of the DDC using German OAI-Data

DDC	Precision	Recall	F1-Measure
000	0.948	0.878	0.915
100	0.906	0.815	0.925
200	0.903	0.720	0.888
300	0.852	0.691	0.871
400	0.828	0.621	0.896
500	0.868	0.819	0.922
600	0.856	0.764	0.770
700	0.812	0.631	0.299
800	0.805	0.620	0.775
900	0.878	0.745	0.355
Overall	0.866	0.730	0.791

Table 4. Results of SVM classification on the first level of the DDC using English OAI-Data

DDC	Precision	Recall	F1-Measure
000	0.932	0.887	0.909
100	0.959	0.911	0.934
200	0.954	0.757	0.844
300	0.951	0.890	0.919
400	0.943	0.858	0.899
500	0.827	0.808	0.817
600	0.807	0.735	0.768
700	0.887	0.496	0.636
800	0.833	0.492	0.619
900	0.911	0.642	0.753
Overall	0.900	0.747	0.810

Fig. 3. Results of SVM classification on the second level ordered by F1-Measure (y-axis) and SVM-Index (x-axis) using English OAI-Data

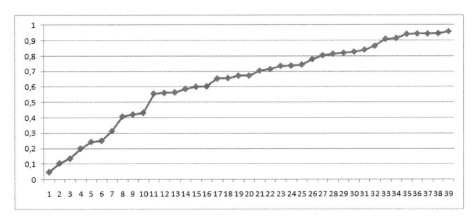

Table 5. Results of SVM classification on the second level within division 30−39 of the DDC using German OAI-Data

DDC	Precision	Recall	F1-Measure
300	0.795	0.619	0.696
310	0.633	0.432	0.513
320	0.904	0.761	0.826
330	0.936	0.893	0.915
340	0.930	0.847	0.886
350	0.947	0.882	0.913
360	0.845	0.722	0.779
370	0.885	0.816	0.849
380	0.881	0.642	0.743
390	0.860	0.711	0.779
Overall	0.862	0.732	0.790

Table 6. Results of SVM classification on the second level within division 50−59 of the DDC using English OAI-Data

DDC	Precision	Recall	F1-Measure
500	0.479	0.163	0.243
510	0.970	0.947	0.958
520	0.880	0.768	0.820
530	0.933	0.897	0.915
540	0.841	0.768	0.803
550	0.858	0.773	0.814
560	—	—	—
570	0.879	0.850	0.864
580	0.381	0.136	0.200
590	0.852	0.418	0.561
Overall	0.786	0.635	0.686

Table 7. Results of SVM classification on the third level within division 610−619 of the DDC using German OAI-Data

DDC	Precision	Recall	F1-Measure
610	0.910	0.836	0.871
611	0.833	0.217	0.345
612	0.167	0.026	0.045
613	0.500	0.139	0.218
614	—	—	—
615	0.533	0.127	0.205
616	0.817	0.606	0.696
617	0.857	0.481	0.617
618	—	—	—
619	—	—	—
Overall	0.659	0.347	0.428

Table 8. Results of SVM classification on the second level within division 000 − 009 of the DDC using English OAI-Data

DDC	Precision	Recall	F1-Measure
000	0.982	0.965	0.973
001	—	—	—
002	—	—	—
003	—	—	—
004	0.929	0.914	0.921
005	—	—	—
006	0.454	0.217	0.294
007	—	—	—
008	—	—	—
009	—	—	—
Overall	0.788	0.698	0.729

Table 9. Average F1-Measure results of SVM classification within three-level depth of the DDC using German OAI-Data

Level	No	Precision	Recall	F1-Measure
1	10	0.866	0.730	0.791
2	31	0.841	0.682	0.744
3	87	0.763	0.545	0.611

Table 10. Average F1-Measure results of SVM classification within three-level depth of the DDC using English OAI-Data

Level	No	Precision	Recall	F1-Measure
1	10	0.900	0.747	0.810
2	39	0.784	0.556	0.631
3	39	0.769	0.545	0.616

Fig. 4. Results of SVM classification on the third level ordered by F1-Measure (y-axis) and SVM-Index (x-axis) using English OAI-Data

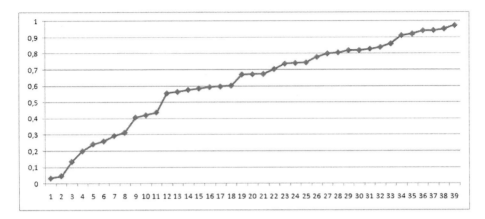

Fig. 5. Distribution of German OAI records within the second-level of DDC by corpus size (y-axis) and SVM-Index (x-axis) (ordered by F1-Measure)

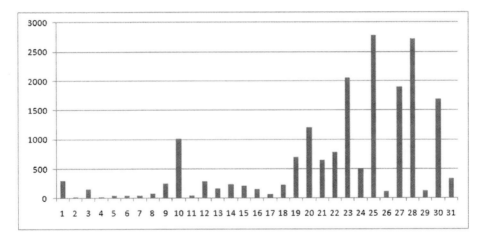

German language. With reference to previous results [22], we could improve the performance of the classifier to a nearly acceptable level. Obviously, increasing the size of the feature set, in terms of using a larger corpus of OAI records, also increases classification accuracy.

The results of the entire classification experiments utilizing the entire DDC taxonomy are depicted in Table 9 and Table 10. With an average F1-Measure of 0.74 (German) and 0.63 (English) for the second level, and an average F1-Measure of 0.61 (German) and 0.62 (English) on the third level, promising results can be achieved (see Figures 1, 2, 3, and 4). However, even though the entire DDC taxonomy comprises 1,110 different categories in total, we were only able to use 128 for the German and 88 categories for the English language. The reason

Fig. 6. Distribution of English OAI records within the second-level of DDC by corpus size (y-axis) and SVM-Index (x-axis) (ordered by F1-Measure)

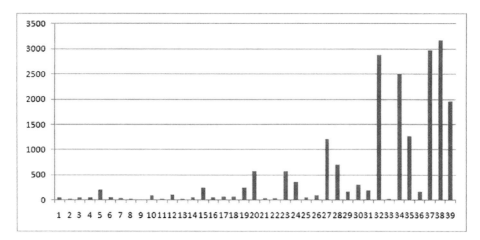

for this is that we could not populate all the categories with positive training examples. Note that we predefined that each trained DDC category must have at least 15 metadata records assigned in order to be successful trained. As Table 5 and 6 depict, categories with sufficient training examples assigned show good results in terms of classification accuracy. However, on the third level (see Table 5 and 6) only few categories are covered with a sufficent number of positive examples. More precisely, the used corpus features show an asymmetric distribution (see Figure 5 and 6) of documents across the classes (issues of data sparseness). That is, while some disciplines have a stronger document representation (e.g. natural science), others (e.g. humanistic) do not even exist. Considering only the second DDC level, we were only able to populate not even about half of the classes with enough positive examples. While our general approach seems promising, we need to overcome problems of data sparseness in our future work.

5   Conclusion

This contribution addressed an automatic enhancement of OAI metadata by means of the *Dewey Decimal Classification*. We explored the hierarchical structure of the DDC taxonomy within a three-level-based specificity using kernel-based Support Vector Machines to classify OAI metadata records. For document representation, only the contents of the Dublin Core *title*, *subject* and *description* fields were used. The results show an asymmetric distribution of documents across the hierarchical structure of the DDC taxonomy. The hierarchical machine learning classifier showed with an average $F1$-Measure of 0.61–0.81 promising results.

Acknowledgement

We gratefully acknowledge financial support of the German Research Foundation (DFG) through the DFG LIS project *Automatic Enhancement of OAI Metadata by means of Computational Linguistics Methodology and Development of Services for a Content-based Network of Repositories* and through the EC 277 *Cognitive Interaction Technology* at Bielefeld University.

References

1. Lagoze, C., Van de Sompel, H.: The open archives initiative: Building a low-barrier interoperability framework. In: Proceedings of the 1st ACM/IEEE-CS Joint Conference on Digital Libraries, pp. 54–62. ACM, New York (2001)
2. Dublin Core Metadata Initiative, Dublin Core Metadata Element Set, Version 1.1 (2008)
3. Stvilia, B., Gasser, L., Twidale, M.B., Shreeves, S.L., Cole, T.W.: Metadata quality for federated collections. In: Proceedings of the 9th International Conference on Information Quality, ICIQ 2004, Cambridge, MA, pp. 111–125 (2004)
4. Tennant, R.: Digital libraries: Metadata's bitter harvest. Library Journal 12 (2004)
5. Pieper, D., Summann, F.: Bielefeld Academic Search Engine (BASE): An end-user oriented institutional repository search service. Library Hi Tech. 24(4), 614–619 (2006)
6. Dewey, M., Mitchell, J.S., Alex, H.: Dewey Dezimalklassifikation und Register: DDC 22, 22 edn. Saur, München (2005)
7. Koller, D., Sahami, M.: Hierarchically classifying documents using very few words. In: ICML 1997: Proceedings of the Fourteenth International Conference on Machine Learning, pp. 170–178. Morgan Kaufmann Publishers Inc., San Francisco (1997)
8. Cutting, D., Karger, D., Pedersen, J., Tukey, J.W.: Scatter/gather: A cluster-based approach to browsing large document collections. In: Proceedings of the 15th Annual International ACM/SIGIR Conference, Copenhagen (1992)
9. Hearst, M.A., Pedersen, J.O.: Reexamining the cluster hypothesis:scatter/gather on retrieval results. In: Proceedings of SIGIR 1996, 19th ACM International Conference on Research and Development in Information Retrieval, Zurich, pp. 76–84 (1996)
10. Zamir, O., Etzioni, O.: Grouper: a dynamic clustering interface to web search results. In: Proceedings of the Eighth International World Wide Web Conference, Toronto (1999)
11. Stefanowski, J., Weiss, D.: Carrot^2 and language properties in web search results clusterings. In: AWIC 2003. LNCS (LNAI), vol. 2663, Springer, Heidelberg (2003)
12. zu Eissen, S.M.:On Information Need and Categorizing Search. Dissertation, University of Paderborn (February 2007)
13. Stein, B., Meyer zu Eißen, S.: Automatic Document Categorization: Interpreting the Perfomance of Clustering Algorithms. In: Günter, A., Kruse, R., Neumann, B. (eds.) KI 2003. LNCS (LNAI), vol. 2821, pp. 254–266. Springer, Heidelberg (2003)
14. Li, T., Zhu, S., Ogihara, M.: Topic hierarchy generation via linear discriminant projection. In: SIGIR 2003: Proceedings of the 26th Annual International ACM SIGIR Conference on Research and Development in Informaion Retrieval, pp. 421–422. ACM, New York (2003)

15. Li, T., Zhu, S., Ogihara, M.: Hierarchical document classification using automatically generated hierarchy. J. Intell. Inf. Syst. 29(2), 211–230 (2007)
16. Zhu, C., Ma, J., Zhang, D., Han, X., Niu, X.: Hierarchical document classification based on a backtracking algorithm. In: Proceedings of the Fifth International Conference on Fuzzy Systems and Knowledge Discovery, FSKD 2008, Jinan, Shandong, China, October 18-20, pp. 467–471 (2008)
17. Dumais, S., Chen, H.: Hierarchical classification of web content. In: SIGIR 2000: Proceedings of the 23rd Annual International ACM SIGIR Conference on Research and Development in Information Retrieval, pp. 256–263. ACM, New York (2000)
18. Hubrich, J.: CrissCross: SWD-DDC-Mapping. Mitteilungen der Vereinigung Österreichischer Bibliothekarinnen & Bibliothekare 61(3), 50–58 (2008)
19. Krowne, A., Halbert, M.: An initial evaluation of automated organization for digital library browsing. In: Proceedings of the 5th ACM/IEEE-CS Joint Conference on Digital Libraries, pp. 246–255. ACM, New York (2005)
20. Hagedorn, K., Chapman, S., Newman, D.: Enhancing search and browse using automated clustering of subject metadata. D-Lib Magazine 13(7/8) (2007)
21. Wang, J.: An extensive study on automated Dewey Decimal Classification. Journal of the American Society for Information Science and Technology (JASIST) 60(11), 2269–2286 (2009)
22. Mehler, A., Waltinger, U.: Enhancing document modeling by means of open topic models: Crossing the frontier of classification schemes in digital libraries by example of the DDC. Library Hi Tech. 27(4), 520–539 (2009)
23. Dimitrov, D., Holst, M., Knauer, C., Kriegel, K.: Computing principal components dynamically. CoRR abs/0912.5380 (2009)
24. Mehler, A., Gleim, R., Ernst, A., Waltinger, U.: WikiDB: Building interoperable wiki-based knowledge resources for semantic databases. International Journal for Language Data Processing Sprache und Datenverarbeitung 32, 47–70 (2008)
25. Joachims, T.: Learning to Classify Text Using Support Vector Machines: Methods, Theory and Algorithms. Kluwer Academic Publishers, Norwell (2002)
26. Salton, G., Buckley, C.: Term-weighting approaches in automatic text retrieval. Information Processing and Management 24(5), 513–523 (1988)

Moving towards Adaptive Search in Digital Libraries

Udo Kruschwitz[1], M-Dyaa Albakour[1], Jinzhong Niu[1], Johannes Leveling[2], Nikolaos Nanas[3], Yunhyong Kim[4], Dawei Song[4], Maria Fasli[1], and Anne De Roeck[5]

[1] University of Essex, Colchester, UK
{udo,malbak}@essex.ac.uk
[2] Dublin City University, Dublin, Ireland
[3] Centre for Research and Technology, Thessaly, Greece
[4] Robert Gordon University, Aberdeen, UK
[5] Open University, Milton Keynes, UK

Abstract. Search applications have become very popular over the last two decades, one of the main drivers being the advent of the Web. Nevertheless, searching on the Web is very different to searching on smaller, often more structured collections such as digital libraries, local Web sites, and intranets. One way of helping the searcher locating the right information for a specific information need in such a collection is by providing well-structured domain knowledge to assist query modification and navigation. There are two main challenges which we will both address in this chapter: acquiring the domain knowledge and adapting it automatically to the specific interests of the user community. We will outline how in digital libraries a domain model can automatically be acquired using search engine query logs and how it can be continuously updated using methods resembling ant colony behaviour.

1 Introduction

Document retrieval systems have been around for more than fifty years, and early systems exploited similar structures to those we have in modern digital libraries, such as author name, book title, and keywords [33]. With the advent of the Web things have changed however and searchers are now very used to simple search interfaces that take a few keywords and return a list of matches. In fact, this is the type of search paradigm we might expect nowadays no matter what collection is being searched for. The problem is that Web search is fundamentally different to searches where users are not just interested in getting *some* matching documents but where they are looking for specific documents, memos, spreadsheets, books, etc. Such information requests are not necessarily best served by a single-shot unstructured query. This type of search is very common in enterprise search which runs on smaller, often more structured collections [21,48,39]. This suggests that search over digital libraries with their inherently structured contents resembles enterprise search much more than generic Web search and we argue that offering some guidance in an interactive search process could actively help the user find the actual documents he or she is after.

How can a user be guided in the search process? Library classification schemes like the *Universal Decimal Classification*[1] (UDC) have been used for decades and have

---

[1] http://www.udcc.org/

R. Bernardi et al. (Eds.): NLP4DL/AT4DL 2009, LNCS 6699, pp. 41–60, 2011.

been demonstrated to be very useful when classifying books. The drawback that these manually encoded classification schemes have is that they lack flexibility. Furthermore, they represent a structured view of the world but that view may not be the view that an *online* searcher has. Suppose, a university's digital library contains a large number of books on information retrieval. They might all be classified under the same code but this will not tell us anything about their relevance or about how users would associate them with other books. We could on the other hand rely on automatically acquired knowledge structures (e.g. domain models, taxonomies, association graphs etc) derived from the document collection. But again, without continuously updating the models they will become out of date as the document collection changes or the users start to view it differently. For example, new concepts are introduced, others disappear and the books that are popular today may not have the same relevance in half a year's time.

The approach that we take is to use log data to build an adaptive domain model automatically. We are looking at search as well as navigation and our aim is to satisfy a user's information request effectively by learning from the entire user population and incorporating this learned knowledge in a constantly adapting domain model. This domain model would assist a user in the search process and reflect the collection characteristics. This is different from building *individual* user profiles. In other words, we exploit the "wisdom of the crowd" to build up knowledge structures automatically and update them constantly as new queries come in. Unlike UDC, the emerging structures are not semantically encoded. They will however encode relations between query terms that reflect how users see and navigate the collection and should represent a bridge between the users' vocabulary and the contents of the collection. To use the earlier example, a user who searches for *"information retrieval"* might be given suggestions to narrow down (or modify) the search such as *"rijsbergen"*, *"bruce croft"*, *"modern information retrieval 2nd edition"* or *"manning and schütze"*. This will allow users to benefit from each other by incorporating *social search* in digital libraries *without* trying to semantically interpret the actual relationships that might hold between a query and its refinement suggestions.

The chapter will be structured as follows. We will start with an overview of some related work (Section 2) before formulating our research questions (Section 3). Section 4 will focus on the domain model construction process and will outline how we use an ant colony optimization algorithm which keeps the domain model in a continuous update cycle. In Section 5 we will describe the log files we are going to use to build the domain model. These log files represent real user needs as they have been collected on the search engine of a digital library catalogue.The experimental setup is explained in Section 6. Results are presented in Section 7 which is followed by a discussion (Section 8). We will finish with some conclusions and an outlook on future work.

2   Related Work

Many ideas have been proposed to address the problem of information overload when searching or exploring a document collection. One very promising route is *Social Search* which combines ideas from personalization and social networking so that a searcher can benefit from past users' search experiences [41]. Applied to the digital libraries context, this idea can also be expressed as *Social Navigation* which adds a social dimension to browsing by guiding future users with the navigation experiences learned collectively from the crowd [12]. The question is what search trails and information should be exploited in this process. Utilizing explicit user judgements about items or search terms seems to be most useful. The problem is however that users are reluctant to leave any explicit feedback when they search a document collection [34]. Nevertheless, implicit feedback, e.g., the analysis of log records, has been shown to be good at approximating explicit feedback. There is a wealth of related work in log analysis, interactive search and other areas [24,40]. For example, users often reformulate their query and such patterns can help in learning an improved ranking function [26]. The same methods have shown to improve an adaptive domain model on a local Web site [32]. Log analysis has in fact developed into an entire research strand and it has been widely recognised that query log files represent a good source for capturing implicit user feedback [24,40].

The next question is how such feedback should be applied to improve the search process. One possibility is to exploit it in order to build knowledge structures that can assist in interactive search. But do users want assisted search? First of all, digital libraries are characterized by much more structured knowledge than Web sites. This makes system-guided search a natural option as evidenced by the success of Aquabrowser² as a tool to access digital libraries. More generally though, there is also evidence that users want support in proposing keywords but they ultimately want to stay in control about what is being submitted as a query [50]. Furthermore, despite the risk of offering irrelevant suggestions in a system-guided search system, users might prefer having them rather than not [49]. On the other hand, it has also been shown that users are more inclined to submit new queries or resubmit modified queries than to navigate from the result set in a search environment that supports search and navigation [35]. Perhaps the best evidence for the usefulness of interactive search systems is the fact that even the big Web search engines have recently added more and more interactive features, e.g., Google's Wonderwheel³.

Belkin calls the move beyond the limited, inherently non-interactive models of IR to truly interactive systems the *challenge of all challenges* in IR at the moment [9]. This is in line with what we propose, i.e. to go beyond static interaction patterns and move to adaptive retrieval exploiting the implicit feedback that users leave when searching and navigating a document collection. Building adaptive domain models for digital libraries and other collections is our approach to capturing and utilizing "collective intelligence" [45].

We wish to build a model that captures user interactions with a digital library and consolidates them to provide a dynamic model that will enable the combined knowledge to be examined e.g., a *learning network* in which algorithms build and extend network representations by acquiring knowledge from examples [43], in that we wish to capture user experience to update the model. One motivation could be that a large proportion of queries submitted to a search engine can be exact repeats of a query issued earlier by the same user [46]. However, our main motivation is to use the model to help make suggestions that can be used by other users.

---

² http://www.serialssolutions.com/aquabrowser/
³ http://www.googlewonderwheel.com

There are many different ways of structuring such models. Models can be built by extracting term relations from documents, e.g. [38,31,51], or from the actual queries that users submit to search the collection by building query flow graphs, e.g. [11], or mining term association rules [16]. Past user queries appear to be preferred by users when compared to terms extracted from documents [29], which is one motivation for using log files in our work. Various Web log studies have been conducted in recent years to study the users' search behaviour, e.g. [5,47,14,23], and log files have widely been used to extract meaningful knowledge, e.g. relations between queries [7], or to derive query substitutions [28]. Much of this work however is based on queries submitted on the *Web* and thus presents a very broad view of the world. Our work is different in that we start with a specific document collection for which suitable knowledge structures are typically not readily available (that collection could but does not have to be a digital library), extract relations from queries submitted within this collection to build and *evolve* a domain model automatically. It has been demonstrated that such an approach has the potential to learn useful relations over time in an intranet environment [15].

Digital libraries are however much more structured and represent a very different type of collection compared to the Web as a whole, a local Web site or an intranet. The question is whether domain knowledge can be acquired automatically from user queries within digital libraries, whether such relations can be improved over time and how this compares to alternative approaches. This leads us to our research questions.

3   Research Questions

The research questions we are trying to answer are as follows:

1. Can we employ the paradigm of the "wisdom of the crowd" to log files of digital libraries to extract useful query term relations that can assist in searching the collection?
2. How do these relations compare to sensible baseline approaches?
3. How do log files collected on digital libraries compare with intranet logs?

4   The Domain Model

Our domain model takes the form of a graph structure where nodes are query phrases and edges represent possible query refinements, higher weights denoting more common selections. Figure 1 gives an example of part of the domain model as it has been derived from our log data. Of inspiration for this model is the Nootropia system [36] for user profiling. This determines hierarchies of terms and disseminates energy using a method based on Artificial Immune Systems. We, however, take a related, if conceptually opposite method, to provide a model based on a *consolidated user* as opposed to learning differences between individuals.

As a reminder, the relation between two terms in the model is purely some form of association link that has been extracted from the logs and is therefore different from (and complementary to) the use of semantically encoded relations as used, for example, in the *Europeana* project[4], or the use of controlled vocabularies, e.g. [18,10].

---

[4] http://eculture.cs.vu.nl/europeana/session/search

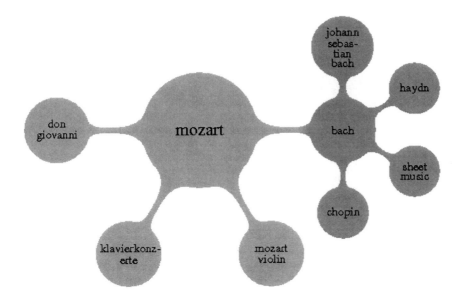

Fig. 1. Partial Domain Model Derived from TEL Log Data

Using such an internal representation allows numerous potential display and interrogation techniques to be presented to the user. In this work we focus on using relations encoded in the model as query modification suggestions in guided search. Applied differently, the domain model could also be used to browse or navigate the collection.

A range of adaptation algorithms have been developed but models that are able to capture *evolving* trends in search query graphs are only just starting to emerge, e.g. [8]. We will use the analogy of ant colony optimization (ACO) to first populate and then adapt the graph. The user traverses a portion of the graph by using query refinements (analogous to the ant's journey), the weights on this route are reinforced (increasing the level of pheromone). Over time all weights are reduced by a set proportion (pheromone evaporation). To reduce noise we only associate immediate refinements, e.g., for a session containing a query modification chain q_1 to q_4, associations will be created between q_1 and q_2, q_2 and q_3, and q_3 and q_4 only (see Algorithm 1). The specifics are as follows:

- At the end of each day all edge weights are normalised to sum to 1 and the mean weight of all edges is then calculated.
- For the next day, all queries in the log are extracted for that day where there are multiple queries in a particular user session.
- The queries are then time ordered and for each query phrase that follows an earlier phrase in the session an edge is created, or updated if it already exists, by the mean association weight of the previous day.
- A nominal update value of 1 is used for our first day, however, any positive real number could have been chosen without affecting the outcome of normalisation.

Algorithm 1. The ACO-based algorithm to build and evolve the domain model

---

Input: domain model as a graph G, daily query log L, number of days DAY_NUMS
Output: G

```
1   τ ← 1
2   for d ← 1 to DAY_NUMS do
        /* update weights of traversed edges                          */
3       foreach (q,q') ∈ L_d do
            /* Query q' immediately follows q in a session on day
               d.                                                      */
4           n ← FindNode (G, q)
5           if n = NULL then n ← AddNode (G, q)
6           n' ← FindNode (G, q')
7           if n' = NULL then n' ← AddNode (G, q')
8           e ← FindEdge (G, n, n')
9           if e = NULL then
10              e ← AddEdge (G, n, n')
11              SetWeight (G, e, τ)
12          else
13              SetWeight (G, e, τ + GetWeight (G, e))

        /* normalize weights of edges                                 */
14      T ← TotalWeights (G)
15      c_e ← 0
16      foreach e ∈ G do
17          c_e ← c_e + 1
18          SetWeight (G, e, GetWeight (G, e) /T)
19      τ ← T/c_e
```

By normalising the weights at the end of each day we reduce the weight of non-traversed edges, hence, over time, penalising incorrect or less relevant phrase refinements. In addition we expect outdated terms to be effectively removed from the model, i.e., the refinement weight will become so low that the phrase will never be recommended to the user.

One would expect to use the model to provide suggested terms by first finding the original query phrase in the graph, then list the linked terms ordered by weight. To use an example, if a user searches for *"mozart"*, then the domain model can propose query modifications such as *"don giovanni"*, *"klavierkonzerte"*, *"mozart violin"* and *"bach"*. Although not addressed in this chapter, indirect associations could also be used when data is sparse, or if we wish to investigate sub-trees with relatively high weights.

Although we have chosen to run the update in the described algorithm on a daily basis, update sessions could be run hourly or weekly, or even when a certain number of user sessions have completed. In addition, it is possible to run the algorithm from any point in the user log to any other, this allows us to compare how the model performs for particular time periods.

5 Log Files

We have used log data that have been collected on the search engine of The European Library (TEL)[5]. The TEL logs contain an entry for every user interaction with the TEL portal. Log entries contain the type of action performed (e.g. simple or advanced search, changing system options) and attributes such as user ID, session ID, the interface language, query, and timestamp. Figure 2 lists five sample entries, the first one describing a search in English for *"pomegranate fertilization"* submitted through the simple user interface.

```
. . .
903779;guest;83.33.xxx.xxx;83et8b7j010eh4vlht3ucj8dll;en;
        ("pomegranate fertilization");search_sim;;0;-;;;2007-10-05 13:52:30
. . .
1889115;guest;71.249.xxx.xxx;8eb3bdv3odg9jncd71u0s2aff6;en;
        ("mozart");search_url;;0;-;;;2008-06-24 22:02:52
. . .
1889118;guest;71.249.xxx.xxx;8eb3bdv3odg9jncd71u0s2aff6;en;
        ("mozart");view_full;;1;;;;2008-06-24 22:03:03
. . .
1889120;guest;71.249.xxx.xxx;8eb3bdv3odg9jncd71u0s2aff6;en;
        Klavierkonzerte;search_res_rec_all;;0;-;;;2008-06-24 22:03:55
1889121;guest;71.249.xxx.xxx;8eb3bdv3odg9jncd71u0s2aff6;en;
        ("klavierkonzerte");view_full;;1;;;;2008-06-24 22:04:10
. . .
```

Fig. 2. Sample entries in the TEL log

The logs record not just all queries submitted to the search engine but also other activities such as viewing a result. We are only interested in search queries (which make up about a quarter of all actions). We use the log file that has also been used in LogCLEF 2009 and 2010[6]. This log covers the period from 1 January 2007 till 30 June 2008 [2]. In the logs there is a great inclination towards using simple search compared to using advanced search [19]. In our experiments we do not consider queries submitted via the advanced search interface. We use the session numbers recorded in the log files to identify search sessions.

We processed the files as follows:

1. Discard all actions that are not simple search queries
2. Remove all queries that do not have English specified as the query language
3. Remove all queries that contain non-ASCII characters
4. Case-fold all queries, replace all non-alphanumeric characters by space
5. If a query contains one or more Boolean operators, trim the query so that the left-most operator and everything that follows gets removed.
6. Delete all queries which have no session number specified
7. Finally, only keep those sessions that consist of at least two search queries.

The last point in particular reduces the number of selected queries dramatically because there is a large proportion of sessions that involve only a single user query. We end up with 152,863 queries. Figure 3 presents two sample entries in the processed query logs.

---

[5] http://www.theeuropeanlibrary.org
[6] http://www.uni-hildesheim.de/logclef/

```
. . .
8eb3bdv3odg9jncd71u0s2aff6 xxxx 1889115 xxxx mozart xxxx 2008-06-24 22:02:52
8eb3bdv3odg9jncd71u0s2aff6 xxxx 1889120 xxxx klavierkonzerte xxxx 2008-06-24 22:03:55
. . .
```

Fig. 3. Sample session records after processing the TEL logs

Note that we make the simplifying assumption that all queries within a session are related to the same search request. This is not always true and a session can easily consist of a number of *search goals* and *search missions* [27]. However, identifying exact session boundaries automatically is an inherently difficult task [20,22].

Finally, we use the processed log file to build and adapt the domain model. The log records are ordered by session and in chronological order. Each consecutive query pair within a session is processed as outlined in Algorithm 1.

6   Experimental Setup

We assume that a high-quality domain model is one that makes sensible suggestions to the user. We employ two evaluation methods to assess the quality of the domain model. Our first evaluation method, *AutoEval*, is fully automated, in the second evaluation method we asked users to assess the quality of domain model relations that have been learned. These methods aim at evaluating the quality of term relations that emerge from the adaptation process.

As part of the automated evaluation we conducted two sets of experiments, one using all queries submitted to TEL. The second experiment only looked at frequently submitted queries. The first experiment will tell us how well the algorithm learns the relations covering the entire domain. The second approach targets high-frequency queries only. The reasoning behind this is that an interactive search system might go for either high recall (offer suggestions whenever there is any relation in the domain model, i.e. cover all possible queries) or for high precision (only suggest "reliable" terms, i.e. focus on highly frequent queries only). The high recall approach runs the risk of offering a lot of noise, the other approach will not offer any suggestions for the long tail of infrequent queries.

For the second evaluation which involved actual assessors we only looked at frequent queries as we will discuss in more detail further down.

Clearly, our experimental settings are necessarily approximations of the real world. They will only be able to give us an indication of the usefulness of term relations learned from the log files. Any such findings will need to be validated by large-scale experiments that are used in realistic user search tasks. This will be left as future work.

6.1   Automatic Evaluation Method: AutoEval

Our first evaluation method, *AutoEval* [4], is based on the idea that we can assess the quality of a domain model by comparing suggestions derived from the model to query modifications actually observed in the log files. We use Mean Reciprocal Rank (MRR) to measure this. Given some initial search request, if a query modification observed in

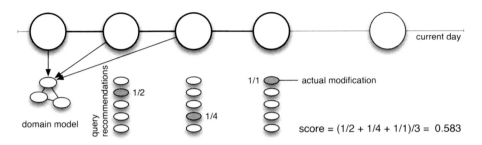

Fig. 4. Daily Model Evaluation

a session matches the suggestion derived from the model, we will reward the model, the highest reward is paid for a suggestion that comes top in the model, smaller rewards (MRR) for suggestions further down the list.

The model's evaluation is performed on an arbitrary interval basis as depicted in Figure 4 where the evaluation takes place on a daily basis. It only takes place for days with at least one query modification pair. For example, let us assume that during the current day, three query modifications have been submitted (Fig. 4). For each query modification pair, the domain model is provided with the initial query and returns a ranked list of recommended query modifications. We take the rank of the actual modified query (i.e., the one in the log data) in this list, as an indication of the domain model's accuracy. The assumption here is that an accurate domain model should be able to propose the most appropriate query modification at the top of the list of recommended modifications. This is based on the observation that users are much more likely to click on the top results of a ranked list than to select something further down [25], and it seems reasonable to assume that such a preference is valid not just for ranked lists of search results but for lists of query modification suggestions as well.

So for the total of three query modifications in the current day, we can calculate the model's accuracy score as $(1/r_1 + 1/r_2 + 1/r_3)/3$, where r_1 to r_3 are the ranks of the actual query modifications in the list of modifications recommended by the model in each of the three cases. In the figure's example the model's score would be 0.583. More generally, given a day d with Q query modification pairs, the model's Mean Reciprocal Rank score MRR_d for that day is given by Equation 1 below.

$$MRR_d = (\sum_{i=1}^{Q} \frac{1}{r_i})/Q \tag{1}$$

Note that in the special case where the actual query modification is not included in the list of recommended modifications $1/r$ is set to zero. The above evaluation process results in an accuracy score for each logged day for which at least a query modification pair exists. So overall, the process produces a series of scores for each domain model being evaluated. These scores allow the comparison between different domain models. A model M_1 can therefore be considered superior over a model M_2 if a statistically significant improvement can be measured over the given period.

The described process fits perfectly a static model, but in the case of dynamic experiments as we are conducting here, the experimental process is similar. We start with an initially empty domain model, or an existing domain model. Like before, the model is evaluated at the end of each daily batch of query modifications, but unlike the static experiments it uses the daily data for updating its structure. This is essentially a continuous learning problem, where the domain model has to learn from temporal query modification data (applying the ACO algorithm in our specific example). Again, we treat a model as superior over another (possibly static one) if an improvement can be observed that is significant.

When testing our ACO algorithm we decided to compare the results against a simple alternative based on association rules [17]. Fonseca's approach represents a sensible baseline for a different way of adapting the search because it accesses exactly the same resources as our proposed method and it has been shown to work well on Web log data. The idea is to use session boundaries and to treat each session as a transaction. Related queries are derived from queries submitted within the same transaction.

6.2   User-Based Evaluation Method: Mechanical Turk

The next evaluation was user-based to find out how users would assess the relevance of query modification suggestions learned by the adaptive model and how they compare against alternative approaches for constructing such suggestions. To do so we adopted a methodology proposed in the literature [38]. An online form was prepared, and participants were asked to determine whether queries and their refinements were relevant.

Table 1. Most frequent queries

Rank	Query Phrase	Rank	Query Phrase
1	mozart	11	dante
2	harry potter	12	zagreb
3	meisje met de parel	13	bible
4	einstein	14	poland
5	shakespeare	15	history
6	bach	16	france
7	music	17	chopin
8	europe	18	paris
9	goethe	19	italy
10	london	20	cervantes

To avoid data sparsity issues we used the top 20 most frequently submitted queries as found in our processed log files (see Table 1) to derive suggestions. For each query we selected the three best (highest weighted) related terms using three different methods:

- **ACO:** For each query we selected the top three suggestions that have been learned after running the full log file through our ant colony optimization algorithm.
- **Fonseca:** Applying the same methods as in the *AutoEval* run, we selected the top three association rules for the given query applied to the full log file.

- **Baseline:** As a baseline we selected a method that does not rely on log data. We assume that the top matching results of a commercial search engine will be a useful resource to derive query modification suggestions. To restrict the results to a collection comparable to the digital library catalogue at hand we decided to search only for matches within the world library catalogue WorldCat[7]. We derived nouns and noun phrases from the top ten snippets returned by *Yahoo!* (restricting the search to the WorldCat Web site). We identify nouns and noun phrases using text processing methods applied in previous experiments, e.g. [31].

Therefore users had to judge 60 individual query suggestions derived for each of the three methods.

We recruited assessors using Amazon Mechanical Turk[8], a crowdsourcing market place that has been shown to work effectively, and it has been demonstrated that its aggregated results approximate expert judgement for a variety of tasks, e.g. [42,13,3]. Obviously, the recruited users might never use the digital library search functionality of TEL, but they do represent potential users as anybody can access the TEL portal and we wanted to learn to what extent potential users would find term suggestions extracted from the domain model useful *if* they were searching a digital library.

CrowdFlower[9] was used to build the assessment task and control access to Amazon Mechanical Turk. The task was built as an online form similar to the one used in [30], where assessors were asked to determine whether queries and their refinements were relevant.

The instructions gave the users a hypothetical context as follows:

Suppose that you are a user of a digital library's search engine. The digital library allows you to access all collections of libraries available on the Internet worldwide. You issue queries on the search engine to find what you are looking for. In addition to returning the best matching books or articles for any given query, this search engine also suggests modified queries that you could use to refine or replace the original one.

The form below gives a list of term pairs. For each pair, imagine the first term was your original query, and that the second is one of the terms proposed by the search system, which you could use to refine or replace the search. Please judge for each pair whether you think the second term is:

- *relevant (Choose 'Relevant').*
- *not relevant (Choose 'Not Relevant').*
- *If you do not know, then choose 'Don't know'.*

Here, 'relevant' means that you can imagine a situation where the second term is an appropriate refinement or replacement of the query given by the first term.

We also pointed out that if they found it difficult to judge the pair, that they might want to consult some online resources, e.g.Wikipedia or The European Library.

---

[7] http://worldcat.org
[8] http://www.mturk.com
[9] http://www.crowdflower.com

Subjects were not told that various different techniques have been used to generate these query pairs. The form contained a list of all query pairs in random order.

We asked 20 Mechanical Turk workers to do the assessment task and restricted the location of those workers to be UK-based. The reason for this restriction is that we know that UK searchers form a significant proportion of actual TEL users [2].

We paid 2 US dollars for each assessment task.

7   Results

For all significance testing we used paired t-tests (where appropriate) with confidence value $p < 0.001$ unless otherwise specified.

7.1   AutoEval Results

Figure 5 illustrates the results of applying *AutoEval* over the entire period covered by the log file. We use monthly batches to update the domain model. Fonseca's association rules approach was evaluated with different settings. The minimum support parameter (MinSup) is the threshold used to infer an association. Fonseca *et al.* conducted their experiments on Web log data using *MinSup=3* [17]. However, due to the much smaller data set we are dealing with here we also provide a run using a weaker support of *MinSup=2* (in other words association rules may be selected even if the query pair has only been found in two sessions). A lower minimum support therefore increases the chance of inferring an association for any given query.

The main observation is that our ACO method is significantly more effective than learning based on association rules (with either minimum support setting). We see that

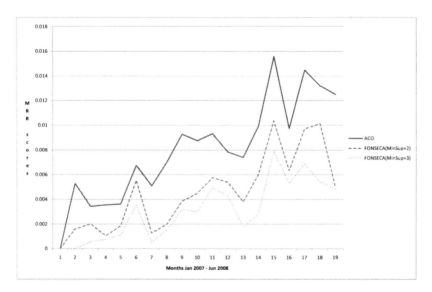

Fig. 5. ACO *vs.* Fonseca-Baseline

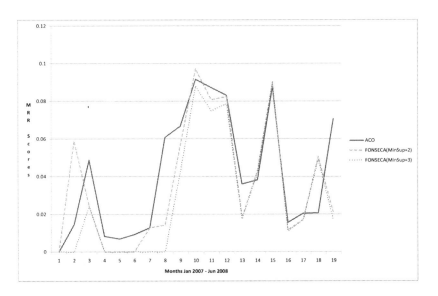

Fig. 6. ACO *vs.* Fonseca-Baseline (Frequent Queries)

despite a few spikes the general trend is upwards indicating that our adaptive learning method (and to a smaller extend the association rules) are able to learn from past log data over time. However, we also observe that the absolute score is relatively low and we will get back to that later.

The second round of *AutoEval* runs considered only the top 20 most frequent queries extracted from the query logs. Those queries are listed in Table 1. Note that these are the most frequent queries in our processed log files. One frequent query (*"sange for claveret"*) was not considered because the baseline failed to produce a single result.

In this case, the MRR scores in Equation 1 were calculated for query modification pairs Q_{top} where the first query in the pair is one of those listed in Table 1. Figure 6 displays the obtained scores for ACO and Fonseca's association rules when we restrict the evaluation to the top 20 queries. The average scores are much higher (and for ACO they remain at a higher level throughout the learning period). Again we observe that ACO is better on average over the entire period (0.041 > 0.035) but there is no significant difference.

7.2   User Assessment Results

The assessments obtained from Mechanical Turk were aggregated and the results are shown in Table 2. For each user we calculated the percentage of pairs that were judged relevant using different criteria and then we aggregated the results among the 20 assessors. The 'Total Relevant' row gives the average judgement of query pairs considered relevant over all users and all three suggestions for each method. If we only take into account the top suggestion (i.e. the one highest ranked by the corresponding method) for each query, then we get the results listed under 'First Relevant'. Finally, the

Table 2. A comparison of user-judged relevant query suggestions for the 20 most frequent TEL queries generated by three different systems

	Ant Colony Optimization	Fonseca's Association Rules	Yahoo! Snippet Baseline
Total Relevant	45.67%	44.08%	57.17%
First Relevant	51.75%	47.75%	58.25%
At Least One Relevant	74.25%	76.00%	84.50%

percentage for which the system in question had provided at least one suggestion that was judged relevant is shown in the bottom row ('At Least One Relevant').

The user assessment indicates that ACO and Fonseca's association rules have a comparable performance on top queries although ACO is slightly better in learning query suggestions from query logs. This is in line with the *AutoEval* scores shown in Figure 6 as we see an improvement though not statistically measurable. The user assessment also shows that both learning methods were considered less effective than the baseline approach.[10] We will discuss the results in the next section.

Note, that for Fonseca's association rules we set the minimum support parameter to 2 in this experiment. The reason for that is we have already shown in the *AutoEval* experiments that this value yields a better performance. More importantly, when we increase this value to 3 no refinements were actually generated for some of the most frequent queries.

8   Discussion

The main finding is that our continuous learning model is capable of learning useful relations from digital library query logs as evidenced by the results of the *AutoEval* runs. Using the automatic evaluation over the entire logs has furthermore shown the superiority of the ACO approach over a method that extracts association rules from query pairs found in the same session. This superiority is less measurable when learning on top queries only.

However, when discussing the results we need to start with an interesting observation regarding data sparsity. Queries submitted to search engines approximately follow the power-law distribution [6]. That means that we can capture a large proportion of user requests with a relatively small number of unique queries. Now, we found that TEL queries are particularly sparse. Whereas the top 20 most frequently submitted queries on a university Web site can make up as much as 15% of the entire query corpus [15], we observe that in a TEL log file of a comparable size to the university log the top 20 queries only cover about 2% of all queries submitted.[11] In that respect, the TEL queries

---

[10] The results closely correlate with an assessment that was conducted by an independent digital libraries expert and can be seen as another successful example of obtaining expert judgements by exploiting the wisdom of the crowd.

[11] For this comparison we used another TEL log file used in LogCLEF covering the period from January 2009 till December 2009.

appear to be more similar to Web queries than intranet queries [44]. The difference of course is that Web logs are magnitudes larger which means that the actual count of even less frequent Web queries may still be large. In our processed query logs we found the most frequent query occurs only 414 times and the 20th-most-frequent query only 70 times! Learning on the TEL logs is therefore particularly challenging. This is reflected in the low *MRR* scores we obtained in the automatic evaluation and possibly also in the assessors' relevance judgements. The sparsity of the data and the open nature of the library domain makes it harder to learn useful query refinement suggestions from the logs.

One possible way forward is to make use of more of the log data (we reduced the log file of more than one million interactions to a fraction of the size). What we have shown here is that the general idea of an adaptive domain model gives very promising results. A more customized and fine-tuned algorithm is likely to improve the learning rate.

Regarding our experiments with top queries, we argue that even after deleting known test queries we still find a number of queries that are unlikely to be typical user requests. One example is *"sange for claveret"* which is frequent but only delivers a single result (from the Danish national library). Furthermore, there are a significant number of sessions in which *"sange for claveret"* co-occurs with other frequent (and perhaps unusual queries) such as *"meisje met de parel"*.

In any case, the experiments we conducted on the top queries nicely correlate with the earlier experiments. On *AutoEval* we see that the ACO method slightly outperforms an association-based approach and this is mirrored when asking users to assess the top three (or the top one) suggestions derived from each model. The user assessments also tell us that almost half of the query suggestions derived by ACO for top queries are considered relevant. Another finding is that users found the query refinement suggestions provided by the baseline more relevant than the ones learned from the logs. This confirms other experiments run on the same data [1]. Interestingly however, the suggestions derived from the logs and the ones found in the snippets appear to be complementary. In fact, there is only a 3% overlap when considering the suggestions derived from the query log learning approaches (ACO and association rules) on the one hand and the snippets baseline on the other hand. For example, for the query *"europe"*, ACO has learned *"europe map"* as the refinement with the highest weight. The top baseline suggestion is *"council of europe"*. Both suggestions were considered relevant by 90% of our assessors.

To put the results in context, running ACO on a university intranet log file results in relations that are considered more relevant by users (above 60% when considering all suggestions or just the top one) [15]. We argue that this is largely due to the aforementioned data sparsity issue.

9   Conclusions

In this chapter we outlined how log files collected on a digital library portal can be exploited to learn query suggestions which can assist users of the portal. We shall now return to our research questions and will try to draw conclusions based on the results we obtained.

1. *Can we employ the paradigm of the "wisdom of the crowd" to log files of digital libraries to extract useful query term relations that can assist in searching the collection?*
   We have demonstrated that an ant colony optimization learning algorithm is capable of learning useful query relations over time. There is certainly a lot of hidden knowledge in log files of digital libraries that should allow us to move towards adaptive system-guided systems in digital libraries.
2. *How do these relations compare to sensible baseline approaches?*
   A sensible baseline approach that does not rely on log data can be difficult to beat. However, the suggestions derived from query logs and those derived dynamically from top matching documents appear to complement each other.
3. *How do log files collected on digital libraries compare with intranet logs?*
   An important finding of this study related to our third question is that digital library logs appear to be much more sparse than for example search engine logs of an intranet or a local Web site. This in itself might not be surprising but the implication is that an effective learning algorithm will either have to rely on large log files or will have to exploit the logs much more effectively than what is needed when extracting relations from intranet or Web logs.

An additional conclusion we would like to draw is that our automatic evaluation methodology *AutoEval* has been shown to be a useful evaluation framework to compare the performance of different approaches for building domain models to provide query suggestions (in the fairly restricted evaluation settings employed here).

10 Future Work

There are a number of areas that will need to be addressed in future. First of all, we have so far not involved *real* users in *realistic* search tasks. Furthermore, and related to that point, in our experiments we simplified the evaluation task by collecting user judgements once only at a fixed point in time. To get more realistic assessments the adaptive algorithms need to be incorporated in a live search engine of a digital library catalogue to allow longitudinal studies. In any case, we would assume that an automatically acquired (and evolving) domain model will allow users to find relevant information more quickly and allow a better navigation experience over time, in particular when deriving query modification suggestions using a variety of approaches. These experiments are on our agenda for future work.

One way of addressing data sparsity is to extract more knowledge from the logs. So far we kept the pre-processing of the log files deliberately simple. A large proportion of queries do however make reference to specific fields in the structured data entries (e.g. author name, topic etc). A natural modification to the simple domain model building described in this chapter will make more use of the query structure as well as other actions recorded in the logs. Furthermore, our domain model is not linked to the actual documents in the collection. By using clickthrough information it will be straightforward to link the model into the collection.

Regarding the ACO algorithm, the approach we applied to automatically adapt the domain model is the simplest possible way of using ACO in this context. Here we assume that the weight of a relation between two queries increases as soon as this query pair is observed, or to use the ants analogy, a pheromone trail is left every time an ant moves from A to B. However, we could modify that in a number of ways. Pheromone might, for example, only be placed if the ant has discovered some valuable resource. Applying this to search we could strengthen the relation only between any query that is part of a session and the final query given that this final query is followed by viewing some result set as the final action. Similar ideas have been shown to work effectively when associating queries with landing pages in Web search [37].

Acknowledgements

This research is part of the AutoAdapt research project. AutoAdapt is funded by EPSRC grants EP/F035357/1 and EP/F035705/1. We would also like to thank Sally Chambers and The European Library as well the organisers of the LogCLEF track for providing the log files, in particular we would like to thank Thomas Mandl. Without realistic log data we would not have been able to conduct this research. We would also like to thank Vivien Petras for helping with the expert assessments and finally we thank the anonymous reviewers for valuable feedback.

This material is based upon works supported by the Science Foundation Ireland under Grant No. Grant 07/CE/I1142.

References

1. Agosti, M., Cisco, D., Di Nunzio, G.M., Masiero, I., Melucci, M.: i-TEL-u: A Query Suggestion Tool for Integrating Heterogeneous Contexts in a Digital Library. In: Lalmas, M., Jose, J., Rauber, A., Sebastiani, F., Frommholz, I. (eds.) ECDL 2010. LNCS, vol. 6273, pp. 397–400. Springer, Heidelberg (2010)
2. Agosti, M., Crivellari, F., Di Nunzio, G.M., Ioannidis, Y., Stamatogiannakis, L., Triantafillidi, M.-L., Vayanou, M.: Report on Search Engines and HTTP Log Analysis. Technical report TELplus D5.2, TELplus Project (2009)
3. Albakour, M.-D., Kruschwitz, U., Lucas, S.: Sentence-level attachment prediction. In: Cunningham, H., Hanbury, A., Rüger, S. (eds.) IRFC 2010. LNCS, vol. 6107, pp. 6–19. Springer, Heidelberg (2010)
4. Albakour, M.-D., Kruschwitz, U., Nanas, N., Kim, Y., Song, D., Fasli, M., De Roeck, A.: AutoEval: An evaluation methodology for evaluating query suggestions using query logs. In: Clough, P., Foley, C., Gurrin, C., Jones, G.J.F., Kraaij, W., Lee, H., Mudoch, V. (eds.) ECIR 2011. LNCS, vol. 6611, pp. 605–610. Springer, Heidelberg (2011)
5. Anick, P.: Using Terminological Feedback for Web Search Refinement - A Log-based Study. In: Proceedings of the 26th Annual International ACM SIGIR Conference on Research and Development in Information Retrieval, Toronto, Canada, pp. 88–95 (2003)
6. Baeza-Yates, R., Saint-Jean, F.: A Three Level Search Engine Index Based in Query Log Distribution. In: Nascimento, M.A., de Moura, E.S., Oliveira, A.L. (eds.) SPIRE 2003. LNCS, vol. 2857, pp. 56–65. Springer, Heidelberg (2003)
7. Baeza-Yates, R., Tiberi, A.: Extracting semantic relations from query logs. In: Proceeding of the 13th ACM SIGKDD International Conference on Knowledge Discovery in Data Mining, San Jose, California, pp. 76–85 (2007)

8. Baraglia, R., Castillo, C., Donato, D., Nardini, F.M., Perego, R., Silvestri, F.: The Effects of Time on Query Flow Graph-based Models for Query Suggestion. In: Proceedings of RIAO 2010, Paris (2010)

9. Belkin, N.J.: Some(what) grand challenges for information retrieval. SIGIR Forum 42(1), 47–54 (2008)

10. Berghaus, B., Mandl, T., Womser-Hacker, C., Kluck, M.: An entry vocabulary module for a political science test collection. In: Business Information Systems. Lecture Notes in Business Information Processing, pp. 1–11 (2008)

11. Boldi, P., Bonchi, F., Castillo, C., Donato, D., Vigna, S.: Query suggestions using query-flow graphs. In: Proceedings of the 2009 Workshop on Web Search Click Data (WSCD 2009), pp. 56–63 (2009)

12. Brusilovsky, P., Cassel, L., Delcambre, L., Fox, E., Furuta, R., Garcia, D., Shipman, F., Bogen, P., Yudelson, M.: Enhancing digital libraries with social navigation: The case of ensemble. In: Lalmas, M., Jose, J., Rauber, A., Sebastiani, F., Frommholz, I. (eds.) ECDL 2010. LNCS, vol. 6273, pp. 116–123. Springer, Heidelberg (2010)

13. Callison-Burch, C.: Fast, cheap, and creative: Evaluating translation quality using Amazon's Mechanical Turk. In: Proceedings of the 2009 Conference on Empirical Methods in Natural Language Processing (EMNLP), pp. 286–295. Association for Computational Linguistics (2009)

14. Chau, M., Fang, X., Sheng, O.R.L.: Analysis of the Query Logs of a Web Site Search Engine. Journal of the American Society for Information Science and Technology (JASIST) 56(13), 1363–1376 (2005)

15. Dignum, S., Kruschwitz, U., Fasli, M., Kim, Y., Song, D., Cervino, U., De Roeck, A.: Incorporating Seasonality into Search Suggestions Derived from Intranet Query Logs. In: Proceedings of the IEEE/WIC/ACM International Conferences on Web Intelligence (WI 2010), Toronto, pp. 425–430 (2010)

16. Fonseca, B.M., Golgher, P.B., de Moura, E.S., Pôssas, B., Ziviani, N.: Discovering search engine related queries using association rules. Journal of Web Engineering 2(4), 215–227 (2004)

17. Fonseca, B.M., Golgher, P.B., de Moura, E.S., Ziviani, N.: Using association rules to discover search engines related queries. In: Proceedings of the First Latin American Web Congress, pp. 66–71 (2003)

18. Gey, F.C., Buckland, M., Chen, A., Larson, R.R.: Entry vocabulary – a technology to enhance digital search. In: Proceedings of the First International Conference on Human Language Technology (2001)

19. Ghorab, M.R., Leveling, J., Zhou, D., Jones, G.J.F., Wade, V.: Identifying common user behaviour in multilingual search logs. In: Peters, C., Di Nunzio, G.M., Kurimo, M., Mostefa, D., Penas, A., Roda, G. (eds.) CLEF 2009. LNCS, vol. 6241, pp. 518–525. Springer, Heidelberg (2010)

20. Göker, A., He, D.: Analysing web search logs to determine session boundaries for user-oriented learning. In: Brusilovsky, P., Stock, O., Strapparava, C. (eds.) AH 2000. LNCS, vol. 1892, pp. 319–322. Springer, Heidelberg (2000)

21. Hawking, D.: Enterprise Search. In: Baeza-Yates, R., Ribeiro-Neto, B. (eds.) Modern Information Retrieval, 2nd edn., pp. 641–683. Addison-Wesley, Harlow (2011)

22. Jansen, B.J., Spink, A., Blakely, C., Koshman, S.: Defining a session on Web search engines. Journal of the American Society for Information Science and Technology (JASIST) 58(6), 862–871 (2007)

23. Jansen, B.J., Spink, A., Koshman, S.: Web Server Interaction with the Dogpile.com Metasearch Engine. Journal of the American Society for Information Science and Technology (JASIST) 58(5), 744–755 (2007)

24. Jansen, J., Spink, A., Taksa, I. (eds.): Handbook of Research on Web Log Analysis. IGI (2008)
25. Joachims, T., Granka, L., Pan, B., Hembrooke, H., Gay, G.: Accurately interpreting click-through data as implicit feedback. In: Proceedings of the 28th Annual International ACM SIGIR Conference on Research and Development in Information Retrieval, Salvador, Brazil, pp. 154–161 (2005)
26. Joachims, T., Radlinski, F.: Search engines that learn from implicit feedback. IEEE Computer 40(8), 34–40 (2007)
27. Jones, R., Klinkner, K.L.: Beyond the session timeout: automatic hierarchical segmentation of search topics in query logs. In: Proceeding of the 17th ACM Conference on Information and Knowledge Management (CIKM 2008), pp. 699–708 (2008)
28. Jones, R., Rey, B., Madani, O., Greiner, W.: Generating Query Substitutions. In: Proceedings of the 15th International World Wide Web Conference (WWW 2006), Edinburgh, pp. 387–396 (2006)
29. Kelly, D., Gyllstrom, K., Bailey, E.W.: A comparison of query and term suggestion features for interactive searching. In: Proceedings of the 32nd Annual International ACM SIGIR Conference on Research and Development in Information Retrieval, Boston, pp. 371–378 (2009)
30. Kruschwitz, U.: An Adaptable Search System for Collections of Partially Structured Documents. IEEE Intelligent Systems 18(4), 44–52 (2003)
31. Kruschwitz, U.: Intelligent Document Retrieval: Exploiting Markup Structure. The Information Retrieval Series, vol. 17. Springer, Heidelberg (2005)
32. Lungley, D., Kruschwitz, U.: Automatically maintained domain knowledge: Initial findings. In: Boughanem, M., Berrut, C., Mothe, J., Soule-Dupuy, C. (eds.) ECIR 2009. LNCS, vol. 5478, pp. 739–743. Springer, Heidelberg (2009)
33. Manning, C., Prabhakar, R., Schütze, H.: Introduction to Information Retrieval. Cambridge University Press, Cambridge (2008)
34. Markey, K.: Twenty-five years of end-user searching, Part 1: Research findings. Journal of the American Society for Information Science and Technology (JASIST) 58(8), 1071–1081 (2007)
35. Mat-Hassan, M., Levene, M.: Associating Search and Navigation Behavior Through Log Analysis. Journal of the American Society for Information Science and Technology (JASIST) 56(9), 913–934 (2005)
36. Nanas, N., Roeck, A.: Autopoiesis, the immune system, and adaptive information filtering. Natural Computing: an International Journal 8(2), 387–427 (2009)
37. Poblete, B., Baeza-Yates, R.: Query-Sets: Using Implicit Feedback and Query Patterns to Organize Web Documents. In: Proceedings of the 17th International World Wide Web Conference (WWW 2008), Beijing, pp. 41–50 (2008)
38. Sanderson, M., Croft, B.: Deriving concept hierarchies from text. In: Proceedings of the 22nd Annual International ACM SIGIR Conference on Research and Development in Information Retrieval, Berkeley, CA, pp. 206–213 (1999)
39. Sherman, C.: Why Enterprise Search will never be Google-y. In: Enterprise Search Sourcebook, pp. 12–13 (2008)
40. Silvestri, F.: Mining Query Logs: Turning Search Usage Data into Knowledge. Foundations and Trends in Information Retrieval, vol. 4. Now Publisher (2010)
41. Smyth, B., Briggs, P., Coyle, M., O'Mahony, M.: Google shared. A case-study in social search. In: Houben, G.-J., McCalla, G., Pianesi, F., Zancanaro, M. (eds.) UMAP 2009. LNCS, vol. 5535, pp. 283–294. Springer, Heidelberg (2009)
42. Snow, R., O'Connor, B., Jurafsky, D., Ng, A.Y.: Cheap and Fast - But is it Good? Evaluating Non-Expert Annotations for Natural Language Tasks. In: Proceedings of the 2008 Conference on Empirical Methods in Natural Language Processing, pp. 254–263. Association for Computational Linguistics (2008)

43. Sowa, J.F.: Semantic networks. In: Shapiro, S.C. (ed.) Encyclopedia of Artificial Intelligence, pp. 1493–1511. John Wiley & Sons, Chichester (1992)
44. Spink, A., Jansen, B.J.: Web Search: Public Searching of the Web. The Information Science and Knowledge Management Series, vol. 6. Kluwer, Dordrecht (2004)
45. Surowiecki, J.: The Wisdom of Crowds. Anchor, New York (2005)
46. Teevan, J., Adar, E., Jones, R., Potts, M.A.S.: Information Re-Retrieval: Repeat Queries in Yahoo's Logs. In: Proceedings of the 30th Annual International ACM SIGIR Conference on Research and Development in Information Retrieval, Amsterdam, pp. 151–158 (2007)
47. Wang, P., Berry, M.W., Yang, Y.: Mining Longitudinal Web Queries: Trends and Patterns. Journal of the American Society for Information Science and Technology (JASIST) 54(8), 743–758 (2003)
48. White, M.: Making Search Work: Implementing Web, Intranet and Enterprise Search. Facet Publishing (2007)
49. White, R.W., Bilenko, M., Cucerzan, S.: Studying the Use of Popular Destinations to Enhance Web Search Interaction. In: Proceedings of the 30th Annual International ACM SIGIR Conference on Research and Development in Information Retrieval, Amsterdam, pp. 159–166 (2007)
50. White, R.W., Ruthven, I.: A Study of Interface Support Mechanisms for Interactive Information Retrieval. Journal of the American Society for Information Science and Technology (JASIST) 57(7), 933–948 (2006)
51. Widdows, D., Dorow, B.: A Graph Model for Unsupervised Lexical Acquisition and Automatic Word-Sense Disambiguation. In: Proceedings of the 19th Conference on Computational Linguistics (COLING), Taipei, Taiwan, pp. 1093–1099 (2002)

Automatic Gazetteer Generation from Wikipedia

Alessio Bosca and Luca Dini

CELI s.r.l., 10131 Torino, Italy
{alessio.bosca,dini}@celi.it

Abstract. The presence of high quality Named Entity gazetteer within a CLIR system is crucial in order to provide multilingual access to digital resources, particularly in the domain of Digital Libraries. In our paper we investigate an approach for automatically extracting this kind of resources from Wikipedia using an unsupervised approach that leverages the DBpedia classification of the English articles in order to induce the same classification onto encyclopedia pages expressed in other languages. By exploiting the structured information present in Wikipedia we furthermore aim at enriching our standard gazetteer with translations to other languages as well as with the alternative spellings of the entities.

1 Introduction

In the last decade the demand for IT systems capable of integrating and correlating documents expressed in different languages generated a huge effort in the research community, particularly in the world of cultural heritage where mature standards are nowadays available for describing and accessing the digital collections of museums, libraries and archives ([26,19]). Along the direction of this research effort different EU founded projects like EuropeanaConnect ([23]), CACAO ([20]) or MICHAEL([25]) focused on the challenge of supporting multilingual resources and Cross-Language Information Retrieval (CLIR) systems.

This diffuse effort evidences that research on CLIR systems is becoming more and more important for global information exchange (like foreign patent information access) and knowledge sharing in multilingual environments like the Web or transnational digital collections. CLIR is a multidisciplinary topic and involves researchers from various fields: information retrieval, natural language processing, machine translation and summarization, document image understanding.

CLIR systems primary goal consists in mapping the informational needs of users (usually expressed by a monolingual query in the form of a bag of words) to all the documents that satisfy such needs regardless to their language. The approach of querying in one language and retrieving documents in all the available languages is particularly significant whenever the contents of the exposed resources are not textual (images, audio, etc) and the constraint of being expressed in a specific language only concerns the meta-data.

Historically two different approaches are available when designing a CLIR system: either to translate the queries submitted by users or the documents

R. Bernardi et al. (Eds.): NLP4DL/AT4DL 2009, LNCS 6699, pp. 61–71, 2011.
© Springer-Verlag Berlin Heidelberg 2011

contained in the search index. According to the design approach chosen, different strategies for the translation should be considered; corpus based, statistical machine translation is the most common choice for document translation while dictionary based translations could be preferred in the context of queries translation. In fact typical MT systems under-perform in syntactically poor contexts such as search queries and with ambiguous translations most MT systems make a choice, thus limiting the retrieval of potentially interesting digital items. Dictionary based techniques instead allow for search of (possibly disambiguated) multiple candidate translations.

Within the scope of this paper we focus on CLIR systems adopting the queries translation strategy (based on dictionaries) and investigate how to automatically generate linguistic resources needed by these systems. In particular we aim at automatically extracting Named Entities (NEs) gazetteers from Wikipedia; these gazetteers constitute in fact a very important resource for the performances of CLIR systems with respect to queries analysis.

The linguistic analysis of search queries constitutes one of the major issues a CLIR system must face; in fact the contextual information available is scarce, function words (grammar particles, highly connotative of a specific language like prepositions, pronouns, conjunctions, etc) are usually missing and there is a relevant presence of Named Entities that increases the complexity of the analysis. With such a scarce contextual information the gazetteers constitute the only viable option for NEs detection and the capability of detecting them directly impacts important CLIR tasks:

- the identification of the language used in the query, when this information is not explicitly provided by users, see [17] (i.e. *"William Shakespeare théâtre"* would probably trick a language guesser, if it is not capable of discriminating between common terms and NEs).;
- the term translation, since they constitute a special category of terms and should be treated differently from common ones (i.e. they can be left untranslated without it necessary being a failure caused by a lack of resources);
- the query expansion, since these terms should not be enriched with synonyms but rather variations of the named entity (i.e. alternative spellings, nicknames, ..)

In this paper we investigate how to leverage the DBpedia classification of the English Wikipedia pages in order to induce the same classification onto the Wikipedia articles expressed in other languages in order to automatically generate Named Entities gazetteers and domain terminology dictionaries.

Exploiting user generated content as the information source for enhancing CLIR system is particularly significant, since it allows to tune the search systems to real users informational needs and interests. In fact, starting from the so-called Web 2.0 revolution, the academic and research community showed an increasing interest towards the analysis of user generated contents: blogs, forums and collaborative environments like Wikipedia (see [15] or [11]). Moreover, explicit user contributions are increasingly integrated in very specific, task-dependent activities like query disambiguation and translation refinements (i.e. the 'Contribute a better translation' strategy in Google Translate services); such trend underlines that capitalizing user generated data is a key challenge in tuning and tailoring search system performances to real users needs.

The paper is organized as follows: section 2 presents motivations and aims for our work, section 3 present an overview on related works on Named Entities extraction from Wikipedia. Section 4 presents our Automatic Gazetteer Generation approach, while 5 details on the techniques applied in order to extract classification features from the Wikipedia pages and 6 shows some experimental results. Finally section 7 draws conclusion and future work guidelines.

2   Motivations and Aims

Motivations for our investigations stem from research works in the field of Log Analysis and in particular it leverages the experiences from the past LogCLEF tracks from the CLEF conference ([4]). Analysis of search log data in fact is an important strategy in order to tailor the performances of a CLIR system to users needs and also for mining new resources ([5]).

Log data constitute a relevant aspect in the evaluation process of the quality of a search engine and of a multilingual search service; log data can be used to study the usage of a search engine, and to better adapt it to the objectives the users were expecting to reach. In this research field, significant efforts have focused on the analysis of data stored in the transaction logs of Web search engines, Intranets, and Web sites as a means to provide a valuable insight for understanding how search engines are used and the users interests and query formulation patterns ([9]).

These efforts are directed towards specific goals like inferring the search intents of users, identifying user categories through their search patterns and facilitating the personalization of contents or inferring semantic concepts or relations by clustering user queries. Therefore the most frequent queries in a retrieval system offer a valuable indication of the contents that user are expecting to find and on the prevalent query formulation patterns. In particular the LogCLEF task ([24]) proposes to its participants to deal with logs from The European Library (TEL action log 2009) which is an highly representative sample of the Digital Library domain.

The authors of [17] analyzed a sample set of 510 queries from this corpus in order to explore the challenges for queries languages identification and categorization in the context of Digital Libraries. From their work emerges an interesting statistic on the presence of Named Entities within search queries, summarized in 1. A further analysis of the frequencies of NE types involved in the queries evidences that they mainly fall in one of the following categories: Person, Location and Work Title see 1. Their work on the TEL query logs categorization highlights a clear tendency in user search trends and evidences the importance of a Named Entity recognition system for providing multilingual access to Digital Libraries, particularly for what concerns the Language Identification of search queries.

Table 1. Query Types

Only NE	279	egon schiele
NE + other terms	37	conrad huber coat of arms
Non NE	194	translation

However, besides Language Identification, Named Entities also constitute a special category of terms in the process of query translation, as many works underline ([18,1]). Wu et al. in their work demonstrate that NEs and their translations play a critical role in improving CLIR effectiveness and adding a specific module for Named Entities translation obtain a performance gain of 18% in terms of precision over their baseline CLIR system .

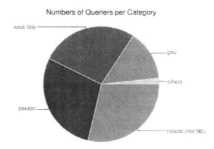

Fig. 1. Search Queries Categorization

From the previous results and considerations it emerges that the presence of high quality Named Entity resources within a CLIR system is crucial in order to provide multilingual access to digital resources, particularly in the domain of Digital Libraries. Therefore in our paper we investigate an approach for automatically extracting a Named Entities gazetteer from Wikipedia using an unsupervised approach that leverages the DBpedia classification of the English Wikipedia pages in order to induce the same classification onto the Wikipedia pages expressed in other languages. In our opinion in the context of search queries analysis gazetteers constitute a better solution with respect to proper NER system since they are designed for extracting references to NE from a syntactically and contextually richer textual input.

3   Related Works

Wikipedia articles have many different useful structures for knowledge extraction: for example, articles are interconnected by hyperlinks carrying relations, articles about similar topics are categorized under the same labels or grouped in lists; categories are organized as taxonomies, interlingual links correlate pages describing the same entity in different languages and title variations lists the different alternative spellings or rephrasing available for the same page title (i.e. *Edison Arantes do Nascimento, Edson Arantes do Nascimiento, Edson Arantes do Nascimento, Pelé, Pelè*).

Different work ([16,11,15]) evidence that a collaboratively constructed resource like Wikipedia is a valuable lexical semantic knowledge base with a high potential in diverse Natural Language Processing (NLP) tasks.

Nothman et al. in [13] propose to transform links between Wikipedia articles into Named Entities annotations and collect the sentences marked with these annotations into a training corpus for NER systems. In order to create the annotations the encyclopedia pages must be previously classified into entity types. The authors used a bootstrap approach to pages classification with heuristics on category head nouns and opening sentences of articles. In a successive work ([2]) they create a gold standard corpus for NER evaluation from Wikipedia pages.

Torisawa et al. ([10]) instead use Wikipedia in order to improve the performances of a CRF-based NE tagger by extracting a category label from the first sentence of the page and using the CoNLL 2003 dataset they demonstrate an improvement of the NER accuracy. The same authors in [14] instead focus on the challenge of enriching multilingual resources by discovering missing cross-language links between English and Japanese Wikipedia articles.

These works demonstrate that Wikipedia is a fruitful choice for Named Entity extraction and in the following section we describe our strategy for automatic Wikipedia pages classification and Named Entities extraction. Unlike previous methods our approach is totally unsupervised, it exploits the various structural elements of Wikipedia, and does not rely on language or domain specific knowledge. By exploiting the structured information present in a Wikipedia article we furthermore aim at enriching our standard gazetteer with the translations of the entities (where cross-lingual links are available) as well as with the alternative spellings or rephrasing of the entity.

4   Automatic Gazetteer Generation

Our approach to automatic gazetteer generation consists in leveraging the results from the DBpedia community project as a means to automatically create a consistent and sound training set in a given language. The training set is used to learn a classification model exploiting a supervised classification techniques from the Machine Learning (ML) field; such a model is then used to classify the Wikipedia pages not present in the training set, thus populating the gazetteer.

The combination of these steps allows for the generation of a typed gazetteer starting from a Wikipedia encyclopedia in a given language and does not require any human intervention or manual annotation of the data.

DBpedia is a community project started in 2007 by the Free University of Berlin and the University of Leipzig; its goal consists in extracting structured information from the English version of Wikipedia and making it publicly available on the Web in the form of a knowledge base. Specifically the Wikipedia entries have been enriched with annotations referring to a shallow, cross-domain ontology. The DBpedia Ontology ([21]) has been manually created within the DBpedia project and is based on the most commonly used infoboxes within Wikipedia. The ontology currently covers over 259 classes hierarchically structured and contains about 1,478,000 instances. With respect to the native Wikipedia classification the DBpedia ontology present a more compact classification and organizes instances according to their types rather than according to their domain or topic as can be evidenced by the respective lists of their top nodes:

- Wikipedia Top Categories: *General reference, Culture and the arts, Geography and places, Health and fitness, History and events, Mathematics and logic, Natural and physical sciences, People and self , Philosophy and thinking, Religion and belief systems, Society and social sciences, Technology and applied sciences.*
- DBpedia Top Categories: *Activity, AnatomicalStructure, Award, Beverage, ChemicalCompound, Currency, Device, Disease, Drug, EthnicGroup, Event, Infrastructure, Language, MeanOfTransportation, MusicGenre, Organisation, Person, Place, Planet, Protein, Species, Website, Work.*

The number of entities semantically labeled by DBpedia is considerable (see 2) and directly provides a valuable gazetteer, unfortunately these resources are only available for the English version of Wikipedia. However exploiting the interlingual links it is possible to partially reuse the same classification for other languages. In fact each Wikipedia page contains links to other pages about the same entity and expressed in other languages; therefore by selecting all the pages in a given language that are related via interlingual links to an English page provided with a semantic label is possible to collecting a set of entities in order to train a classifier. In our experiments we applied this approach to the Italian version of Wikipedia and the table below reports the number of instances for a few classes within the ontology both for the original DBpedia ontology and for the Italian training set.

The number of Italian entities retrieved via the DBpedia mappings (see 2) is significantly less with respect to the original ones; partially because of missing interlingual link between pages but mainly because some of the Named Entities instances (like Person or ArtWork categories) are specific to a given culture and Wikipedia documents describing the same entity in other languages simply don't exist (i.e the English version of Wikipedia contains no entries about the Italian writer *Giuseppe Culicchia* or the novel *"I ventitre giorni della città di Alba"* although they are both very likely to be present in the archives of an Italian library).

Table 2. Instances number by Class

Class	Instances(en)	Instances(it)
Resource (overall)	1478000	692000
Place	413000	97109
Person	312000	43259
Work	320000	33493
Organization	140000	10700

The number of elements collected via the DBpedia mappings and summarized in 2 is enough for avoiding any further manual annotation on the data and apply ML techniques like Decision Trees or Support Vector Machine in order to learn a classification model (more details on the techniques exploited are reported in 6). A crucial aspect in the process of learning such a model is the activity of features selection that consists in extracting from the input data an array of values that represent the elements characteristics.

In the context of a Wikipedia page these values can be extracted both from its textual and structural contents (i.e. interlingual links, titles, alternate spellings). As our approach to automatic gazetteer generation aims at being language agnostic and independent from specific linguistic resources like lemmatizers or POS taggers, for the process of features extraction we decided to rely purely on terms frequency analysis and keyword detection techniques. The process of features extraction is details in 5.

We finally applied a few ML techniques to the collections of features extracted from the training set pages (retrieved via the DBpedia mappings) obtaining classification models that we then used for automatically associating the Italian Wikipedia pages not present in the training set to the DBpedia categories, thus inducing on them the same ontological classification available for the English resources. The classification process and the experimental results we obtained are described in 6.

5   Features Extraction

Since our approach to automatic gazetteer generation aims at being language agnostic in order to be replicable with any natural language (if Wikipedia resources in that language are available), we decided to perform feature selection on textual contents without relying on any language specific knowledge or resources (i.e. lemmatizers or POS taggers) and exploiting measures of terms frequencies distribution across the encyclopedia corpus.

By means of Keyword Extraction techniques, grounded on corpus-based term frequency measures, we preprocessed the data in order to detects lists of terms specific to the DBPedia categories; thus we extracted a set of keywords from each collection of documents associated to a DBpedia category and used the frequencies of all these terms within the encyclopedia pages as features for the classification model.

In order to extract the keywords from the textual contents we adopted the Log Odds Ratio measure (LOR) to evaluate the specificity of a given term for the domain under analysis ([3,6]); the LOR measure is based on the comparison of the frequencies of the same term within different corpora: a domain corpus and a general one. The idea behind this approach is that if the normalized frequency of a term in the domain corpus significantly surpasses the normalized frequency of the same term in a general corpus then such a term is connotative of the domain under exam and can be formalized in the following formula:

$$- \; lor(termX) = ln(\frac{domainFreq(termX)*(GeneralTermsFreq-generalFreq(termX))}{generalFreq(termX)*(DomainTermsFreq-domainFreq(termX))})$$

where *domainFreq(termX)* and *generalFreq(termX)* represent the frequencies of a given term respectively in the domain corpus and in the general one, while *DomainTermsFreq* and *GeneralTermsFreq* measures the total frequencies of all terms in the two corpora.

In the context of our approach the domain corpus is constituted by all Wikipedia pages included in the training set and pertaining to a specific NE category (i.e. Person) while the general corpus is constituted by all the other pages. Only the terms with a LOR value greater than a given threshold are selected as domain terms. In our experimental setup the threshold used is *0.7* and correspond to a ratio of *2.5* (meaning that only terms with a frequency in the domain corpus 2.5 times greater than the frequency within the general corpus may be selected).

In order to limit the number of features selected by this strategy we decided to collect terms not only specific to the domain of interest but also with a significant document coverage therefore we imposed an additional constraint on domain term selection constituted by a coverage measure; only the terms that appear at least in the *3%* of domain documents are selected. An excerpt of the extracted terms along with their LOR values and grouped by class is reported in table 3.

From the structured data present in encyclopedia pages we extracted and used a couple of additional features:

- the number of title variations available for a given page in the same language(i.e. different alternative spellings or rephrasing expressions);

Table 3. Terms by Class

Organization	Person	Location	Work
band [3.176]	carriera [2.195]	demografica [4.341]	trama [2.720]
calcistiche [3.048]	palmares [2.113]	demografia [3.968]	drammatici [2.688]
demo [2.867]	school [1.915]	circondario [3.272]	tracce [2.296]
records [2.782]	professionista [1.906]	geografia [3.171]	dvd [2.236]
etichetta [2.318]	titolare [1.876]	censimento [3.109]	film [2.208]
football [2.163]	attore [1.767]	comuni [2.7458]	sonora [2.183]
fan [2.117]	cresciuto [1.667]	dipartimento [2.617]	gioco [2.153]
discografica [2.082]	sposato [1.645]	abitanti [2.590]	video [2.142]
marchio [2.049]	infanzia [1.612]	situato [2.486]	canzone [2.122]
aziende [1.985]	college [1.594]	capoluogo [2.464]	girato [2.085]
gruppo [1.911]	trasferisce [1.514]	abitato [2.451]	cover [2.0462]
vendite [1.905]	successi [1.500]	contea [2.440]	brano [1.993]
registrato [1.888]	biografia [1.470]	alpi [2.426]	disco [1.957]
azienda [1.8509]	sposare [1.435]	comunale [2.390]	rilasciato [1.837]
league [1.844]	privata [1.404]	luoghi [2.363]	singolo [1.801]
compagnie [1.741]	lavorare [1.404]	situata [2.177]	uscito [1.787]
classifiche [1.714]	matrimonio [1.333]	autonoma [2.175]	album [1.783]
fondata [1.701]	morire [1.312]	distretto [2.090]	romanzo [1.724]
formazione [1.6163]	figli [1.305]	popolazione [2.067]	episodi [1.712]
compagnia [1.559]	padre [1.304]	economia [2.058]	brani [1.693]

– the label variability across languages, as the ratio between the number of distinct labels from the interlingual links and their total number (i.e. if a page has 4 interlingual links, all with the same label, the ratio would be *0.25*)

The selection of these additional features is motivated by the statistical observation that Named Entities tend to have a greater number of variations available and a lower label variability across languages with respect to common words.

6   Experimental Results

In this section we present the experimental results obtained by applying our Automatic Gazetteer Generation approach to the Italian Wikipedia entries and taking into account the following DBpedia categories: *Person, Location, Organization* and *Work*. Therefore our classification task requires to associate each Italian Wikipedia page (not in the training set) to one of the previous four categories or to the common words group.

By using the training set (labeled with the DBpedia categories) and the features described in the previous sections we built a classification model exploiting a few of the supervised techniques publicly available in the well known Weka suite [8]. In particular, in the experimental setup presented in this work, we decided to adopt an evenly weighted combination of 3 different classifiers:

– a classifier based on the C4.5 decision tree algorithm
  (weka.classifiers.trees.J48)
– a classifier based on Support Vector Machine
  (weka.classifiers.functions.SMO)
– a classifier based on Naive Bayes approach
  (weka.classifiers.bayes.NaiveBayesMultinomial)

These classifiers, besides being publicly available for research purposes, are widely adopted in literature ([12]) and proved to be techniques well fitting to the NER task; furthermore previous works ([7]) have also shown that combining several ML models using voting technique always performs better than any single ML model.

In order to evaluate the performance of the classifier we manually annotated a test corpus of 1000 Wikipedia articles, randomly selected among the ones not included in the training set and composed by:

– 308 Common Words
– 692 Named Entities (198 Locations, 173 Organizations, 179 Persons, 149 ArtWorks)

and analyzed it with our classifier. The performance of this classification task obtained are reported in table 4

Table 5 instead details by NE type the number of Italian Wikipedia pages classified by our approach in comparison to the ones present in the training set induced from DBpedia.

Table 4. Classifier Evaluation

Correctly Classified	956	95.6 %
Incorrectly Classified	44	4.4 %

Precision	Recall	F-Measure	Class
0.931	0.952	0.941	per
0.985	0.983	0.984	loc
0.889	0.847	0.867	org
0.931	0.931	0.931	wrd
0.954	0.944	0.949	wrk

Table 5. New Instances Obtained via Classification

Class	Training Set	Classified	New	Gain in #Instances
Place	97109	204378	107269	110%
Person	43259	170211	126952	293%
Work	33493	120794	87301	260%
Organization	10700	34778	24078	225%

7   Conclusions

In this paper we described a completely unsupervised methodology that leverages the DBpedia classification of the English Wikipedia pages and induces the same classification onto Wikipedia pages expressed in other languages. Exploiting this automated classification an enriched gazetteer of Named Entities is generated. By properly selecting the DBpedia classes that compose the training set the approach can be easily adapted to generate list of domain terms along with their translations and spelling variations.

The proposed approach seems promising as it doesn't require any human intervention and yields very good performances. In future we plan to extend our investigations in order to take into account a wider set of DBpedia categories (the full ontology taxonomy and not only a few specific classes) and the multiple membership of entities through the types hierarchy.

Besides further developments of the proposed approach as we stated in our motivations, we intend to exploit the automatically generated gazetteer to the next LogCLEF task in order to evaluate its effective usefulness in the analysis of Digital Libraries logs.

Acknowledgements

This work has been supported and founded by EuropeanaConnect and Galateas EU projects.

References

1. Babych, B., Hartley, A.: Improving machine translation quality with automatic named entity recognition. In: EAMT (2003)
2. Balasuriya, D., Ringland, N., Nothman, J., Murphy, T., Curran, J.R.: Named entity recognition in Wikipedia. In: People's Web (2009)
3. Baroni, M., Bernardini, S.: BootCaT: Bootstrapping corpora and terms from the web. In: LREC (2004)
4. Bosca, A., Dini, L.: Language Identification Strategies for Cross Language Information Retrieval. In: logCLEF (2010)
5. Bosca, A., Dini, L.: The role of logs in improving cross language access in digital libraries. In: Proceedings of the International Conference on Semantic Web and Digital Libraries (2009)
6. Bosca, A., Dini, L.: Ontology based law discovery. In: Francesconi, E., Montemagni, S., Peters, W., Tiscornia, D. (eds.) Semantic Processing of Legal Texts. LNCS (LNAI), vol. 6036, pp. 122–135. Springer, Heidelberg (2010)
7. Florian, R., Ittycheriah, A., Jing, H., Zhang, T.: Named entity recognition through classifier combination. In: Proceedings of CoNLL (2003)
8. Hall, M., Eibe, F., Holmes, G., Pfahringer, B., Reutemann, P., Witten, I.H.: The WEKA Data Mining Software: An Update. SIGKDD Explorations 11(1) (2009)
9. Jansen, B.J.: Search log analysis: What it is, what's been done, how to do it. Library & Information Science Research 28(3), 407–432 (2006)
10. Kazama, J., Torisawa, K.: Exploiting Wikipedia as External Knowledge for Named Entity Recognition. In: EMNLP-CoNLL (2007)
11. Müller, C., Gurevych, I.: Using wikipedia and wiktionary in domain-specific information retrieval. In: Peters, C., Deselaers, T., Ferro, N., Gonzalo, J., Jones, G.J.F., Kurimo, M., Mandl, T., Peñas, A., Petras, V. (eds.) CLEF 2008. LNCS, vol. 5706, pp. 219–226. Springer, Heidelberg (2009)
12. Nadeau, D., Sekine, S.: A survey of named entity recognition and classification. Journal of Linguisticae Investigationes (2007)
13. Nothman, J., Curran, J.R., Murphy, T.: Transforming Wikipedia into Named Entity Training Data. In: ALTA (2008)
14. Oh, J., Kawahara, D., Uchimoto, K., Kazama, J., Torisawa, K.: Enriching Multilingual Language Resources by Discovering Missing Cross-Language Links in Wikipedia. In: Web Intelligence (2008)
15. Ponzetto, S.P., Navigli, R.: Knowledge-rich Word Sense Disambiguation rivaling supervised systems. In: ACL (2010)
16. Reese, S., Boleda, G., Cuadros, M., Padr, L., Rigau, G.: Wikicorpus: A Word-Sense Disambiguated Multilingual Wikipedia Corpus. In: LREC (2010)
17. Stiller, J., Gde, M., Petras, V.: Ambiguity of Queries and the Challenges for Query Language Detection. In: logCLEF (2010)
18. Wu, D., He, D., Ji, H., Grishman, R.: The Effects of High Quality Translations of Named Entities in Cross-Language Information Exploration. In: IEEE NLP-KE (2008)
19. ANSI/NISO Z39.50, http://www.loc.gov/z3950/agency/
20. CACAO project, http://www.cacaoproject.eu/
21. DBPedia Ontology, http://wiki.dbpedia.org/ Ontology
22. Dublin Core Metadata Initiative, http://dublincore.org/
23. EuropeanaConnect project, http://www.europeanaconnect.eu/
24. http://www.uni-hildesheim.de/logclef/index.html
25. MICHAEL project, http://www.michael-culture.eu/
26. OAI-PMH, http://www.openarchives.org/pmh/

Hybrid and Interactive Domain-Specific Translation for Multilingual Access to Digital Libraries

Gareth J.F. Jones, Marguerite Fuller, Eamonn Newman, and Ying Zhang

Centre for Digital Video Processing
School of Computing
Dublin City University, Dublin 9, Ireland
gjones@computing.dcu.ie

Abstract. Accurate high-coverage translation is a vital component of reliable cross language information retrieval (CLIR) systems. This is particularly true for retrieval from archives such as Digital Libraries which are often specific to certain domains. While general machine translation (MT) has been shown to be effective for CLIR tasks in laboratory information retrieval evaluation tasks, it is generally not well suited to specialized situations where domain-specific translations are required. We demonstrate that effective query translation in the domain of cultural heritage (CH) can be achieved using a hybrid translation method which augments a standard MT system with domain-specific phrase dictionaries automatically mined from *Wikipedia* . We further describe the use of these components in a domain-specific interactive query translation service. The interactive system selects the hybrid translation by default, with other possible translations being offered to the user interactively to enable them to select alternative or additional translation(s). The objective of this interactive service is to provide user control of translation while maximising translation accuracy and minimizing the translation effort of the user. Experiments using our hybrid translation system with sample query logs from users of CH websites demonstrate a large improvement in the accuracy of domain-specific phrase detection and translation.

1 Introduction

The growth in Digital Libraries (DLs) is offering access to increasing numbers of document collections from around the world. The full potential of these resources for applications such as research, study and cultural exchange can only be realised when users have efficient and reliable access to them. Such access poses many challenges for the designers of technologies for DLs. One of these challenges is the development of effective methods to support multilingual access to DLs where the contents may be in multiple languages, one or more of which may be unknown or known only partially to the user of the DLs. In such situations the user must rely on automatic translation technologies to support search

R. Bernardi et al. (Eds.): NLP4DL/AT4DL 2009, LNCS 6699, pp. 72–91, 2011.

of the content and interaction with retrieved items. In working with these systems user must pose their search queries in a language known to them and rely on automatic translation to render their search request into the document language or languages, and, depending on their reading skills in the target language, possibly rely on automatic translation of retrieved documents. The effectiveness with which their search is conducted depends to a large extent on the quality of the translation of the domain-specific concepts.

Reliable translation is thus a key component of effective cross language information retrieval (CLIR) and multilingual information retrieval (MLIR) systems. Various approaches to translation have been explored at evaluation workshops such as TREC[1], CLEF[2] and NTCIR[3]. While extensive sets of experiments have been reported at these workshops, they have been based on laboratory information retrieval (IR) test collections consisting of news articles or technical reports with "TREC" style search queries[4] with a minimum length of a full sentence. With document sets such as these, general purpose translation resources based on bilingual dictionaries or standard machine translation (MT) have been shown to be effective for translation in CLIR.

This approach to translation using general resources will however frequently not be sufficient for multilingual DLs which often contain domain-specific terms or phrases related to the specific content that the user is seeking to locate within the library. In these cases content, and in particular the sections of the content related to the specific domain of interest, must be translated accurately if effective access to relevant information is to be achieved. One DL domain of which this is true is cultural heritage (CH). The CH domain is of interest to many organisations, including museums and national institutions engaged in the preservation of cultural content. Developing tools to make this content available to larger numbers of potential users than is the case at present is of interest to all such organisations. This desire is driven partially by a desire to increase societal awareness of their cultural assets, but also more pragmatically to justify the resources currently being invested in the development of DLs and their cultural holdings. Search tools for CH content may take the form of standard search engines producing ranked lists for users, but may also look towards more sophisticated applications incorporating personalisation of content selection and delivery of dynamically composed personal responses.

A number of projects in recent years have explored technologies to advance multilingual access to DLs. Among these projects was the EU FP6 *MultiMatch*[5] project which was concerned with information access for multimedia and multilingual content for a range of European languages in the domain of CH. In this paper we briefly review the principle approaches taken to translation in CLIR and MLIR systems, namely dictionary-based methods and machine translation

---

[1] http://trec.nist.gov

[2] http://www.clef-campaign.org/

[3] http://research.nii.ac.jp/ntcir/

[4] Referred to at TREC as search *topics*.

[5] http://www.multimatch.org

(MT). We then use this to motivate our proposal of a hybrid translation service for CLIR and MLIR developed within the MultiMatch project to facilitate effective domain-specific translation in the CH domain. This combines a commercial MT service with a domain-specific dictionary gathered automatically from the multilingual *Wikipedia*. The basic form of this service operates automatically in the form of an augmented MT service which outputs its best available translation of the text input. We demonstrate the effectiveness of this service using sample CH request logs in English, Spanish and Italian provided to us by organisations providing access to in DLs in the area of CH. We translate the requests and examine the quality of the translated output using human assessors. This study demonstrates how using a domain-specific phrase dictionary to augment a general MT system can improve the coverage and reliability of translation of these requests within this domain.

The automatic hybrid service is then extended to provide an interactive translation service enabling users with some knowledge of the target translation language to check the elements of the hybrid translated output and to correct or augment those which they judge to be inaccurate or limited using alternative possible translations taken from the bilingual dictionary.

The remainder of this paper is organized as follows: Section 2 overviews the topic of translation in CLIR and MLIR, Section 3 introduces our hybrid approach to translation and the translation resources used in this study, Section 4 describes our experimental investigation of the effectiveness of the hybrid translation service, Section 5 then describes the extension of the hybrid service to enable interactive user adjustment of the translated output, and finally Section 6 summarizes our conclusions and considers directions for further work.

2 Translation Approaches in CLIR and MLIR

The majority of early work in CLIR concentrated on the translation of search queries using bilingual dictionaries. These were typically the largest general purpose electronic dictionaries available to the investigators. Simple request translation using these dictionaries replaced each word in the source language with all possible alternatives in the target language. The significant ambiguity introduced into the request by this approach was quickly shown to have a significant adverse impact on retrieval effectiveness [9]. Much research in CLIR then focused on methods to remove or reduce the impact of this ambiguity in translation of search queries. One of the most important factors introduced which improved CLIR effectiveness was translation of phrases rather than their individual words [3]. This is particularly important for idiomatic phrases, but also reduces ambiguity in the case of compositional phrases.

A logical alternative translation method in CLIR is the use of MT. It was often argued that search requests lack sufficient grammatical structure to be reliably translated by MT systems, which are traditionally designed for the translation of linguistically well formed text. However, experiments applying MT to CLIR tasks rapidly showed that while the lack of structure in the requests can result in translation errors, overall CLIR effectiveness is often as good as or better than that achieved by using the most complex dictionary-based methods [10]. Until recently MT systems were only available for a very limited number of language pairs due to the very high cost of development. However, MT systems for many more language pairs are now appearing, greatly increasing its appeal for CLIR. For the translation of documents either for use in the retrieval process (by translating documents instead of the queries [11]), or for reading by users after retrieval with query translation, MT is the only realistic option.

While MT systems can provide sufficient translations for general language expressions, they are often not sufficient for domain-specific phrases that contain personal names, place names, technical terms, titles of artworks, etc. In addition, certain words and phrases hold special meanings in specific domains. For example, the Spanish phrase "Canto general" was translated by a standard MT system used in our work into English as "general song", which is arguably correct. However, in the CH domain, "Canto general" refers to a book title from Pablo Neruda's book of poems and should be translated directly into English as the phrase "Canto general". Multiple word phrases are more information-bearing and more unambiguously represented than single words; they are also often domain-specific and typically absent from static general lexicons. Effective translation of such phrases is particularly critical for the short search queries that are typically entered by non-expert users of search engines. It should be clear that failure to translate these important expressions correctly will often have a disastrous impact on search effectiveness.

An advantage of dictionary-based translation methods for search queries is that bilingual dictionaries can be constructed for new language pairs or domains at comparatively very low cost, and easily be adjusted to add new translation entries, and, of particular importance for CLIR, new phrase translation pairs.

Overall then it would be desirable to have a translation service for CLIR which was well specified for the domain of interest, e.g. CH, and could be easily further adapted as new vocabulary is encountered, but also did not introduce the ambiguity associated with dictionary-based translation. The next section proposes a hybrid translation method that combines these features.

3   A Hybrid Approach to Translation in Information Retrieval

Our novel hybrid translation service aims to improve translation effectiveness in the CH domain by improving the translation of phrases previously untranslated or inappropriately translated by a standard MT system. In this work we combine a standard non-domain specific MT system with domain-specific phrase dictionaries mined from Wikipedia combined with a small standard bilingual dictionaries. Our hybrid service aims to simultaneously address problems of words or phrases which are outside the domain of the MT system, prevent the problems of introducing translation ambiguity associated with dictionary-based translation models, and to improve the reliability of CH phrase translation. Figure 1

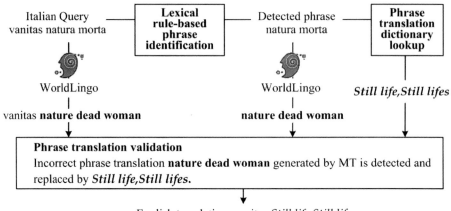

Fig. 1. An example of Italian–English hybrid translation of a search query

illustrates the stages of our hybrid query translation process for the translation of an Italian search query into English. The basic idea is that rather than passing the text for translation directly to the MT system, we first analyse it to locate phrases in a bilingual dictionary, and handle these specially so that the statistically most likely phrases can be included in a hybrid translation output by combining them with the output of the MT system.

Three methods of multiple-word phrase identification have been commonly used in text analysis: lexical rule-based [3][9], statistical [5], and syntactical methods [5][15]. The lexical rule-based approach with maximum forward matching is adopted in our hybrid translation process due to its robust performance and computational simplicity. The input text is sequentially scanned to seek matches in the phrase dictionary. Where more than one phrase translation is available in the bilingual dictionary, the most frequent translation in the training corpus is selected for inclusion in the final translation. The longest matched sub-sequence is taken as a phrase and translated via a domain-specific dictionary lookup. This process is recursively invoked on the remaining part of the text until no further matches are found. The effectiveness of this approach depends strongly on the completeness of the coverage of the adopted dictionary.

The text for translation is then processed to replace the identified phrases with their corresponding translation from the dictionary-based translation service. The translated phrase is then annotated in the text to be translated to prevent any mistranslation that might occur during translation by the MT system. The demarcation marks indicate to the MT system that content between these marks should not be translated by the MT system. The augmented text is passed to the MT system and its response is processed to remove markup before the combined hybrid output is presented as the translation. One important practical feature for an MT system selected to be used in this service is that it must support text markup to leave marked items untranslated in the output. After informal analysis of a number of possible online MT systems we selected the WorldLingo[6] system for our work since it provided good support for content markup and translation for a good number of language pairs.

The next section describes the construction of our CH domain-specific bilingual dictionaries.

3.1   CH Domain-Specific Dictionary Construction

Our CH domain-specific dictionaries combine bilingual wordlists downloaded from the XDXF Dictionaries[7] webpage combined with.domain-specific bilingual wordlists built by mining interdocument links from Wikipedia[8] for documents on the same topic. The downloaded XDXF dictionaries contained between 950,000 and 250,000 word pairs depending on the language pair and direction of translation being considered.

In recent years Wikipedia has emerged as a major online source of information. While the largest proportion of content is in English, varying amounts of content are available in other languages. As might be expected since the content is community contributed, the amount of context is somewhat correlated with the number of speakers of the language, but is continuing to grow for all languages. There are many instances of pages on the same topic in different languages within Wikipedia. Although not directly relevant here, it should be noted that while these pages are on the same topic in different languages, they are not generally parallel texts or even close translations of each other, but rather individual pages on the same topic authored separately by speakers of the relevant languages. This means that they generally reflect the cultural perspective and vocabulary use associated with the speakers of the language in question. As a multilingual hypertext medium, Wikipedia has been shown to be a valuable source of translation information [1,2,4,6]. Wikipedia is structured as an interconnected network of articles, in particular, Wikipedia page titles in one language are often linked to a multilingual database of corresponding articles in other languages. Unlike the web, most hyperlinks in Wikipedia have a more consistent pattern and meaningful interpretation. For example, the English Wikipedia page http://en.wikipedia.org/wiki/Cupid_and_Psyche hyperlinks to its counterpart written in Italian http://it.wikipedia.org/wiki/Amore_e_Psiche, where the basenames of these two URLs ("Cupid and Psyche" and "Amore e Psiche") are an English–Italian translation pair. Thus, the URL basename can be considered to be a term (single word or multiple-word phrase) that should be translated as a unit.

Utilizing the multilingual linkage feature of Wikipedia, we used a three-stage automatic process to mine Wikipedia pages as a translation source and construct phrase dictionaries in the culture heritage domain:

---

[6] http://worldlingo.com
[7] http://xdxf.revdanica.com/down/
[8] http://wikipedia.org

1. We performed a web crawl from the English Wikipedia, Category: Culture. This category contains links to articles and subcategories concerning arts, religions, traditions, entertainment, philosophy, etc. The crawl process in the category of culture included all of its recursive subcategories. In total, we collected 458, 929 English pages.
2. For each English page the hyperlinks to each of the translation languages to be used were extracted. For the study reported here, the languages mined for links were Italian and Spanish.
3. The basenames of each pair of hyperlinks (English–Italian, English–Spanish) were selected as translations and then added into our domain-specific dictionaries. Multiple-word phrases were added into the phrase dictionary for each language.

Our Wikipedia mined dictionaries contained about 90, 000, 70, 000, and 80, 000 distinct multiple-word phrases in English, Italian, and Spanish respectively. The majority of the phrases extracted were CH domain-specific named entities and the rest of them general noun-based phrases, such as "Music of Ireland" and "Philosophy of history". We did not apply any classifier to filter out the general noun-based phrases since such phrases can be useful additions for accurate query translation.

Where multiple translations of a phrase were located in the Wikipedia archive, the alternative translations were ranked in the bilingual dictionaries by frequency of occurrence in the Wikipedia pages. This ranking enables us to select a single most likely translation for use in the single best output of the hybrid translation system. Combining the Wikipedia mined dictionaries with the general purpose ones gathered from XDXF Dictionaries gave CH-biased dictionaries with good coverage of general and domain-specific concepts.

4 Experimental Investigation

In order to investigate the effectiveness of our hybrid translation service for CH search request translation, we performed an experimental investigation to compare request translation accuracy of our domain-specific hybrid approach with the output of WorldLingo standard MT. The goal here was to measure the degree to which output translations were judged suitable as translated search queries by human assessors. Thus rather than using a standard IR test collection, we based our experiments on real user query log data.

4.1 Query Log Test Sets

The query logs used in our experiments were all provided by real users sending CH related queries to websites provided by or associated with CH organisations. One of the sets consists of queries in Spanish, the second is in Italian and the third is in English. The Spanish queries came from a DL based in Spain whose focus is on poetry and ancient and modern literature in the Spanish language. The

Table 1. Query translation examples

Original	WorldLingo MT	Hybrid Translation
Plinio il giovane	Plinio the young person	Pliny the Younger
Pittura a tempura	Painting to moderates	Egg tempera
Literatura infantil y juvenil	Infantile and youthful Literature	Children's literature
Al andalus	To andalus	Islamic Spain
Still life paintings	Pinturasde la vida inmovil	Bodegon pinturas

Italian queries are taken from the "Cultural" section of a large Italian Internet Service Provider's website. The queries in English were extracted from the query logs of the website for a well-known art gallery based in London, U.K. There were 1423 Italian queries (with an average length of 2.49 words), 1088 Spanish queries (3.39 words on average) and 100 English queries (1.67 words on average).

Each query was translated separately using the standard WorldLingo MT system and the hybrid system. We translated the Spanish and Italian queries to English (and the English to Spanish and Italian) since we had bilingual evaluators available for these language pairs. When both systems produced the same translation for a given text, the results were discarded since for this evaluation we were interested in the disagreements between the systems. The sets of translations are denoted *Es-En*, *It-En*, *En-Es* and *En-It*. The translations were collated so that the evaluators could make a side-by-side comparison between the original text, the MT output and hybrid translation. Some examples are given in Table 1. A single bilingual evaluator judged the suitability of each translated query set. The details of instructions given to each evaluator for the experiment are described in the following section. It should be noted that it was not possible to directly compare the lexical coverage of our domain-specific dictionaries and the built-in phrase dictionaries of WorldLingo since we did not have access to the internal WorldLingo dictionaries.

4.2 Human Evaluation of Translation Quality

For each query where the WordLingo MT and hybrid outputs differed, the bilingual evaluators were asked to mark which of the two translation results they "considered to be better", that is more accurate to a native speaker. As there was only one evaluator per set, we were not able to consider inter-annotator agreement on this subjective measure. Any possible bias due to a single evaluator will result in a skew of the results for one set, rather than the whole evaluation. Table 2 summarises the results of the experiments. There were 2711 queries to be translated in total. The same translated output was produced for 1919 queries leaving 792 to be examined by the assessors.

The results in Table 2 show that the hybrid translation system was generally regarded as providing a better translation than the WorldLingo MT system. For Spanish-English, the hybrid translation was correct in 79% of the cases where there was a disagreement between the systems. "No preference" results

Table 2. Results of analysis of alternative translations

Language Pair	Number of Translations	Number of Disagreements	Hybrid Correct	Both Correct	WorldLingo MT Correct	No Preference
It - En	1423	482	288	63	75	56
Es - En	1088	281	222	0	58	1
En - It	100	15	9	1	2	3
En - Es	100	14	11	0	3	0

Table 3. Results of analysis of hybrid translations including all dictionary entries

Language Pair	Number of Translations	Number of Disagreements	Hybrid Correct	Both Correct	WorldLingo MT Correct	No Preference
It - En	1423	482	353 (+65)	71 (+8)	2 (-73)	56
Es - En	1088	281	273 (+51)	0	7 (-51)	1
En - It	100	15	10 (+1)	2 (+1)	0 (-2)	3
En - Es	100	14	12 (+1)	2 (+2)	0 (-3)	0

indicate that the evaluator felt that neither translation was appropriate. For Italian to English, when we remove "no preference" results and those where both systems were deemed correct (leaving 482-(56+63) = 363 instances), we achieve a very similar score of 79.3% correctly translated by the hybrid system. Situations where both are deemed "correct" raise the interesting issue for CLIR of which one should be preferred in order to be most likely to retrieve relevant documents. The small number of English queries means that we cannot attach significance to the results, however for the sake of completeness, we can report correct translation rates of 81.8% for English to Italian and 78.5% for English to Spanish, which are similar to the results from the larger sets. The similarity of these results, across different language pairs, different evaluators and different set sizes suggests that there was no significant bias inherent in any of the evaluations.

These results show that our method of enhancing MT by incorporating domain-specific dictionaries is successful for query translation. By identifying phrases and named entities with specific interpretations in the CH domain, we are able to improve on standard MT output in around 80% of cases.

Having native speakers as evaluators allows further analysis of the actual quality of the translations, rather than just comparing them to the baseline. In order to make a more detailed comparison, the evaluators were also asked to highlight any translations which they thought were "particularly good" or "particularly bad". For example, the evaluator for translations between Spanish and English thought a translation of "poema del mio cid" was particularly good as it inserted the full name of the work ("Cantar de Mio Cid") into the translation (giving "poem of Cantar de Mio Cid") making it much better than the literal translation provided by the MT system ("poem of mine cid").

In CLIR, unlike conventional MT tasks, there is no need to produce a single best translation, and indeed including multiple possible translations has the potential to retrieve a set of relevant documents where information is described in alternative equally correct ways in different documents. This alternative descriptions of the relevant information may match well with different versions of a query. In order to assess the potential of the hybrid system to be used in CLIR, including all the possible translations available in the domain-specific dictionaries, the results were re-examined showing all the alternative translations available in the hybrid dictionary to the evaluators. In many cases, one of the alternative hybrid translations matched the MT system translation exactly, or matched it when stopwords were removed. Table 3 shows the updated results of adding these alternative translations. The new results show that including the alternative translations produces a large increase in the number of translations produced by the hybrid system deemed correct. In this case where the hybrid system was preferred, the evaluator felt that the expanded output of the hybrid system was better for CLIR than the MT system on its own in almost all cases. The few cases where both results were judged to be correct arose in situations where the output from the two systems was so similar as to effectively be functionally identical.

Analysis of the output of the hybrid translation system showed that at least one phrase is detected in 90% of the evaluation queries. These included, personal names, geographic locations, and titles of various types of artworks. This indicates that our phrase dictionaries have good coverage of phrases to be translated.

While we were not able to manually evaluate the accuracy of all translation pairs in our bilingual dictionaries due to limited resources, our experiments using the hybrid translation tool for sample queries in the CH domain demonstrate that our translations are generally regarded as very accurate by bilingual assessors.

4.3   Related Experiments

The practical objective of our hybrid translation system is to improve CLIR effectiveness in a specific domain of interest. Since we did not have access to a suitable IR test collection consisting of set of documents with corresponding relevance data for the user search topics provided by the CH organisations, we conducted a set of CLIR experiments using a different domain-specific IR test collection. We used the CLEF 2007 Cross Language Speech Retrieval (CLSR) English language task. This task consists of a small collection of about 8000 spoken "documents" and 42 search queries with corresponding relevance data indicating which of the documents are relevant to each query. The documents were formed from English language interviews with survivors of the Holocaust which were divided into topically coherent segments by subject matter experts. The audio segments were automatically transcribed using automatic speech recognition. The speech recognition was adapted to the domain of the audio recordings, and produced transcripts with an error rate on the order of 20%. This error rate may appear high, but is generally found to be sufficiently accurate to support effective retrieval of the content based on the transcriptions [7]. This test collection provided an interesting test for search technologies within the MultiMatch project since it is a (non-CH) domain-specific cross language multimedia retrieval task. One limitation of this dataset is that the query statements are generally rather longer than those typically entered into a web search engine. They are typically a full sentence of text, rather than the two or three words often entered into a search engine. However, this task is sufficient to explore the efficacy of our hybrid translation method.

For the CLEF task we trained new bilingual dictionaries in the domain of the CL-SR data set (issues relating to World War Two). These were then used in combination with the WorldLingo MT system to perform a set of comparative experiments exploring alternative translation strategies for search queries originating in French, German and Spanish. The full results of these experiments are reported in [16]. Results from these experiments showed that combining our domain-specific dictionaries with MT methods improves the CLIR effectiveness in terms of Mean Average Precision (MAP) and Precision at rank 10 (P@10) for the CL-SR task. While best retrieval accuracy was achieved using a monolingual evaluation task where the queries were English, our results for the cross language task were the best among those making formal submissions to the CLEF 2007 CL-SR task, showing the lowest decrease relative to monolingual performance when queries were translated from their source language to English [12]. These results are encouraging for us since they demonstrate that our approach can work well for ad hoc retrieval and when working with errorful transcribed output from speech recognition systems, as is often encountered when working with multimedia DL archives.

5   Interactive Hybrid Translation Service

The hybrid translation service described so far provides a single best or most likely translation of the input text. The experimental analysis in the previous section shows that when there is a difference between them, this "best" translation often improves on the standard WorldLingo MT output, and additionally that including alternative translations available in the dictionary improves the coverage of correct translations in the output. Users of CLIR systems typically have differing skills in the languages concerned. Thus users with some knowledge of the language into which the text is being translated will be able to identify some of the mistakes in the hybrid output, i.e. users with some level of reading or at least word recognition skill, but not sufficient productive skills to write the query in the target language. In order to take advantage of these users's language abilities and where possible to eliminate or at least reduce translation errors, an interactive version of the hybrid translation service was developed.

The intention of this system is to provide a translation service which provides an effective integration of the strengths of the separate MT and dictionary-based translation services, and exploits any linguistic knowledge of the users. The MT service provides a single automatic output, similar in form and functionality to the new hybrid service. In this approach the user only has to enter the text which is translated automatically. This is thus low cost to the user and fast, however using this strategy the user has no control over the output and is thus

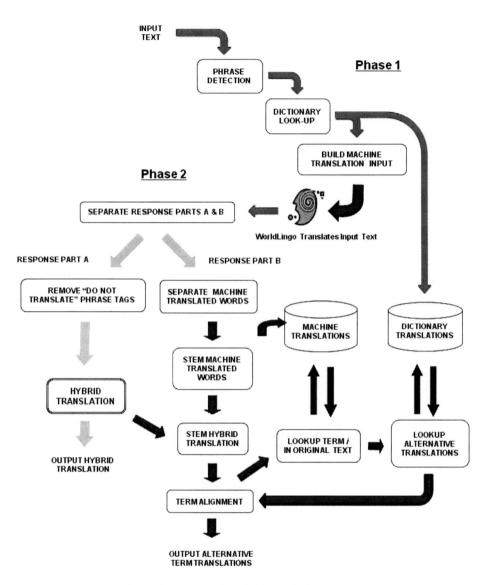

Fig. 2. Interactive Hybrid Translation Process

entirely dependent on the suitability of the design and parameter settings of the translation system. A simple dictionary-based approach uses all the available translations of each word, however, as outlined earlier, this has been shown to be ineffective in many experimental studies since it introduces ambiguities, effectively translation errors, some of which can have substantial impact on retrieval behaviour. However, dictionary-based translation potentially offers the user the possibility to select from all the available translations. These translations can be presented to the user in many different ways, for example presenting possible translations in order of frequency or alphabetically, or recommending the first sense in a dictionary as the default translation, with other possibilities shown to the user for selection. Whatever translation ranking design choice is made here, the key point is that the process is interactive with the user having complete free choice of which translations should be used in the CLIR process.

User studies generally show that users who are suitably linguistically qualified like to have control of the translation process in CLIR [8][13]. However, this requires work from the user to perform the translation selections in the CLIR process, and it is generally understood that users do not like to expend more effort than necessary in undertaking the search process. The objective of the interactive hybrid translation service is to increase user control of the translation while maximising translation accuracy and minimizing the average amount of work to be carried by the user to achieve this. To achieve this, the hybrid translation service described in the previous section was extended to facilitate a user's possible desire to find alternative translations for words and phrases within their query to those proposed by automatic translation. The nature of the dictionary translation system lent itself to this extension since many of the terms translated by the MT system also appear in the dictionary with alternative translations. The aim of the hybrid translation system is to provide the single "best" translation to the user as the default translation. If the user is happy with this, they can then proceed directly to the CLIR phase. If, however, they are not satisfied with the accuracy or coverage of the translation, the interactive hybrid system enables them to access the alternative translations available in the dictionary and to select items from among those available to replace or augment elements of the single "best" default translation.

While perhaps appearing a very simple process, incorporating the interactive aspect to the hybrid translation service is actually quite complex due to the use of multiword phrases and the characteristics of MT. For example, if a word sequence is sent to WordLingo for translation, it is often highly problematic to match each word in the original text with its translation as is required for simple dictionary-based translation. There are a number of reasons for this, the word order many differ, a single term in one language may translate into multiple words in another language, multiple words in one language may form compound words in another language, or additional words may be added to the translation which have no equivalent translation in the source language. A simple approach to overcoming this problem would have been to send each word separately to the MT system for translation. However this would have defeated the purpose of using an MT system since it would have performed simple single word translation of isolated words in the same manner a dictionary-based translation service and any context data contained in the text, important for exploitation of the full linguistic resources of the MT system, would have been ignored. Our solution to this problem is to augment the text sent to the MT system. The augmented text contains the original text fused with a tagged version of the text. The tagged version of the text contains each query word separated by demarcated tags. The MT system translates the text as a whole entity and each word as an entity. This allows a mapping of translated words to original words, this mapping enables the combination of a translation component containing the full hybrid translation along with possible alternative translations for each word in the translation. The complete process to produce the output for the interactive translation system is illustrated in Figure 2.

5.1 Interactive Hybrid Translation Process

This section describes the stages of the complete process for generating the output components of the interactive hybrid translation service. This description assumes use of our CH phrase translation dictionary with the WorldLingo MT system, but the model could in principle be applied with another domain-specific dictionary for an alternative domain or another MT system with similar features.

The process comprises 6 stages at the end of which the output includes the automated single best hybrid translator and the available alternative translations from the CH bilingual dictionary.

Step 0: Request Pre-Processing

Remove excess white space, convert request to lower case.

Step 1: Cultural Heritage Phrase Detection

Detection of words and phrases contained in the input text found in the word and phrase list in the bilingual dictionaries. Greedy-parsing algorithms are used to identify the longest sequences of dictionary words in the input.

Step 2: Dictionary Look-Up

Dictionary look-up is performed on each word in the input text. If the word is present in the dictionary, the word and its corresponding translations are placed in a table. This dictionary table is referenced later during the alignment process ub Step 5(iv). Where a phrase translation is identified in the dictionary, the translation of the phrase replaces the original phrase in the text to be translated.

For example, the text `Mona Lisa Louvre` becomes `<-- La Gionda --> Louvre`, since the phrase `Mona Lisa` appears in our CH dictionary with the translation `La Gionda`.

Step 3: Build Machine Translation Request

The text is formatted for input to the WorldLingo MT system. The formatted text consists of two components:

- First component: the full text with identified CH phrases marked as "do not translate" (the input to the automatic hybrid translation service);
- Second component: two copies are made of each individual word in the text input one of them marked with "do not translate" tags. The purpose of this is to identify the translation of each word generated by the MT service.

Step 4: Formatted text is sent to the WorldLingo MT system.

Step 5: The response from WorldLingo MT system is processed to align the hybrid and alternative translations.

Step 5(i): The two components of the MT response are separated:

- First component: the automatic hybrid translation of the text input (output of the automatic hybrid translation service);
- Second component: individual words and their translations.

Step 5(ii): The tags are removed from the hybrid translation and the individual words and their translations.

Step 5(iii): The words in the hybrid translation and individual translated words are stemmed.

The application of stemming is required on the translated output since word forms in the hybrid translation may be different to those appearing in the translated individual words.

Stemming algorithms are a standard approach in IR which enable alternative word forms, e.g. single and plural, to be matched. Our hybrid system uses the popular rule-based Porter stemming algorithm [14]. The Porter algorithm was originally developed for English, alternative versions for a large number of other languages are now available from Snowball[9].

Step 5(iv): Term Alignment

- Look up each stemmed term in the hybrid translation from the first component in the stemmed individual terms in the second component.
- Look up the corresponding word in the source language.
- Look up the alternative translations of the source word in the dictionary table formed in Step 2.

Example of Generation of Interactive Translation Output

Query: `Storia del teatro Greco`
Source Language: Italian
Target Language: English

Step 0: Request Pre-Processing

Remove excess white space, convert request to lower case.

`storia del teatro greco`

Step 1: Cultural Heritage Phrase Detection

The request is converted to a list of terms and phrases.

`storia`	- single word found in domain-specific dictionary
`del`	- single word not in domain-specific dictionary
`teatro Greco`	- phrase found in domain-specific phrase dictionary

---

[9] `http://snowball.tartarus.org/`

`del` is a common Italian function word and not found in the CH domain-specific dictionary.

Step 2: Dictionary Look-Up

Form dictionary table of translations found in domain-specific dictionary.

```
storia        - Historie; Historic; History;
teatro greco - Theatre of ancient Greece; Ancient Greek
               theatre; Greek theater; Greek theatre;
```

Where a term is located as a phrase in the domain specific dictionary, it is replaced with its most frequent translation phrase. Other words are left untranslated and untagged in the input to the WorldLingo system.

```
storia
del
Theatre of ancient Greece
```

Step 3: Build Machine Translation Request

The MT request consists of two parts:

Part 1: Complete query for translation, enables use of all available context information in the query using the hybrid translation service.

```
storia del <-- Theatre of ancient Greece -->
```

Part 2: Individual words copied twice. One copy marked "do not translate".

```
<--[storia]--> storia <--[del]--> del <--[teatro greco]-->
<--Theatre of ancient Greece --> <--teatro greco-->
<--[ -->teatro greco <-- ]-->
```

`<-- xxx -->` and `<--[xxx]-->` are WorldLingo markup syntax for pass through unchanged and ignore item.

The two parts are fused together to form a request to be passed to WorldLingo.

Step 4: Send Machine Translation Request to the WorldLingo MT System

Step 5: Process response from WorldLingo MT system to align the hybrid and alternative translations

Step 5(i): Separate Response from WorldLingo

Part 1: history of `<--Theatre of ancient Greece-->`

Part 2: `<--[storia]--> history <--[del]--> of <--[teatro greco]-->`
`<--Theatre of ancient Greece--> <--teatro greco-->`
`<--[ --> Greek theatre <-- ]-->`

Step 5(iia): Remove tags from Part 1

```
history of Theatre of ancient Greece
```

Step 5(iib): Extract words in Part 2

Separate words and phrases into original words and their translations.

```
history - storia
of - del
Theatre of ancient Greece - teatro greco
Greek theatre - teatro greco
```

Step 5(iiia): Stem Hybrid Translation

```
Histori of Theatr of anci Greec
```

Step 5(iiib): Stem Machine Translated Words

```
Histori - Storia
Theatr of anci Greec - teatro greco
of - del
teatro greco - Greek theatre
```

Step 5(iv): Term Alignment

- Split the hybrid translation into its constituent stemmed terms.
- For each term i in the hybrid translation.
- Look up original text of i in the machine translation table.

```
Histori → Storia
of → del
Theatr of anci Greec → teatro greco
Greek theatre → teatro greco
```

Look up alternative translations in the dictionary table.

```
Storia → Historie
Storia → Historic
Storia → History
```

```
Del → null **Not in dictionary table
```

```
teatro Greco → Theatre of ancient Greece
teatro Greco → Ancient Greek theatre
teatro Greco → Greek theater
teatro Greco → Greek theatre
```

Note: A look-up is also performed on the MT table for the machine translated output of the dictionary translated phrases. This allows for the inclusion of cases where the MT output is different and potentially more appropriate than those contained in the hybrid components of the complete interactive translation.

The automated primary hybrid output shows the selected "best" translation at each point. The alternative translations at each point proposed by the MT system and CH dictionary are also made available to the user. The best translation is shown to user as the selected translation. The user is then free to make use of alternative translations as displayed to them in the user interface.

Source Lanaguage: ITALIAN
Target Language: ENGLISH

Position:	0	1	2
Original Query:	storia	del	teatro greco
Best Hybrid Translation:	history	of	Theatre of ancient Greece

Elements available for use in the interactive translation interface.

position: 0

originalTerm: storia
Type: STANDARD MT
Translation: history
Type: DICT
Translation: Historie
Type: DICT
Translation: Historic
Type: DICT
Translation: History

position: 1

originalTerm: del
Type: STANDARD MT
Translation: of

position: 2

originalTerm: teatro greco
Type: HYBRID MT
Translation: Theatre of ancient Greece
Type: STANDARD MT
Translation: Greek theatre
Type: DICT
Translation: Theatre of ancient Greece
Type: DICT
Translation: Ancient Greek theatre
Type: DICT
Translation: Greek theater
Type: DICT
Translation: Greek theatre

6   Conclusions

In this paper we have described and demonstrated our hybrid text translation service developed with the MultiMatch project for use in multilingual Digital Libraries. This combines a standard MT system with a domain-specific bilingual dictionary gathered automatically from Wikipedia. An experimental investigation using a query log file from the CH domain illustrated the ability of this approach to improve the suitability of translated queries for this domain. The automatic hybrid translation service was extended to an interactive service enabling users with some knowledge of the translation target language to adjust and augment the "best" automatically generated hybrid translation. The main objective of the interactive service is to incorporate the user's knowledge in order to improve translation quality for their search while minimising the time and effort that they must expend in doing this.

In further work we plan to extend the coverage of our dictionaries by exploring the mining of other translations pairs from within the linked Wikipedia pages. The interactive translation service could also be extended to record the translation adjustments made by the users, and to incorporate these in future translation of similar queries with the objective of increasing the likelihood of more often produced "best" translations which do not require user adjustment. Hence improving the average quality of translations provided to users with no knowledge of the target language who are not able to make corrective adjustments to the proposed translation. The service could be further extended to enable users to add additional entries to the bilingual dictionaries, although this would require participation of users able to suitable dictionary additions.

Acknowledgement

Work supported by the European Community under the Information Society Technologies (IST) programme of the 6th FP for RTD — project MultiMATCH contract IST−033104. The authors are solely responsible for the content of this paper.

References

1. Adafre, S.F., de Rijke, M.: Discovering Missing Links in Wikipedia. In: Proceedings of the 3rd International Workshop on Link Discovery, Chicago, USA, pp. 90–97 (2005)
2. Adafre, S.F., de Rijke, M.: Finding Similar Sentences Across Multiple Languages in Wikipedia. In: Proceedings of EACL 2006, Trento, Italy, pp. 62–69 (2006)
3. Ballesteros, L., Croft, W.B.: Phrasal Translation and Query Expansion Techniques for Cross-Language Information Retrieval. In: Proceedings of SIGIR 1997, Philadelphia, USA, pp. 84–91 (1997)
4. Bouma, G., Fahmi, I., Mur, J., van Noord, G., van der Plas, L., Tiedemann, J.: Using syntactic knowledge for QA. In: Peters, C., Clough, P., Gey, F.C., Karlgren, J., Magnini, B., Oard, D.W., de Rijke, M., Stempfhuber, M. (eds.) CLEF 2006. LNCS, vol. 4730, pp. 318–327. Springer, Heidelberg (2007)
5. Coenen, F., Leng, P., Sanderson, R., Wang, Y.J.: Statistical identification of key phrases for text classification. In: Perner, P. (ed.) MLDM 2007. LNCS (LNAI), vol. 4571, pp. 838–853. Springer, Heidelberg (2007)
6. Declerck, T., Pèrez, A.G., Vela, O., Gantner, Z., Manzano-Macho, D.: Multilingual Lexical Semantic Resources for Ontology Translation. In: Proceedings of LREC 2006, Genoa, Italy, pp. 28–32. ELDA (2006)

7. Garofolo, J.S., Auzanne, C.G.P., Voorhees, E.M.: The TREC Spoken Document Retrieval Track: A Success Story. In: Proceedings of RIAO 2000, Paris, France, pp. 1–20 (2000)
8. He, D., Wang, J., Oard, D.W., Nossal, M.: Comparing User-Assisted and Automatic Query Translation. In: Peters, C., Braschler, M., Gonzalo, J. (eds.) CLEF 2002. LNCS, vol. 2785, pp. 400–415. Springer, Heidelberg (2003)
9. Hull, D.A., Grefenstette, G.: Querying Across Languages: A Dictionary-Based Approach to Multilingual Information Retrieval. In: Proceedings of SIGIR 1996, Zurich, Switzerland, pp. 49–57 (1996)
10. Jones, G.J.F., Sakai, T., Collier, N., Kumano, A., Sumita, K.: A Comparison of Query Translation Methods for English-Japanese Cross-Language Information Retrieval. In: Proceedings of SIGIR 1999, Berkeley, CA, USA, pp. 269–270 (1999)
11. Lam-Adesina, A.M., Jones, G.J.F.: Exeter at CLEF 2003: Experiments with machine translation for monolingual, bilingual and multilingual retrieval. In: Peters, C., Gonzalo, J., Braschler, M., Kluck, M. (eds.) CLEF 2003. LNCS, vol. 3237, pp. 271–285. Springer, Heidelberg (2004)
12. Pecina, P., Hoffmannová, P., Jones, G.J.F., Zhang, Y., Oard, D.W.: Overview of the CLEF-2007 cross-language speech retrieval track. In: Peters, C., Jijkoun, V., Mandl, T., Müller, H., Oard, D.W., Peñas, A., Petras, V., Santos, D. (eds.) CLEF 2007. LNCS, vol. 5152, pp. 674–686. Springer, Heidelberg (2008)
13. Petrelli, D., Hansen, P., Beaulieu, M., Sanderson, M.: User Requirement Elicitation for Cross-Language Information Retrieval. New Review of Information Behaviour Research 3, 17–35 (2002)
14. Porter, M.F.: An Algorithm for Suffix Stripping. Program 14(3), 130–137 (1980)
15. Van de Cruys, T., Villada Moirón, B.: Semantics-Based Multiword Expression Extraction. In: Proceedings of the Workshop on A Broader Perspective on Multiword Expressions, Prague, Czech Republic, pp. 25–32. ACL (June 2007)
16. Zhang, Y., Jones, G.J.F., Zhang, K.: Dublin city university at CLEF 2007: Cross-language speech retrieval experiments. In: Peters, C., Jijkoun, V., Mandl, T., Müller, H., Oard, D.W., Peñas, A., Petras, V., Santos, D. (eds.) CLEF 2007. LNCS, vol. 5152, pp. 703–711. Springer, Heidelberg (2008)

Metadata Enrichment via Topic Models for Author Name Disambiguation

Raffaella Bernardi and Dieu-Thu Le*

DISI
University of Trento, Italy
{bernardi,dieuthu.le}@disi.unitn.it

Abstract. This paper tackles the well known problem of Author Name Disambiguation (AND) in Digital Libraries (DL). Following [14,13], we assume that an individual tends to create a distinctively coherent body of work that can hence form a single cluster containing all of his/her articles yet distinguishing them from those of everyone else with the same name. Still, we believe the information contained in a DL may be not sufficient to allow an automatic detection of such clusters; this lack of information becomes even more evident in federated digital libraries, where the labels assigned by librarians may belong to different controlled vocabularies or different classification systems, and in digital libraries on the web where records may be not assigned neither subject headings nor classification numbers. Hence, we exploit Topic Models, extracted from Wikipedia, to enhance records metadata and use Agglomerative Clustering to disambiguate ambiguous author names by clustering together similar records; records in different clusters are supposed to have been written by different people. We investigate the following two research questions: (a) are the Classification Systems and Subject Heading labels manually assigned by librarians general and informative enough to disambiguate Author Names via clustering techniques? (b) Do Topic Models induce from large corpora the conceptual information necessary for labelling automatically DL metadata and grasp topic similarities of the records? To answer these questions, we will use the Library Catalogue of the Bolzano University Library as case study.

Keywords: Digital Libraries, Topic Models, Author Name Disambiguation.

1   Introduction

Multiple authors can have the same exact name or share the surname and first initial, library catalogues may record the author names either fully or only with

---

* We would like to thank Massimo Poesio and Marco Baroni for their constant and valuable help during the different phases of this work, and the three anonymous reviewers for their interesting suggestions. This work started as MSc Thesis of the second author during her studies as EMLCT students at the Free University of Bozen-Bolzano. The thesis had been supervised by the first author and by Massimo Poesio.

R. Bernardi et al. (Eds.): NLP4DL/AT4DL 2009, LNCS 6699, pp. 92–113, 2011.

partial information (surname and initials). This fact can cause problems in several situations, for instance, it can be a problem for the user when searching for relevant books by using the author's name, or it can cause wrong citation index measure assignments. Authors' ambiguous names are quite frequent as it has been observed in [9,3] by looking at ACM Portal, Citeseer and DBLP as case studies; exact figures have been reported in [13] whose case study database is MEDLINE, the oldest and best curated biomedical research database: almost 2/3 authors have an ambiguous name, their last name and first initial is shared with one or more other authors. On average, an ambiguous name comprises around eight different individuals.

The importance of Author Name Disambiguation (AND) becomes even stronger when one notices that author name searching is one of the most used search strategy. [5] reports that of 2.7 million daily PubMed queries, 23% were formulated using author names exclusively.

Against this scenario, we aim at building a system able to alert the users when they have searched for an author's name that may refer to different authors and provide the books retrieved clustered by topics. For example, when a user searches for books by "R Smith", the results will show books clustered into two blocks with labels "Finance" and "Ecology" so to alert the user that the "R Smith" authors of these two blocks of books could be two different persons and disambiguate them.

To this end, we first review relevant works to set up the ground of our proposal introducing the main aspects of it, in particular the idea of using Topic Models extract from an external source, Wikipedia, to enrich topic information in the metadata records. Hence, Section 3 provides background information to the statistical methods used in our proposal which is tested against a dataset extracted from the University Library of Bolzano. Information about the Library Catalogue and its metadata is provided in Section 4. Section 5 explains the framework of our proposal and the specific methods we tested. Evaluation results are presented in Section 6 where it is shown that (a) Classification number and Subject Headings do provide important information for document metadata similarity, and (b) the automatic annotation we propose via Topic Models is a good alternative to such manual annotation: pairwise precision, recall and accuracy measures of the two methods are in fact comparable.

2   Related Works

The problem of AND has been traditionally addressed within the librarians community by means of Authority Control files, namely files created and updated manually with cross-references and consistent forms of fields. In particular, attention has been put on the cases of different names referring to the same person, instead of the same name referring to different persons as it is in our case. For example, the American Mathematical Society maintains MathSciNet with names disambiguated manually. Creating authority files automatically has been considered too [2].

Recently, the problem has been addressed by means of supervised or unsupervised probabilistic methods. We decided to follow the unsupervised trend to avoid the use of training sets to be created manually, since they are not suitable for large DLs which are our target. Within the solutions based on the unsupervised method, the standard practice is to look at the AND problem as a clustering problem. To this end, one has to (i) select features significant for the records and decide similarity measures to compare the representation of the records, (ii) choose a clustering method, (iii) define evaluation measures.

(i) The features mostly used to represent records are: co-author names, paper titles, publication venue titles (viz. titles of Proceedings, Journals, etc.) as well as the language of the paper, author's affiliation, and subject headings [14,3,13]. A collection of records is then represented as a matrix whose rows are the records, and whose columns (dimensions) are the relevant parts of the chosen features (Figure 1). For each record and each dimension, it is assigned a 1 vs. 0 value indicating simply whether the dimension is present in the records or not, respectively; alternatively, using some statistical methods, a weight can be assigned estimating the relevance of the dimension for the record. In [3], it has been shown that a good feature weighting is important to the performance of AND, however we won't put attention on accurate weights and focus on the impact of automatic topic metadata field enrichment.

In [8], on the one hand it has been shown that federated digital libraries need enhanced subject metadata since the subject headings assigned by librarians for local use end up being not homogeneous in the federated scenario and as such less useful for searching; on the other hand, it has been shown that Topic Models are successful for metadata enrichment also in large and heterogeneous collections.

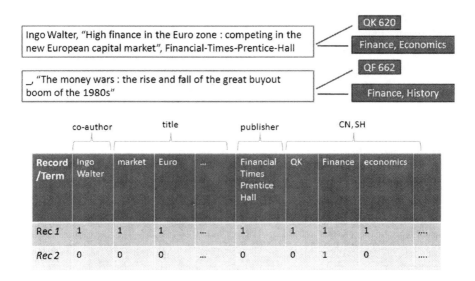

Fig. 1. Matrix representation of records

In [7,11], it has been claimed that common hidden topics discovered from large external datasets (universal datasets like Wikipedia), when included, can make short documents less sparse and more topic-oriented. Furthermore, hidden topics from universal datasets help handle unseen data better. Interesting results have been shown to be achieved on two online applications, web search result classification and matching/ranking for contextual advertising.

We will build our work on these three lines of research by enriching the features in the records metadata with hidden topics discovered from Wikipedia and assigned automatically to the records; we use the enhanced metadata information for clustering books by the same author.

(ii) Once the records have been represented as features, usually a blocking method is applied so to retrieve candidate classes of authors with similar names and a clustering algorithm clusters papers by author. First, a similarity function compares the vector dimensions in record pairs, then a clustering method clusters the pairs based on a pairwise distance [9,6,13]. We will use a simple blocking method, without considering author name variation and gathering in the same block only records with the exact author surname and initial. As for the clustering method, we will follow [13] and employ the maximum-likelihood agglomerative clustering solution since it has been shown to adequately cluster records in MEDLINE.

(iii) Finally, how to evaluate the results is a research question per se. In [13] three measures are considered: recall (number of pairwise comparisons in the dataset that refer to the same individual/number of pairs of articles written by the same individual across the Library database), "lumping" (percentage of author-individual clusters that contain articles by 2 or more individuals) and "splitting" (percentage of articles written by one individual that fail to be assigned to their major author-individual cluster). In [6] a two level measure disambiguation performance is proposed to evaluate the precision/recall of the pairwise similarity as well as the precision/recall of the clusters. We will follow the latter solution and focus on the pair-wise level.

3 Distributional Semantic Models

A general view which is spreading around the Computational Linguistics community and it is behind many Language Technologies is the assumption that semantic information can be derived from a word-document co-occurrence matrix. Statistical methods that share this research hypothesis may differ then on how words and documents are represented. In this paper we will exploit Vector Space Models to represent and compare records' metadata and Topic Models to enrich the metadata with further information about the record's topic.

Vector Space Models represent documents as vectors. Vectors are just a formal way to represent the matrix view introduced above. To explain the connection, we will see how the information about the number of times two words co-occur recorded in a matrix can be seen as vectors. Take the matrix below saying that e.g. "dog" occurs 1 time with "runs" and 4 times with "legs"

	runs	legs
dog	1	4
cat	1	5
car	4	0

the words can be seen as vectors as shown in Figure 2.

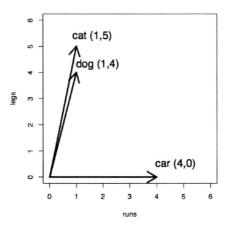

Fig. 2. Vectors standing for cat, dog, car

When we look at documents as vectors, each dimension of the vector corresponds to a separate term. If a term occurs in the document, its value in the vector is non-zero. Several different ways of computing these values, also known as (term) weights, have been developed. The definition of term depends on the application. Typically terms are single words, keywords, or longer phrases. If the words are chosen to be the terms, the dimensionality of the vector is the number of words in the vocabulary (the number of distinct words occurring in the corpus). Vector operations can be used to compare documents. A standard similarity measure is the cosine of the angle between the document vectors.

Topic Models represent documents as a mixture of topics, where a topic is a probability distribution over words. Here we provide a brief overview, the reader is referred to [12] for a clear and detailed introduction. Topic Models can be used either to generate documents out of given topics or to infer the topic distribution within given documents. The method is based on bayesian inferences: it posits a hidden structure in the documents and then learns that structure by iterating the process of checking the probability that the hypothesis may be true or not. Hence, two important parameters are those indicating which words are important for which topic (multinomial distribution over words for a topic) and which topics are important for a particular document (multinomial distribution over topics for a document). In [1] a method for smoothing the topic distribution is introduced, the resulting model is called Latent Direchlet Allocation (LDA) since it relays on a statistical technique known as "Dirichlet distribution". We will use this model in our analysis.

Efficient algorithms have been implemented to discover the hidden topical structure, Gibbs Sampling algorithm is one of them. It considers each word token in the text collection in turn, and estimates the probability of assigning the current word token to each topic, conditioned on the topic assignments to all other word tokens. From this conditional distribution, a topic is sampled and stored as the new topic assignment for this word token. Once many tokens of a word have been assigned to a topic j (across documents), it will increase the probability of assigning any particular token of that word to topic j. At the same time, if topic j has been used multiple times in one document, it will increase the probability that any word from that document will be assigned to topic j. Therefore, words are assigned to topics depending on how likely the word is for a topic, as well as how dominant a topic is in a document. The iterative sampling function as a disambiguation process too, since the assignment of each word token to a topic depends on the assignments of the other words in the context. We conclude this introduction by presenting an example taken from [12] which conveys clearly and intuitively the aspects of Topic Models relevant to our presentation.

Figure 3 shows fragments of three documents in which the ambiguous word "play" occur with three different senses. The superscript numbers show the topic assignments for each word token. The gray words are stop words or very low frequency words that were not used in the analysis. The sampling process assigns the word "play" to topics 77, 82, and 162 in the three documents contexts. The presence of other less ambiguous words builds up evidence for a particular topic in the document.

Figure 4 shows three topic labels with their word distribution inferred from the texts.

4   Case Study: University Library Catalogue

As our case study, we exploit the Bolzano University Library looking at the English collection which amounts to 29,203 records. For each record, besides the information about author, title and publisher, we use the Classification number and the Subject Headings assigned manually by the librarians. The Classification System used in the Bolzano University Library is the RVK (Regensburger Verbundklassifikation). Each number is made up of 2 letters, followed by 4 decimal digits (e.g. DP 1982, where D stands for "Pedagogy", DP is the sub-node Didactic and Teaching Methods, and 1982 stands for the specific projects carried out in the USA and Canada – the 1980-1989 node is "Projects"). Top Classification categories are given in Table 1.

Furthermore, English records of the Library are manually assigned Library of Congress Subject Headings (LCSH). For instance, the two books in Figure 1

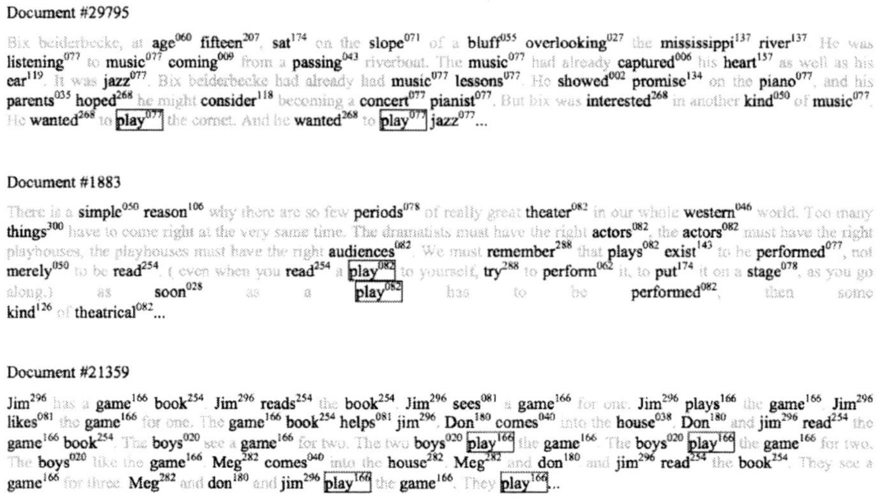

Document #29795

Bix beiderbecke, at age[060] fifteen[207], sat[174] on the slope[071] of a bluff[055] overlooking[027] the mississippi[137] river[137]. He was listening[077] to music[077] coming[009] from a passing[043] riverboat. The music[077] had already captured[006] his heart[137] as well as his ear[119]. It was jazz[077]. Bix beiderbecke had already had music[077] lessons[077]. He showed[002] promise[134] on the piano[077], and his parents[035] hoped[268] he might consider[118] becoming a concert[077] pianist[077]. But bix was interested[268] in another kind[050] of music[077]. He wanted[268] to play[077] the cornet. And he wanted[268] to play[077] jazz[077]...

Document #1883

There is a simple[050] reason[106] why there are so few periods[078] of really great theater[082] in our whole western[046] world. Too many things[300] have to come right at the very same time. The dramatists must have the right actors[082], the actors[082] must have the right playhouses, the playhouses must have the right audiences[082]. We must remember[288] that plays[082] exist[143] to be performed[077], not merely[050] to be read[254]. (even when you read[254] a play[082] to yourself, try[288] to perform[062] it, to put[174] it on a stage[078], as you go along.) as soon[028] as a play[082] has to be performed[082], then some kind[126] of theatrical[082]...

Document #21359

Jim[296] has a game[166] book[254]. Jim[296] reads[254] the book[254]. Jim[296] sees[081] a game[166] for one. Jim[296] plays[166] the game[166]. Jim[296] likes[081] the game[166] for one. The game[166] book[254] helps[081] jim[296]. Don[180] comes[040] into the house[038]. Don[180] and jim[296] read[254] the game[166] book[254]. The boys[020] see a game[166] for two. The two boys[020] play[166] the game[166]. The boys[020] play[166] the game[166] for two. The boys[020] like the game[166]. Meg[282] comes[040] into the house[282]. Meg[282] and don[180] and jim[296] read[254] the book[254]. They see a game[166] for three. Meg[282] and don[180] and jim[296] play[166] the game[166]. They play[166]...

Fig. 3. Document with topic distributions

are annotated with the following strings of SHs: "Europe / Economic conditions / 20th century Finance / European Union" and "Consolidation and merger of corporations / United States / Finance / History / 20th century Leveraged buyouts / United States / History / 20th century United States / Economic conditions / 1981-", respectively.

To create an ambiguous dataset and have a gold standard for the evaluation, we randomly choose only records that have full information (i.e., author full name, book title, classification numbers, subject headings and publisher). We consider optional the availability of co-author names. We extract records from the library index and group them by author first name initial and last name. We first use author full name as a gold standard for disambiguating those authors. For example, all records written by authors with name abbreviation "R Smith" (such as: Ricky Smith, Robert Smith, Richard Smith, Roy Smith, etc.)

Table 1. Top RVK Categories

CN	Categories	Number of Records
ST	Computer Science, Artificial Intelligence	2,746
QP	Business Administration	2,498
AP	Media and Communication Studies	1,042
LH	General Art History	765
QC	Economic Theory, Monetary Theory	739
QQ	Special Business Administration	635
QM	International Trade	510
LI	Artist Monographs	398

Topic 77

word	prob.
MUSIC	.090
DANCE	.034
SONG	.033
PLAY	.030
SING	.026
SINGING	.026
BAND	.026
PLAYED	.023
SANG	.022
SONGS	.021
DANCING	.020
PIANO	.017
PLAYING	.016
RHYTHM	.015
ALBERT	.013
MUSICAL	.013

Topic 82

word	prob.
LITERATURE	.031
POEM	.028
POETRY	.027
POET	.020
PLAYS	.019
POEMS	.019
PLAY	.015
LITERARY	.013
WRITERS	.013
DRAMA	.012
WROTE	.012
POETS	.011
WRITER	.011
SHAKESPEARE	.010
WRITTEN	.009
STAGE	.009

Topic 166

word	prob.
PLAY	.136
BALL	.129
GAME	.065
PLAYING	.042
HIT	.032
PLAYED	.031
BASEBALL	.027
GAMES	.025
BAT	.019
RUN	.019
THROW	.016
BALLS	.015
TENNIS	.011
HOME	.010
CATCH	.010
FIELD	.010

Fig. 4. Topics with word distributions

are mixed together. Then we manually read again to remove some cases that we cannot decide whether they refer to only one author or more than one (e.g., two authors named Robert Smith). Our goal is to cluster all books within this block so that each cluster contains only books by the same author. The data set has 26 blocks containing 256 books and 115 distinguished authors. The average number of books per individual is 2.2; and the average number of distinguished authors per each cluster is 4.4 (115/26). Most of the blocks contain from 2 to 4 ambiguous authors ($\approx$ 60%) and $\approx$15% of the blocks contain more than 8 ambiguous authors.

5 Author Name Disambiguation: Our Framework

Figure 5 shows our system architecture for disambiguating author names. The metadata extraction module extracts from the index all records associated with author names. After that, the blocking module groups ambiguous candidates into blocks that contain only records with the same first name initial and same last name. The records in these blocks of ambiguous candidates are enriched by the Metadata enriching module that we will describe later. The texts in the metadata are preprocessed before being clustered. This step includes normalization, word segmentation and stop word removal. Different attributes are preprocessed differently (e.g., in *SH*, we only remove punctuations but not stop words since each phrase in *SH* is tagged by librarians from a pre-defined set of *SH*, hence related books might share the same *SH* phrase). Finally, the Clustering Module clusters the records within each block. The results are clusters of records which are meant to have been written by the same author. In the following, we will describe our methods that we will evaluate in the next section.

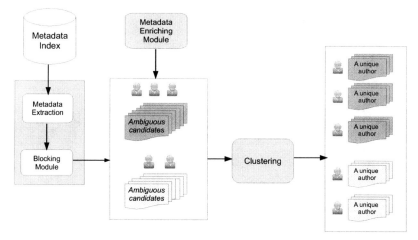

Fig. 5. Disambiguation system overview

5.1   Metadata Enrichment

One of the main challenges when comparing metadata information about books is the sparsity problem. Books by the same author could have no overlapping words, even if they are about the same or related topics. The information provided in the classification number and subject heading fields should overcome this lack of similarity. Still it may very well be that similar books do not share this information either. In the example of Table 2, the two books by the same author are about related topics but share only the Classification number (the alphabetic part of it).

The information shared is too little for the two books to be considered similar by a clustering algorithm based on the features at disposal. Furthermore, in federated libraries the classification systems and the subject heading vocabularies used by the libraries with the local catalogue may be even different. Finally, Digital Libraries on the web, may not contain these two fields at all. Hence, we investigate two ways to enrich the metadata information focusing in particular on the topic of the books.

Metadata enrichment via SH induction. To further exploit the information provided by SH and CN, we try a shallow mapping between the two information:

Table 2. An example of two books of the same authors that do not share any common words

Author	David C. Hay
Books	1. Requirements analysis: from business views to architecture (ST 230 / System analysis / Object-Oriented methods)
	2. Data model patterns: conventions of thought (ST 270 / Database Design / Data structures / Computer Science)

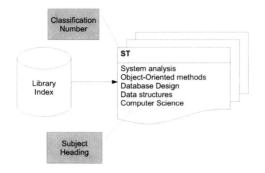

Fig. 6. Grouping *SHs* by *CNs*

Table 3. Sample *SHs* grouped by *CNs*

CN	SHs
AH	Terms and phrases, Abbreviations, Examinations, study guides, New words, Acronyms, Dictionaries English language, United States, English, 20th century, Synonyms and antonyms, Signs and symbols...
AK	Research, Middle East, Proposal writing in research, Internet, Philosophy, Technical writing, Business meetings, Post-graduate studies, Dissertations, Academic, Directories, Scholarly publishing, Endowments, Public speaking, Public relations ...
AM	Illumination of books and manuscripts, Typographers, Alphabet, Book design, Alphabets Graphic arts, Netherlands, Lettering, Signs and symbols, Logotypes (Printing)...
AP	Pattern books, Fashion design, Rock musicians, Motion picture producers and directors, Movie posters, Railroad travel, Advertising t-shirts, Advertising layout and typography, Lighting, Directories, Communication and technology, Miscellanea...
CC	Religion, Addresses, essays, lectures, Civilization, Imagination (Philosophy), Philosophy, Realism, Ethics, Cognition, Evolution (Biology), Animal welfare, Truth, Emotions (Philosophy), Ecology, Art, Intellectual life ...
CF	17th century, Essay concerning human understanding, Ethics, Modern, Reason, Ethics, History, 18th century, Metaphysics, Virtue, Teleology, Philosophy, Modern, Economics, Aesthetics ...
DK	Observation (Educational method), Research, Great Britain, Project method in teaching, Educational evaluation, Educational change, School improvement programs, Active learning, School management and organization, Day care centers, Child development, Educational leadership, Early childhood education ...
ET	Phonetics, Systemic grammar, Lexicography, Consonants, Philosophy, Study and teaching, Tense, Data processing, Typology (Linguistics), Semantics, Cognition, Phonology ...
ST	PHP (Computer program language), XSLT (computer program language), Microsoft Excel for Windows, Design and construction, Microsoft software, , Metadata, Business, SAP R/3, Smart cards, Word processing, Distributed processing, Lighting ...
WF	Microbiology, Transgenic organisms, Government policy, Soil microbiology, Food industry and trade, Crops, Standards, Technological innovations, Food Microbiology, Nitrogen, Microbial biotechnology ...

First, we extract all the English books ($\approx$ 29,000 books) and group all *SHs* that are associated with a *CNs* together (Figure 6), we only consider the highest level of *CN*, i.e., the first two capital letters. Then, only *SHs* that appear in a *CN* with high frequency are kept (in this experiment, we filter all *SHs* that appear less than 15 times in a *CN*). Examples of most frequent *SHs* in each *CN* are given in Table 3.

After grouping *SHs* by *CNs*, each book in the index is enriched with *SHs* in the same *CNs*. For example, a book assigned with a *CN* will be enriched with the first τ *SHs* that appear most often with that *CN* (τ is a cutoff threshold). In our experiments, we will refer to this method as *CNSH_Enriched*.

Metadata enrichment via Topic Models induction. *CNs* and *SHs* are two important topic indicators for records in the library index. However, this manual annotation is not available in most digital libraries on the Internet, and especially in federated libraries, where different *CS* may be used. To detect and label the topics of the record automatically, we introduce a framework that takes advantage of available large scale background knowledge-base (Figure 7).

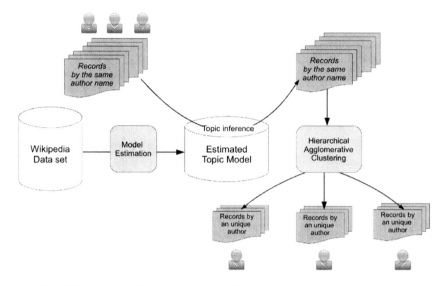

Fig. 7. Framework for author name disambiguation using topic models

Model Estimation from the Wikipedia dataset. In this work, we choose Wikipedia as our large-scale data set since it contains a lot of concepts in different domains, thus it is reasonable to assume it provides hidden topics that are neither too narrow nor too broad and are associated with frequent significant words. To model the hidden topic analysis of the Wikipedia dataset, we use Latent Dirichlet Allocation (LDA) to estimate the multinomial observations by unsupervised learning. To estimating parameters for LDA, we use Gibbs Sampling, a special case of Markov-chain Monte Carlo that often yields relatively simple algorithms for approximate inference in high-dimensional models like LDA [4].

In this framework, we estimate a topic model with 100 topics and 500 Gibbs sampling iterations as it has been shown in [11] that model estimation for around 70K documents from Wikipedia is quite stable with the changes of the number of topics (from 20 to 100 topics) and after the "burn-in" period of Gibbs Sampling iterations (around 200 iterations).

- **Data preprocess:** We download English-language Wikipedia[1] and pre-process the data, filtered to 80,000 random documents in different topics.

---

[1] Wikipedia dumps in SQL and XML: http://en.wikipedia.org/wiki/ Wikipedia_database

Table 4. An illustration of sample topics extracted from hidden topic analysis

Topic 0: company business services market companies million bank corporation service management industry financial products investment trade sold price finance tax sold price
Topic 8: album music band song released songs records single rock guitar first live new recorded vocals love one version group
Topic 16: software data system computer systems code information windows digital used network web use using memory users internet file user server
Topic 19: language english languages word words arabic spoken latin used names written meaning letters alphabet dialect letter pronounced speakers vowel verb
Topic 23: cells disease medical patients treatment cell blood health medicine dna brain protein cancer drug human therapy proteins syndrome cause symptoms
Topic 27: engine aircraft car design vehicle cars engines model war built used production air united vehicles mm speed cold fuel designed
Topic 39: law court act police states case legal rights state public justice united laws federal judge supreme criminal trial under
Topic 41: food wine beer rice meat made milk tea oil sugar coffee fruit drink cuisine served foods cream bread popular alcohol
Topic 45: water energy used light surface gas nuclear pressure earth temperature mass chemical high air carbon power heat material metal acid
Topic 48: team season first won game league world games year championship played football player teams race one two second baseball national
Topic 55: city area town river located park one north south built part east building village west many local site known two
Topic 68: storm hurricane tropical malaysia damage depression winds typhoon atlantic cyclone storms malaysian pearls caused malay landfall pearl tornado season pacific
Topic 71: station line railway london train service rail trains road bus services north south railroad west new east street between class
Topic 75: church god christian catholic jesus st religious holy christ saint bishop pope roman bible faith religion churches john life orthodox
Topic 86: war army force battle military air during forces navy ships ship command british attack service division general naval corps fire
Topic 96: school university college high students schools education student institute year national program public campus science center research arts community academy

The preprocessing step includes HTML tag removal, normalization, punctuations and stop word removal (Figure 8). We use our own HTML patterns, tokenization defined by regular expression and the list of stop words to preprocess the data.

- **Analysis and outputs:** After preprocessing, we analyze hidden topics for this dataset using GibbsLDA++ and JGibbsLDA.[2] It takes totally around 14 hours to estimate the model. Table 4 shows some sample topics derived from the estimated model with 100 topics. The topics are typically interpretable as those shown here.

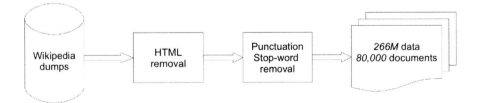

Fig. 8. Wikipedia dataset preprocessing

---

[2] http://gibbslda.sourceforge.net/

Hidden Topic Analysis and Inference. After estimating the topic model from Wikipedia dataset, we use this model to do topic inference for each record in the library index and integrate topic labels with highest probability $\vartheta_{\underline{m},k}$ to records $\underline{m}$ containing one or more of the words in the set associated with that topic. We expand their vocabularies with their most likely hidden topics. Technically, the weight of each topic is determined by two parameters *cut-off* and *scale* :

$$Frequency_{\underline{m},k} = \begin{cases} round\left(scale \times \vartheta_{\underline{m},k}\right), \text{if } \vartheta_{\underline{m},k} \geq cut\text{-}off \\ 0, \text{if } \vartheta_{\underline{m},k} < cut\text{-}off \end{cases} \tag{1}$$

where *cut-off* is the topic probability threshold, *scale* is a parameter that determines how many times the topic is added. For example, using *cut-off* = 0.05 with *scale* = 20, if $\vartheta_{\underline{m},k} = 0.1$, the weight of topic k is 20 x 0.1 = 2.

An example of topic integration into a record is illustrated in Figure 9, the metadata of the two books will be enriched with the inferred topic "Topic 0" since, though they do not share any word, both contain words – "market", "investment" and "finance", respectively – that are in the set of most important words associated with "Topic 0" . This example shows how Topic Model can help handling the limitation of word choice and make the metadata more topic-focused.

In general, the main advantages of this approach are: (1) it does not require manual annotators from librarians (e.g., *SHs, CNs*), (2) it is easy to implement and not *expensive*: with the availability of many knowledge based resources like Wikipedia, it is easy to collect and take advantage of these resources automatically, (3) it can help reduce the difference between vocabularies by exploiting the semantic relations of words in documents from the analysis of a large scale dataset.

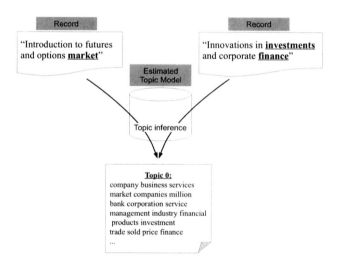

Fig. 9. An example of two records with titles that do not share common words, but share the same hidden topic

5.2   Agglomerative Clustering

To represent records, measure the similarity of records within a same block and then cluster them as belonging to the same author, we use the following features from the metadata: co-author names (**c**), titles (**t**), publisher information (**p**) and the two alphabets of the classification numbers (**CN**) and the subject headings (**SH**). A record is then represented as a vector of word co-occurrences in a Vector Space Model: $\overrightarrow{r_m} = \{w_{tm}\}_{t \in V}$, where V is the vocabulary that contains all terms in the corpus.

After that, the cosine similarity is computed with:

$$cosin\_sim(\mathbf{r}_i, \mathbf{r}_j) = \frac{\overrightarrow{\mathbf{r}_i}.\overrightarrow{\mathbf{r}_j}}{|\overrightarrow{\mathbf{r}_i}|.|\overrightarrow{\mathbf{r}_j}|} = \frac{\sum_{t \in V} w_{ti}.w_{tj}}{\sqrt{\sum_{t \in V} w_{ti}^2}.\sqrt{\sum_{t \in V} w_{tj}^2}} \tag{2}$$

where w_{ti}, w_{tj} is the weight of the term t in the vector of $\mathbf{r}_i$, $\mathbf{r}_j$ (its frequency in the document).

After the similarity between each pair of records is computed, we use our java implementation of Hierarchical Agglomerative Clustering (JHAC) to group together books with the highest similarity. The algorithm starts out with all articles in singleton clusters and iteratively merges the most similar pairs of clusters into larger ones. As distance measure between two clusters $\mathcal{A}$ and $\mathcal{B}$, we use the *average linkage*, namely the average distance between every record x and y in those clusters:

$$d(\mathcal{A}, \mathcal{B}) = \frac{1}{|\mathcal{A}|.|\mathcal{B}|} \cdot \sum_{x \in \mathcal{A}} \sum_{y \in \mathcal{B}} d(x, y) \tag{3}$$

where $d(x, y)$ is the distance between two elements x and y in these two clusters.

The clustering process stops when it reaches a *cutting point* τ, the similarity threshold for grouping related books. The most important functions of *JHAC* are given in Algorithm 1 and Algorithm 2.

The main procedure of the algorithm is the function *updateMatrix*, where M is the similarity matrix, N is the number of input elements. Hence, the input matrix M has the size N x N. The merging procedure continues when there are still more than two clusters left and when the maximum similarity we find is still smaller than our cutting point threshold τ. Function *subMatrix* builds a sub matrix by deleting 2 rows and 2 columns in the position x and y. Function *findClosestCluster* returns the indexes of two closest clusters in the database. Function *newSimAvg* calculates the new similarity between two merged clusters using *average linkage*.

5.3   Dimensionality Reduction via PCA

The term-document matrix that represents each record contains several hundreds to thousands dimensions and it is rather sparse – recall that each column, viz. each word in the metadata fields, corresponds to a dimension. Hence, we

Algorithm 1. Main functions of JHAC (1)

```
updateMatrix(M,N):
while N ≥ 1 do
  (x, y) ← findClosestClusters()
  if sim(Cluster x, Cluster y) ≥ τ then
    Merge Cluster x and Cluster y
    double[][] subMatrix ← subMatrix(x, y)
    Update similarity matrix
    min ← min(x, y)
    max ← max(x,y)
    for i = 1 to N do
      if i ¡ min then
        subMatrix[i][N-1] = subMatrix[N-1][i]
        = newSimAvg(M[i][min], M[i][max])
      else {i ≥ max - 1}
        subMatrix[i][N-1] = subMatrix[N-1][i]
        = newSimAvg(M[i+2][min], M[i+2][max])
      else
        subMatrix[i][N-1] = subMatrix[N-1][i]
        = newSimAvg(M[i+1][min], M[i+1][max])
      end if
    end for
    M ← subMatrix
    N = N-1
  else
    Finished Clustering (Reach τ)
  end if
end while
```

try to overcome the sparsity of the data by reducing the number of dimensions. To examine whether traditional dimensionality reduction techniques help reducing noise and complexity while persevering the most important information, we employ Principle Component Analysis (*PCA*) [10].

In our experiment, we use the *NIPALS* (Nonlinear Iterative Partial Least Squares) algorithm to find the eigenvectors in the *PCA* module[3] in Python. The number of dimensions k is determined by a scale value s: $k = n/s$, where n is the original number of dimensions in the data set. The new matrix is constructed from the Scores part (T) of the *PCA*, where column i in T is the score of the corresponding principle component i, $i = \{1... k\}$.

6   Experiments

We set up several experiments to answer the two research questions introduced in Section 1, namely (a) are the Classification Systems and Subject Heading labels manually assigned by librarians general and informative enough to disambiguate Author Names via clustering techniques? (b) Do Topic Models induce from large

---

[3] http://folk.uio.no/henninri/pca_module/

Algorithm 2. Main functions of JHAC (2)

---

subMatrix(x, y,M,N):
double subM[N][N]
$nW = 0$
for $nR = 0$ to N **do**
  if $nR \neq x$ and $nR \neq y$ **then**
    $mW = 0$
    for $mR = 0$ to N **do**
      if $mR \neq x$ and $mR \neq y$ **then**
        subM[nW][mW] = M[nR][mR]
        mW = mW + 1
      end if
    end for
    nW = nW + 1
  end if
end for
return subM

---

findClosestClusters(M,N):
$x \leftarrow 0$
$y \leftarrow 1$
double maxSim $\leftarrow M[0][0]$
for $i = 0$ to N **do**
  for $j = 0$ to N **do**
    if M[i][j] ¿ maxSim and $i \neq j$ **then**
      maxSim $\leftarrow M[i][j]$
      $x \leftarrow i$
      $y \leftarrow j$
    end if
  end for
end for
return (x, y)

---

corpora the conceptual information necessary for labelling automatically DL metadata and grasping topic similarities of the records?

First, we set two different baselines: the first one that does not rely on the clustering step is *No-Cluster*, where we group all ambiguous authors in one single cluster; the second one is *Baseline*, where we use the Hierarchical Agglomerative Clustering method to group together related records using the co-author names, book's title and book's publishers as features (Table 5).

Second, to quantify the importance of *CN* and *SH* in disambiguating author name, we perform two experiments without and with these two attributes (*Baseline* and *CNSH*). After that, to see whether enriching records with more *SH* grouped by *CN* can increase the accuracy of disambiguating author name or not, we perform the third experiment using extended *SH* of the same *CN*. The aim of this method, called *CNSH-Enriched*, is to exploit as much as possible the information coming from the librarians in the dataset.

Table 5. Experimental Settings for disambiguating author name in the library index

Settings	Features
Without-Cluster	using no feature, simply group all ambiguous authors in one cluster
Baseline	$c \cup t \cup p$
CNSH	$(c \cup t \cup p) \oplus (CN \cup SH)$
CNSH-Enriched	$(c \cup t \cup p) \oplus (CN \cup SH) \oplus SH\text{-}enriched$
CNSH-PCA	$[(c \cup t \cup p) \oplus (CN \cup SH)]_{PCA}$
HT	$(c \cup t \cup p) \oplus HT$
HT-CNSH	$(c \cup t \cup p) \oplus HT \oplus (CN \cup SH)$

- c = co-author names
- t = book's title
- p = book's publisher
- CN = book's Classification Numbers
- SH = book's Subject Headings
- $SH\text{-}Enriched$: Set of Enriched Subject Headings
- PCA: applying PCA to reduce dimensions
- HT: Set of most likely hidden topics inferred from the estimated topic model

Third, to examine whether traditional dimensionality reduction techniques like PCA can help overcome the problem of sparsity and synonyms/homonyms and reduce noises in textual data, we implement an experiment combining all features in the records metadata (co-authors, title, publisher, first two letters of the classification number, and the subject headings) then apply PCA to reduce the number of dimensions using a scale value $PCA\text{-}scale$. This method is called $CNSH\text{-}PCA$. In this experiment, we reduce the number of dimensions in each data set 50 times (e.g., if the original dimension $n = 1000$, PCA reduces it to $k = n/PCA\text{-}scale = 1000/50 = 200$ dimensions).

Fourth, to evaluate the contribution of hidden topics without using annotation information like CN and SH, we carry out an experiment using only co-author's name, title and publisher attribute of each record and enrich them with hidden topics analyzed from our estimated model. To control the number of topics and their weights in each record, we set the *cut-off* value = 0.05 and *scale* value = 20 (Equation 1).[4]

Finally, we also report the performance of disambiguating author name combining both hidden topics and $CNSH$ in the method $HT\text{-}CNSH$.

6.1   Evaluation Metrics

We measure disambiguation performance using *pairwise precision, recall* and *F1* as in [6]. **Pairwise precision** $pPre$ is defined as the fraction of pairs in the same cluster belonging to the same author:

---

[4] We tested with different *cut-off* and *scale*, then estimated values that provide a reasonable number of added topics by observing several examples. Adjusting these parameters to optimize the performance is also an open question that we may investigate in future works.

$$pPre = \frac{number\ of\ correct\ pairs\ in\ the\ output\ clusters}{number\ of\ total\ pairs\ in\ the\ output\ clusters} \tag{4}$$

Pairwise recall pRe is defined as the fraction of book pairs of the same author clustered together:

$$pRe = \frac{number\ of\ correct\ pairs\ in\ the\ output\ clusters}{number\ of\ total\ pairs\ in\ the\ truth\ clusters} \tag{5}$$

And **Pairwise F1** $pF1$ as the harmonic mean of $pPre$ and pRe:

$$pF1 = 2.\frac{pPre.pRe}{pPre + pRe} \tag{6}$$

6.2 Results and Analysis

We try different cutting points τ for the Hierarchical Agglomerative Clustering algorithm using similarity thresholds varied from 0.05 to 0.3. We observe that if the threshold is too low, the algorithm tends to cluster more records together (i.e., even books of different authors are grouped together). Hence, the recall value is high while the precision is low in this case. On the contrary, the precision increases and the recall reduces when the threshold increases. Our goal is to

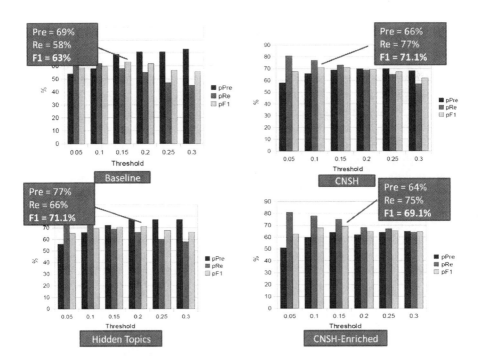

Fig. 10. Disambiguating results: different methods

maximize the $pF1$ value, the harmonic mean of these two values. As the threshold increases, only very similar books are grouped together, hence, the precision increases while the recall value decreases.

In Figure 10, we highlight the best $pPre$, pRe and $pF1$ of our baselines comparing it with those of *CNSH*, *CNSH-Enriched* and the Hidden Topic methods. We will come back to the method *CNSH-PCA* later. As shown in Figure 10, the lower bound baseline created by grouping together all ambiguous authors in one single cluster in method *Without-Cluster* gains 41% in $pF1$ score. Using clustering in the *Baseline*, the maximum $pF1$ we get is around 63% with threshold 0.15. Exploiting subject headings and classification numbers increases the performance significantly, reaching a $pF1$ of 71.1%. Enriching the records with more *SH* of the same *CN* (*CNSH-Enriched*) does not improve the accuracy in comparison with using their *SH* only (*CNSH*). In particular, the highest $pF1$ score this method reaches is 69.1%, slightly lower than that reached by *CNSH* method. Using hidden topics in the *HT* method instead of *CN* and *SH*, we achieve the same accuracy ($pF1$ score is 71.1%).

As for our first research question, i.e., the impact of *CN, SH* in disambiguating author name, we evaluate and compare the performance of the two methods *CNSH, CNSH-Enriched* against our Baseline (Figure 11 (left)). As *CN* and *SH* are two indicators of the topics for each records in the library, they play an important role in clustering documents belonging to different authors. However, when we enrich records with more *SH* of the same *CN*, it does not improve the accuracy. It is likely that this method also adds more noise and makes the records more sparse and less topic-focused. Since we only consider the first level of the classification numbers (e.g., "CC"), it might refer to different unrelated topics. For instance, terms that occur very frequently in "CC" include Religion, Ethics, Evolution (Biology), Emotions (Philosophy) (Table 3), which belong to different areas. Such added terms can cause noises to the dataset although these classes of *CN* defined by *SH* with high frequency might be useful in other cases.

As for our second research question, we quantify the effect of hidden topics, instead of using annotated information (such as *CN* and *SH*). It is shown in Figure 11 (right) that using hidden topics increase the accuracy of clustering books written by different authors. In particular, it increases the $pF1$ score from 63% to 71% and reduces 22% errors. We observe that in many cases in the dataset, relevant books titles do not share any common words. However, those books share the same hidden topic. Combining both *CNSH* and *HT* results in an only slightly higher $pF1$ score (72%). It suggests that both *CNSH* and *HT* provide useful information for clustering records of related topics. However, it is hard to disambiguate author name by only looking into topics of books that they wrote. To avoid these errors, other information related to authors might be needed to further disambiguate cases that do not only depend on the topics of the books.

Figure 12 shows the $pF1$ comparison between the *CNSH* and $CNSH\text{-}PCA_s$ methods, where s denotes the scale value that we use to reduce the number of dimensions. After using *PCA*, since the number of dimensions is reduced, the similarity thresholds are chosen to be lower than that of the method *CNSH*. It

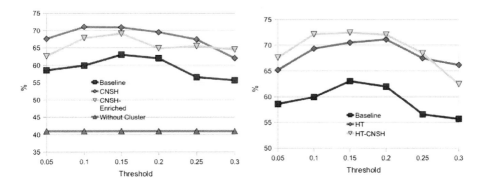

Fig. 11. $pF1$ score comparison: (left) Without-Cluster, Baseline, *CNSH* & *CNSH-Enriched*; (right) Baseline and *HT*, *HT-CNSH*

shows that the highest accuracy this method could reach is lower than that of before reducing dimensions ($\approx 61\%$). It suggests that *PCA* can somehow preserve the most informative features of the dataset, although the number of dimensions (i.e., features) is reduced by a factor of 5, 10, 20. Representing the data in a more compact space also causes the loss of information and reducing the number of dimensions in our dataset reduces the speed and complexity of the clustering task. Therefore, when disambiguating author name in a large scale data set, one might consider using *PCA* to make the clustering task easier and faster.

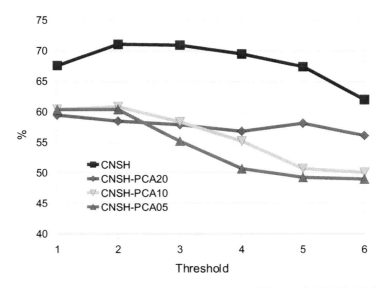

Fig. 12. $pF1$ score comparison between *CNSH* and *CNSH-PCA*

Scalability and Computability issues. In our framework, the most time-consuming task is the estimation of the topic model from Wikipedia. In particular, it took 14 hours[5] to estimate the topic model for 80,000 documents in Wikipedia. However, once the model is estimated, the next step for enriching metadata is to infer the topic distribution for every book in the library. This step is very fast since the titles of books in the library is often very short. Thousands of books are analyzed topics and enriched within several seconds. Hence, inferring and enriching topics for metadata is feasible even for big digital libraries.

In Hierarchical Agglomerative Clustering, it might be expensive to process clustering given a big number of documents. However, in disambiguating author name, using blocking methods, we can significantly reduce the number of books in each block that we need to cluster. For example, in our dataset, the average number of books in each block is 17. Therefore, hierarchical clustering can be practical to apply for clustering books of ambiguous authors.

7   Conclusions and Future Research

We have shown that Classification numbers and Subject Headings encode valuable information for Author Name Disambiguation. Moreover, we have provided evidences that in their absence Topic Models can be used to label records automatically and that with the induced labels the clustering results achieved are comparable to those obtained with the CN and SH.

We leave for the future a qualitative analysis of our results by investigating whether the performance of the clustering is influenced by some parameters of the records, like topic, year of publication, kind of author name. We also leave for further study a comparison of our methods with those presented in the literature and an analysis of our methods on different kinds of DL (e.g. federated DL).

References

1. Blei, D.M., Ng, A.Y., Jordan, M.I.: Latent dirichlet allocation. J. Mach. Learn. Res. 3, 993–1022 (2003)
2. Di Lauro, T., Choudhury, G.S., Patton, M., Warner, J.W., Brown, E.W.: Automated name authority contol and enhanced searching in the levy collection. D-Lib Magazine 7(4) (2001)
3. Han, H., Zha, H., Lee Giles, C.: Name disambiguation in author citations using a k-way spectral clustering method. In: JCDL 2005: Proceedings of the 5th ACM/IEEE-CS Joint Conference on Digital Libraries, pp. 334–343. ACM, New York (2005)
4. Heinrich, G.: Parameter estimation for text analysis, Technical report, University of Leipzig (2008)
5. Herskovic, J.R., Tanaka, L.Y., Hersh, W., Bernstam, E.V.: A day in the life of pubmed:analysis of typical days' query log. J. Amer. Med. Inform. Ass. 14, 212–220 (2007)
6. Huang, J., Ertekin, S., Giles, C.L.: Efficient name disambiguation for large-scale databases. In: Fürnkranz, J., Scheffer, T., Spiliopoulou, M. (eds.) PKDD 2006. LNCS (LNAI), vol. 4213, pp. 536–544. Springer, Heidelberg (2006)

---

[5] We used a laptop with 2GHz Processor and 2GB Memory.

7. Le, D.-T., Nguyen, C.-T., Ha, Q.-T., Phan, X.H., Horiguchi, S.: Matching and rank-ing with hidden topics towards online contextual advertising. In: Web Intelligence, Sydney, NSW, Australia, pp. 888–891 (2008)

8. Newman, D., Hagedorn, K., Chemudugunta, C., Smyth, P.: Subject metadata en-richment using statistical topic models. In: JCDL 2007: Proceedings of the 7th ACM/IEEE-CS Joint Conference on Digital Libraries, pp. 366–375. ACM, New York (2007)

9. On, B.-W., Lee, D., Kang, J., Mitra, P.: Comparative study of name disambiguation problem using a scalable blocking-based framework. In: JCDL 2005: Proceedings of the 5th ACM/IEEE-CS Joint Conference on Digital Libraries, pp. 344–353. ACM, New York (2005)

10. Pearson, K.: On lines and planes of closest fit to systems of points in space. London, Edinburgh and Dublin Philosophical Magazine and Journal of Science 2(11), 559–572 (1901)

11. Phan, X.-H., Nguyen, C.-T., Le, D.-T., Nguyen, L.-M., Horiguchi, S., Ha, Q.-T.: A hidden topic-based framework towards building applications with short web documents. IEEE Transactions on Knowledge and Data Engineering 99 (2010) (prePrints)

12. Steyvers, M., Griffiths, T.: Probablistic topic models. In: Landauer, T., McNamara, D., Dennis, S., Kintsch, W. (eds.) Latent Semantic Anaylsis: A Road to Meaning. Lawrence Erlbaum, Mahwah (2006)

13. Torvik, V.I., Smalheiser, N.R.: Author name disambiguation in medline. ACM Trans. Knowl. Discov. Data 3(3), 1–29 (2009)

14. Torvik, V.I., Weeber, M., Swanson, D.R., Smalheiser, N.R.: A probabilistic similar-ity metric for medline records: A model for author name disambiguation: Research articles. J. Am. Soc. Inf. Sci. Technol. 56(2), 140–158 (2005)

Semantic Disambiguation in Folksonomy: A Case Study

Pierre Andrews, Juan Pane, and Ilya Zaihrayeu

Dipartimento di Ingegneria e Scienza Dell'Informazione,
Università degli studi di Trento, Italy
{andrews,pane,ilya}@disi.unitn.it

Abstract. Social annotation systems such as del.icio.us, Flickr and others have gained tremendous popularity among Web 2.0 users. One of the factors of success was the simplicity of the underlying model, which consists of a resource (e.g., a web page), a tag (e.g., a text string), and a user who annotates the resource with the tag. However, due to the syntactic nature of the underlying model, these systems have been criticised for not being able to take into account the explicit semantics implicitly encoded by the users in each tag. In this article we: a) provide a formalisation of an annotation model in which tags are based on concepts instead of being free text strings; b) describe how an existing annotation system can be converted to the proposed model; c) report on the results of such a conversion on the example of a del.icio.us dataset; and d) show how the quality of search can be improved by the semantic in the converted dataset.

1 Introduction

One of the cornerstones of what we now call the "Web 2.0" is unconstrained user collaboration and creation of content. Some of the first sites to allow such features were del.icio.us and Flickr where users could share resources – bookmarks and photos respectively – and freely annotate them. Both websites allowed the creation of so called Folksonomies: social classification of resources created by the community that have shown to be very important for organising the large amount of content online, but also for, later on, studying the collaborative creation of shared vocabularies and taxonomies.

These folksonomies are now widely studied, in particular with the model of tripartite graphs of *tags-users-resources*. However, in this model, *tags* are free-form terms with no explicit semantic, therefore a number of issues arise from their use, such as:

- the loss in precision due to the ambiguity of tags – for example, the tag "java" can refer to the "Indonesian island", the "programming language", and a "beverage".
- the loss of recall due to the synonymy of terms – for instance, if you search for the tag "travel", you might be interested by the results for the tag "journey".

R. Bernardi et al. (Eds.): NLP4DL/AT4DL 2009, LNCS 6699, pp. 114–134, 2011.

The use of different forms of the same word also exacerbate these issues as some users would, for example, use the tag "running", others would use instead "run", "runs", "torun", etc.

A number of approaches try to disambiguate tags in folksonomies and to create organised formal vocabularies automatically from them [1]. This has shown to be a difficult task and has not yet been fully characterised and evaluated. In this article, we propose a case study of a sample of the del.icio.us tripartite graph that was manually annotated with senses from a controlled vocabulary (Wordnet). We show a number of properties of the vocabulary shared by the users of this folksonomy and identify important features that have been overlooked by previous studies on disambiguation and sense extraction from such folksonomies. Moreover, we provide a quantitative analysis of the impact of the introduction of explicit semantics in folksonomies on the construction of digital libraries on top of them where the data can be more easily accessed and processed by computers.

This article is organised as follows. First, in Section 2, we introduce the issue of folksonomy modelling and how we believe it can be extended to formalise the semantic of tags; we then discuss in Section 3 our case study and the methodology that was used to construct the dataset we examine. In Section 5 we then introduce and analyse a number of features of the vocabulary used, in particular on: *a*) how preprocessing of different forms of the same term can reduce the vocabulary size by ca. 17%, *b*) how a general controlled vocabulary is too static to encode the vocabulary of the folksonomy users as only around 50% of terms can be mapped to a controlled sense. In Section 6, we extend this analysis by showing quantitatively how the disambiguation of tags to senses can improve search. Finally, in Section 7 we discuss the related work and how it compares to the results we have obtained.

2   Semantic Folksonomy Model

2.1   Syntactic Folksonomy

The term folksonomy was coined in 2004 by T. Vander Wal [2] who characterised the new social tagging web sites that were appearing at the time. He defined a folksonomy as *"the result of personal free tagging of information and objects (anything with a URL) for one's own retrieval"*. This "result" is one of the simplest form of annotation of resources with metadata that can serve to help the indexing, categorisation or sharing of such resources: a tag annotation.

Mika[3] introduced a formalisation of this result to ease its processing in multimodal graph analysis. Doing so, the author enables the formal representation of the social network resulting from the folksonomy building activity. Mika represents a folksonomy as a tripartite graph composed of three disjoint types of vertices, the *actors* A (the user creating the tag annotation), the *concepts* C (tags, keywords) used as metadata and the *objects* O or resources being annotated. A tag annotation is thus a triple combining three vertices from each type:

$$T = \langle u, t, r \rangle \text{ where } u \in A, t \in C \text{ and } r \in O$$

According to Mika, such a tripartite graph can be used to describe an ontology representing the knowledge of the community that created this folksonomy. Some recent research have exploited social network analysis and distributional semantic models to extract formal representations of the semantic knowledge encoded in these tripartite graphs (see [1] for a review).

2.2   Semantic Folksonomy

An important point in Mika's [3] description of the folksonomy model is that "tags" or "keywords" are considered to be mapped one-to-one to the *concepts* of the ontology and that these are the semantic units of the language used in the community that created the folksonomy. However, we believe that a more granular model has to be used to represent the conceptual part of folksonomies. This will enable a better understanding of its underlying semantic and of the overlap of vocabularies between the users of the folksonomy.

In fact, tags and keywords, while they represent a specific concept and have a known semantic for the agent that creates them, are just stored and shared in the folksonomy as purely free-form natural language text. Because of the ambiguous nature of natural language [4], a number of issues arise when sharing only the textual version of the annotations:

Base form variation. This problem is related to natural language input issues where the annotation is based on different forms of the same word (e.g., plurals vs. singular forms, conjugations, misspellings) [4].

Homography. Annotation elements may have ambiguous interpretation. For instance, the tag "Java" may be used to describe a resource about the *Java island* or a resource about the *Java programming language*; thus, users looking for resources related to the programming language may also get some irrelevant resources related to the Island (therefore, reducing the precision);

Synonymy. Syntactically different annotation elements may have the same meaning. For example, the tags "image" and "picture" may be used interchangeably by users but will be treated by the system as two different tags because of their different spelling; thus, retrieving resources using only one of these tags may yield incomplete results as the computer is not aware of the synonymy link;

Specificity gap. This problem comes from a difference in the specificity of terms used in annotation and searching. For example, the user searching with the tag "cheese" will not find resources tagged with "cheddar[1]" if no link connecting these two terms exists in the system.

Indeed, as we show in our case study of del.icio.us (see Section 5.2), such issues can be found in a real application of the folksonomy model. We thus propose to replace the simple "Concept"↔"tag" mapping to one that will allow for an explicit formalisation of the intended semantic of the tag. The intuition behind this new formalisation is two-fold:

---

[1] Which is a kind of cheese.

- different tags could represent different forms of the same concept – for instance, "folksonomy" and "folksonomies" or "image" and "picture",
- a tag could represent a composed concept relying on two atomic concepts – for instance "sunny italy".

One suitable formalism for the representation of concepts is the one defined by Description Logics (DL) [5]. Briefly, the semantics (or, the extension) of a concept in DL is defined as a set of elements (or, instances). For example, the extension of the concept **Person** is the set of people existing in some model (e.g., in the model of the world). Because they are defined under a set-theoretic semantics, operators from the set theory can be applied on concepts, e.g., one could state that concept **Organism** *subsumes* (or, is more general than) the concept **Person** because the extension of the former concept is a superset for the extension of the latter concept. Among other things, the subsumption relation can be used for building taxonomies of concepts. These properties lead to a number of useful reasoning capabilities such as computing the instances of concepts through the concept subsumption, computing more specific or general concepts – these capabilities can be used for building services for the end users such as semantic search, as discussed in Section 6. A more complete introduction to DL is out of the scope of this article; interested readers are referred to [5] for details.

We thus introduce two new formalisations in the model to create a quadri-partite graph representing the user-resource-tag-concept link:

- A *controlled tag ct* is a tuple $ct = \langle t, \{lc\} \rangle$, where t is a tag, i.e., a non-empty finite sequence of characters normally representing natural language words or phrases such as "bird", "sunnydays" or "sea"; and $\{lc\}$ is an ordered list of linguistic concepts, defined as follows:
- A *linguistic concept lc* is a tuple $lc = \langle c, nlt \rangle$, where c is a concept as defined in DL (see above); and nlt is a natural language term that denotes the concept c.

Consider an example of a controlled tag: $ct = \langle "sunnydays", \{lc_1, lc_2\} \rangle$, with $lc_1 = \langle \mathsf{Sunny}, "sunny" \rangle$ and $lc_1 = \langle \mathsf{Day}, "day" \rangle$. Note that there can be more than one natural language term that denotes the same concept as in $lc_3 = \langle \mathsf{Sunny}, "bright" \rangle$.

Recall the syntactic folksonomy model definition (see Section 2.1) that we now extend to the definition of a controlled tag annotation, T^C:

$$T^C = \langle u, ct, r \rangle \ \text{where } u \in A, ct \text{ is a controlled tag, and } r \in O$$

In the following section we discuss how controlled tag annotations can be used to "semantify" a social annotation system such as del.icio.us.

3   Semantifying del.icio.us

To analyse our model and a set of natural language technologies that can be used to help the users in specifying the semantic of tags at the time of their creation, we examine the widely used del.icio.us[2] folksonomy as a case study.

---

[2] `http://del.icio.us`

del.icio.us is a simple folksonomy as was defined by [2] and formalised by [3] in that it links resources to users and tags in a tripartite graph. However, these tags are totally uncontrolled and their semantic is not explicit. In the current datasets, for instance the ones provided by Tagora[3] or listed in [6], no-one has yet, to the best of our knowledge, provided a gold standard with such semantics. In that, the del.icio.us dataset is not perfectly what we are looking for, the Faviki[4] website could provide such dataset, however it does not contain so many users and annotations as del.icio.us and the quality of the disambiguations is not guaranteed. To make the del.icio.us dataset fit our problem statement, we have thus decided to extend a subset of a del.icio.us dump with disambiguated tags by manual validation. We used WordNet 2.0 [7] as the underlying controlled vocabulary for finding and assigning senses for tag tokens.

3.1   del.icio.us Sample

We obtained the initial data from the authors of [8] who crawled del.icio.us between December 2007 and April 2008. After some initial cleaning the dataset contains *5 431 804* unique tags (where the uniqueness criteria is the exact string match) of *947 729* anonymized users, over *45 600 619* unique URLs on *8 213 547* different website domains. This data can be considered to follow the syntactic folksonomy model $\langle t, r, u \rangle$ where the resource r is the URL being annotated, containing a total of *401 970 328* tag annotations.

To study the semantic used in these tags, we have thus decided to extend a subset of the data with disambiguated tags; i.e., convert $t \rightarrow ct$. This means that for each tag t in this subset, we have explicitly split it in its component tokens and marked it with the Wordnet synset (its sense) it refers to and thus get to the semantic folksonomy model described in Section 2.2.

The gold standard dataset we have built includes annotations from users which have less than 1 000 tags and have used at least ten different tags in five different website domains to select representative active users. This upper bound was decided considering that del.icio.us is also subject to spamming, and users with more than one thousand tags could potentially be spammers as the original authors of the crawled data assumed [8]. Furthermore, only $\langle r, u \rangle$ pairs that have at least three tags (to provide diversity in the gold standard), no more than ten tags (to avoid time consuming manual validation effort) and coming from users who have tags in at least five website domains (to further reduce the probability of spam tags) are selected. Only URLs that have been used by at least twenty users are considered in the gold standard in order to provide enough overlap between users. A complete random selection out of $\tilde{1}22$ million $\langle r, u \rangle$ pairs would have not yield enough overlap between tag use and bookmarking for an interesting study of the users' tagging habits. After retrieving all the $\langle r, u \rangle$ pairs that comply with the previously mentioned constraints, we randomly selected 500 pairs. We thus obtained 4 707 tag annotations with 871 unique tags on 299 URLs in 172 different web domains.

---

[3] http://www.tagora-project.eu/data/
[4] http://faviki.com/

3.2   Manual Validation

Selecting the right tag split and the right disambiguation for each token in such split is a tedious task for the human annotators and we try to make this task as straightforward as possible. Thus we use some supporting tools to simplify the work of the validators and streamline the annotation process. A team of three annotators have already annotated a sample of one thousand bookmarks from a del.icio.us crawl in less than a week. To enable such streamlined annotation, some pre-annotation is performed automatically so that the most probable splits are already available to the validators and the most probable disambiguation is also proposed. These supporting tools are described in the following sections.

3.3   Preprocessing

The goal of the preprocessing step is to recognise a word sequence in a tag that may consist of several concatenated tokens that might have been written with syntactic variations (e.g,. plurals, exceptional forms). This step is composed of the following sub-steps:

1. **Tag split**: split the tags into the component tokens. This step is needed considering the fact that many annotation systems such as del.icio.us do not allow spaces as word separators and, therefore, users just concatenate multi-words (javaisland) or concatenate them using the Camel case (javaIsland), slashes (java-island), underscores (java_island) or other separator they deem useful. The tag split preprocessing runs a search in WordNet and tries to place *splits* when it recognises valid tokens. This preprocessing can generate different splits for the same tag, for instance, the tag "javaisland" can be split into { "java", "island"} or { "java", "is", "land"}. The output of this step is ranked to present the most plausible split to the annotator first. The ranking prefers proposals with fewer number of splits and with the maximum number of tokens linked to the controlled vocabulary.
2. **Lemmatization**: in order to reduce different forms of the word into a single form (that can later be found in a vocabulary such as Wordnet), a number of standard lemmatization heuristics are applied. For example, "banks" would be preprocessed as "bank".

3.4   Disambiguation

In this step we run an automatic disambiguation algorithm in order to suggest to the validator the possibly correct sense of the word (as preprocessed in the previous step). The algorithm is an extension of the one reported in [9] and based on the idea that collocated tags provide context for disambiguating (as generalised in the survey by Garcia-Silva [1]). In our approach, given a token within a tag split, we consider three levels of context: 1. the other tokens in the tag split provide the first level of context, 2. the tokens in the tag splits for the other tags used for the annotation of the same resource by the *same* user provide the second level, 3. the tokens in the tag splits for the tags used for the annotation of the same resource by *other* users, provide the third level of context.

The possible semantic relations between the senses of the given token and the senses of the tokens from its contexts are then mined to find a disambiguation. When a relation is found, the score of the corresponding word sense is boosted by a predefined value. The relations used are as follows (in decreasing order of their boost value)[5]:

1. synonymy (e.g., "image" and "picture");
2. specificity, measured as the length of the is-a path between two senses (e.g., "dog (Canis familiaris)" is more specific than "animal (a living organism)"); and
3. relatedness, measured as the sum of the lengths of the specificity paths from the two given senses to the nearest common parent sense (e.g., "table (a piece of furniture)" is related to "chair" (a seat for one person) through the common parent sense "furniture (furnishings that make a room)").

For the specificity and relatedness relations, the scores are adjusted according to the length of the path (the shorter the length, the higher the score). The scores for all the relations are also boosted according to the level of the used context (level one leads to higher scores, whereas level three leads to lower scores). The algorithm then uses two other heuristics to boost the scores of word senses, namely: 1. we boost the sense of a word if the part-of-speech (POS) of that sense is the same as the one returned by a POS tagger[6]; and 2. we boost the sense of a word according to the frequency of usage of the sense[7].

The sense with the highest score is then proposed to the validator as the suggested meaning of the token. If more than one sense has the highest score we applied an heuristic were the POS is preferred in the following order: nouns, verbs, adjectives and adverbs – as this follows the distribution of the tag tokens by POS in annotation systems such as del.icio.us as reported in [10] and confirmed in our own analysis (see Figure 5a)). Finally, if more than one candidate remains, then the sense with the highest frequency of usage is selected.

4   Results

In the following paragraphs we describe a first evaluation of the validity of the algorithms we described in the previous section, based on the annotated sample from del.icio.us.

---

[5] For the purposes of our tests we use Wordnet relations, namely: the synonymy relation is explicitly codified in Wordnet's synsets; and the specificity relation is encoded as the hypernym relation.

[6] Which can reach more than 97% in accuracy on metadata labels as shown in [9].

[7] This data is available in linguistic resources such as WordNet [7].

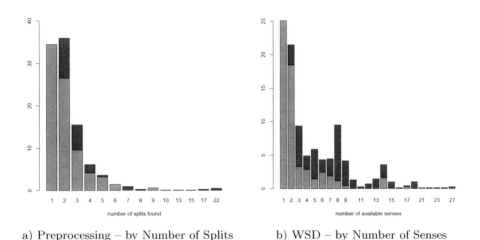

a) Preprocessing – by Number of Splits   b) WSD – by Number of Senses

Fig. 1. Accuracy of the Preprocessing and WSD Algorithms

4.1 Preprocessing

In the current dataset, we have found that 10% of the tags required to be split in more than one token. There are many concatenation methods used in the dataset by users: _, +, - and / are found, for example "teachers.site". However, the majority of the concatenations (71%) are done without any splitting character, for example "searchengine". In this case, the splitting is non trivial and we report the results of our algorithm in this task.

The accuracy of the preprocessing step (see Section 3.3) in this validation task reached 80.31%. In Figure 1a) we provide a detailed analysis of the accuracy of the algorithm for different numbers of possible splits. The Y axis corresponds to the distribution of tags per number of possible splits found by the algorithm, the top box is the amount of wrong splits selected as best split while the bottom one represents the amount of accurate splits that were selected by the preprocessing algorithm. The plot should be read as follows: ∼35% of all the tags have two possible splits and the accuracy of the algorithm for these tags is ∼80% (see the second bar from the left).

We believe that the current accuracy of the preprocessing algorithm can be increased by some improvements on the lemmatization heuristics to be able to lemmatize strings within concatenated words (such as "teachersresources"). In addition, our approach is based on a lexicon to detect existing words, but 22.5% of the tags were unknown lemmas in WordNet, in that sense, using a lexicon of existing words in the English language might improve the preprocessing.

4.2 Word Sense Disambiguation

The average homography of the tag tokens in the dataset is 4.68, i.e., each tag token has 4.68 possible senses on average. The proposed WSD algorithm performed at 59.37% in accuracy. In Figure 1b) we provide a detailed analysis of the accuracy of the algorithm for different levels of homography. The Y axis corresponds to the distribution of tokens per number of possible homographs, the top box is the amount of wrong disambiguations ranked as best while the bottom one represents the amount of accurate disambiguations that were ranked top by the WSD algorithm. The figure should be read as follows: the number of cases with two possible senses in the controlled vocabulary is ∼22% and the accuracy of the algorithm for these cases is ∼90% (see the second bar from the left).

It is worth noting that, on Figure 1b), we can see that the WSD algorithm has an accuracy lower than 50% for the tokens with many available senses, however, the biggest amount of tokens only have two senses available and in this case, the WSD algorithm performs at an accuracy close to 90%.

From the result we conclude that the WSD problem can be harder in its application in the domain of tag annotations than in its application in the domain of web directory labels, which are closer to tags in their structure than well formed sentences but still provide a more specific context for disambiguation. In fact, as reported in [9], the WSD algorithm proposed by the authors reaches 66.51% in accuracy which is only 2.61% higher than the baseline, when the most frequently sense is used.

4.3   Validation

In order to guarantee the correctness of the assignment of tag splits and tag token senses, two different validators validated each $\langle URL, u \rangle$ pair. The "agreement

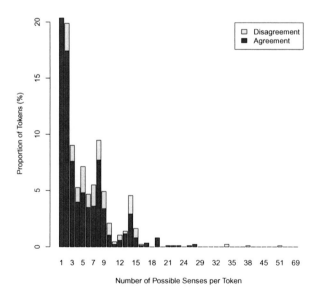

Fig. 2. Agreement between Annotators on Sense Validation, per Number of Available Senses

without chance correction" [11] between users in the task of disambiguation of tokens is of 0.76. As mentioned in [11], there is not yet any accepted best measure for the agreement in the task of sense annotation and thus we currently report only the raw agreement. It is intuitive to think that the agreement will fall when there are more available senses for one token as the annotators will have more chance to choose a different sense. This could also happen because, as we show in Figure 5b), sometimes the annotators cannot decide between too fine grained senses in the controlled vocabulary. Figure 2 shows a more detailed view of the effect of number of available senses on the annotators' agreement.

5   Analysis

5.1   Considerations on the Dataset Uncontrolled Vocabulary

del.icio.us is used in many research groups that work on folksonomies as a large dataset showing how users use tags to organise and share their resources. We have thus started by a basic analysis of how users used tags in the dataset and what we could observe from this. In the following paragraphs, we discuss the analysis that we performed on the whole dataset of 45 600 619 URLs, with all the users and tags available. The analyis and first conclusion on the manual disambiguation batch of 500 $\langle URL, u \rangle$ pairs is discussed in the next section.

While the annotation task on del.icio.us is quite simple as it does not require the specification of semantics, we can already see that the users are not motivated to provide a large amount of annotations. Note that we cannot make any conclusions on why this might be the case as this would require a direct users study, however, as illustrated by Figure 3a), we can see that in 35.5% of the cases, users use only one tag per bookmark and only in 12.1% of the cases they would add more than five tags per bookmark.

This might be because each user only uses very specific tags to classify-categorize the bookmark and thus does not require many indexing terms to find the resource in the future. This assumption would be a "dream" scenario as it would mean that the users are already ready to provide very specific descriptors

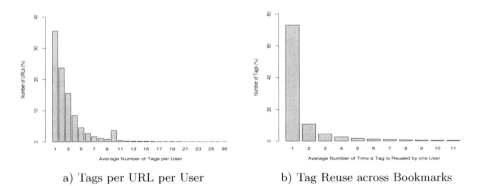

a) Tags per URL per User   b) Tag Reuse across Bookmarks

Fig. 3. Use of Tags in del.icio.us

for their resources and if these descriptors are linked to the underlying controlled vocabulary, we can retrieve them using synonymous and/or more general terms very easily. However, it might just be that the users are not bothered to add more tags as they do not see the value of adding many indexing terms for future retrieval.

An interesting point is that there is an out-of-the-norm peak at ten tags per bookmark that seems too strong to be coincidental. We have not yet studied in details why this happens but hypothesise that it might be created by spambots providing a lot of bookmarks with exactly ten tags.

In Figure 3b), we consider another interesting feature of the tagging behaviour of users on del.icio.us. While an often used assumption in folksonomy study algorithms (see [1] for a review) is that we can learn a lot from tag collocations on different resources, we can see that users do not often reuse the same tag more than once. In fact, from our analysis, in 73% of the cases, a tag is used only once on the whole set of bookmarks by a single user. This means that in a majority of the cases, a tag will not be found located on different resources, at least not by the same user. Only in 7.3% of the cases a tag is reused on more than seven resources.

This might support our previous assumption that the users use very specific tags when they annotate resources and thus they do not use them on multiple documents. However, this might create difficulties when sharing knowledge between users as they might not use the same vocabulary (as they use very specific/personal terms). It might also impair the ontology learning algorithms [1] that are based on the measure of collocation of tags.

When annotating shared goods such as web pages, if there is no agreement between the users on what the resource means, it is difficult to reuse these annotations to improve search and ranking of resources. It is also difficult to learn the meaning of the resource or of the annotations attached to it. We have thus done a preliminary analysis of the general agreement of the users in the del.icio.us dataset

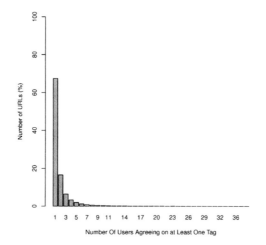

Fig. 4. Average Agreement on Tags for the same Resource

when they tag a resource. Here we are interested to see how many tags are used by more than one user on the same resource.

To do this, we have adopted a naïve measure of agreement where we count how many users have used the same tag on the same resource. For instance, if there is user U_1 who tagged a resource R_1 with T_1 and T_2 while user U_2 tagged this resource with T_3 and T_4, then there is only one user using any of the four tags. If U_3 tagged R_2 with T_5 and T_6, U_4 tagged it with T_6 and T_7 and U_5 with T_8 and T_9, then there are two users agreeing on at least one tag for that resource. Note that we only consider URLs in the dataset bookmarked by at least two users. Figure 4 shows the results of this measure. In 67.5% of the cases, there is only one user "agreeing" on at least one tag, which means different users used different tags on the same resources. In only 9.3% of the cases more than three users agreed on at least one tag.

In a sense this is a good result in that users do provide very diverse tags for the same resource and thus we can learn more about the resource itself. However, if there is no agreement between the users, it is difficult to consider that tags are valid as they might be very personal or subjective.

It is interesting to note that these percentages apply on millions of tags, resources and users and in this, a small percentage still represent a large mass of resources and users on which automatic semantic extraction algorithms can be applied. Also, these figures were computed without any preprocessing of the different forms of tags, or without their disambiguation. As we show in the next section, this might be an important factor for the lack of overlap of tags between resources and users that we are seeing.

However, seeing these results, it is clear that there is a need to create better incentives for the users to provide annotations. In particular, they should be motivated to provide diverse annotation, but also annotations that create a consensus on the meaning of the resources as both these factors are important for leveraging the power of semantic search, navigation and knowledge learning.

5.2   Consideration on the Dataset Controlled Vocabulary

As discussed earlier, we have obtained a quality, disambiguated, sample of the del.icio.us folksonomy for which we know the sense of each tag. In this section, we analyse this subset to see the tagging behaviour when tags are disambiguated to the terms in a controlled vocabulary. In the following paragraphs we present some first conclusions on the use of a controlled vocabulary and how it maps to the users' vocabulary. In the following analysis, we only consider entries that were validated and agreed upon by two validators.

Use of Nouns, Verbs and Adjectives. In a previous study Dutta et al. [10] point out that the users of del.icio.us tend to use mainly Nouns as descriptors of the urls. In the current dataset we have a validated sense (with all its metadata provided by Wordnet) for each term and thus we can easily reproduce such observation.

Figure 5a) shows that we can come to the same conclusions as [10]. In fact, Nouns are used most of the times (88.18%) while Verbs and Adjectives, even if

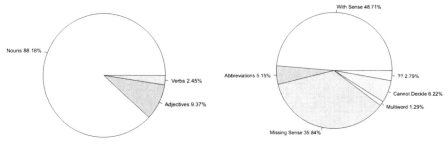

a) Part of Speech   b) Valid vs. Missing Senses

Fig. 5. Properties of Validated Tokens

they are used sometimes cannot be found in great numbers in the annotations. Note that Adverbs seem to be never used, at least in the sample of del.icio.us that we are studying.

Controlled Vocabulary vs. the Users' Vocabulary. While disambiguating the tags to a sense in Wordnet, the manual annotators could decide that no sense provided by the controlled vocabulary was adequate to express the sense meant by the user. For example, the tag "ajax" was found in the dataset and usually referred to the ajax technology used in web applications[8]. However, the only sense present in Wordnet for this tag is "a mythical Greek hero".

As shown in Figure 5b), the case of the missing sense happened in 35.8% of the cases. However, the validators were able to find a matching sense in Wordnet for 48.7% of the terms used in the validated batch. For diverse reasons (the users use abbreviations, there is no sense in wordnet, etc.) less than half of the vocabulary used by the users can be mapped to the WordNet controlled vocabulary.

This is an important observation as it shows the inadequacy of fully automatic folksonomy processing systems based on fixed controlled vocabularies such as Wordnet. For instance, if we consider the issue of Word Sense Disambiguation, the state-of-the-art tools cannot often achieve more that 60% accuracy. However, given the fact that only half of the terms from our dataset can be found in a vocabulary such as WordNet, from the end user perspective, it means that the user will be suggested the right sense for a given tag token in much less than 60% of cases.

Sense Disambiguation. One of the issues presented in the raw tags analysis we discussed in Section 5.1 is that there is not a great agreement between users in the tags they use and there is not a great overlap in their personal vocabularies. One of the hypothesis for this is that there are many lexical variations of the same term that cannot be matched without preprocessing the tags (for example, "javaisland", "java_island", "java" and "island", etc.) and as we have already discussed earlier, there are different terms that can be used for the same concept (for example, "trip" and "journey").

---

[8] http://en.wikipedia.org/wiki/Ajax_(programming)

Table 1. Decrease in the Amount of ambiguities after pre-processing and after sense disambiguation

	tags	tokens	senses	synsets
total	311	265	274	258
decrease (%)		-14.8	-11.9	-17.0

In the validation process for the batch, we have actually cleaned all these issues by collapsing different lexical variations and linking them to their relevant concepts. We can thus evaluate the amount of ambiguity that is added by these different type of variations.

Table 1 shows a summary of this decrease in ambiguity when going from *tags* – that can represent the same word in different forms – to *tokens* – that are pre-processed tags collapsed to the normal form of the world –, to *senses* that a word can take[9] and then to *synsets* – that disambiguate the meaning of the tag.

We can thus see that by preprocessing alone (splitting and lemmatazing tags), the vocabulary size shrinks by 14.8%, thus reducing the ambiguity of the annotations significantly without the need to disambiguate them to the terms in a controlled vocabulary (e.g., a user searching for "blog" will be able to find bookmarks tagged with "blogs", "coolblog", "my_blog", etc.).

The disambiguation provided by the linking to the controlled vocabulary, in the current batch, does not actually provide a great amount of reduction in the vocabulary size. In fact, in the current batch, only seven tokens can be mapped to a smaller set of synsets. This means that there is not a great amount of synonymy in the tags that we have studied.

We believe that this is not a general feature of the full del.icio.us folksonomy and that synonyms and homograph tags will happen in a bigger number in different domains. We are now extending the size of our study batch to observe this hypothesis. In fact, in the current batch, as in del.icio.us in general, the main topic seems to be, from the most used tags, focused on computer and web technologies. These domains use a very restricted vocabulary where words do not often have synonyms (e.g. css, ajax, html). For instance, as of January 2011, 90% of the top ten tags on del.icio.us were except for one, all computer technology related (i.e., design[10], blog, video, software,tools, programming, wed design, reference); only "music[11]" is in another domain. Considering the top 20 tags, we still find 80% of computer technology related tags (e.g. web, howto, javascript, linux, web2.0, development, google), mixed with other topics (e.g. art, free[12], inspiration). We believe that synonymy and homography should appear more often if the dataset is better spread across topics as, for example, the same polysemous term will most

---

[9] Because of homography, one token can have more than one sense and thus there are more senses than tokens.

[10] In the context of webdesing, blog, web, css.

[11] In the context of: free,mp3, download, software.

[12] In the context of: webdesign, download, software, music.

probably happen in different topic with a different sense. However, to observe such effect, a better sampling process has to be designed to spread the entries across topics.

6   Evaluating Semantic Quality of Service

It is often argued that the quality of search would improve if the explicit semantic of the resources were known by the search engine [12]. In order to evaluate this improvement in the Quality of Service (QoS) of search in annotation systems such as del.icio.us, we implemented and evaluated the performance of a semantic search algorithm in the gold standard dataset. The key difference from keywords-based search algorithms is that instead of using strings as query terms, the algorithm uses concepts from the controlled vocabulary and searches results in the semantically annotated dataset of del.icio.us discussed in Section 3.

We built queries from validated tag tokens, i.e., tokens for which an agreement on their meaning was reached amongst the validators. The key intuition here was that if the users used these tags to annotate web resources, then they are likely to use the same tags and in the same meaning to find these and other resources.

In order to implement search, we built two indexes: a *keyword index* and a *concept index*. The keyword index contains mappings from tag tokens (e.g., "java") to all the resources annotated with this tag token (e.g., pages about the Java island but also about the programming language, the coffee beverage, etc). The concept index contains mappings from the concepts of the validated tag tokens to all the resources annotated with this tag token in the meaning represented by the concept (e.g., given the token "java" in the meaning of the Java island, the index would point to all resources about the java island but *not* about the programming language or about the coffee beverage). From the gold standard, we generate 377 entries in the concept index, 369 entries in the keyword index, which both point to 262 resources.

Given a number of tag tokens (which corresponds to the desired number of query terms) we built two queries: a *keyword-based query* and a *concept-based query*. The keywords-based query is the conjunction of the token strings, whereas the concepts-based query is the conjunction of the corresponding validated concepts of the tokens. The results of the keyword-based queries might be incorrect and incomplete due to, among other things, the issues discussed in Section 2.2 such as base form variation, homography, synonymy and specificity gap.

The results of the concept-based queries were computed by matching concepts in the query to those in the index. Thus, a query with a particular concept would return all and only resources that have this concept amongst its tag tokens independently of any linguistic variation used to denote this concept in the tag token (e.g., synonymy, homography, as from above). Therefore, the results of concepts-based queries are *correct* and *complete* as long as the meaning of tag tokens in the resource annotations and of the terms in the concepts-based queries is properly disambiguated, which is the case for the analysed dataset due to its manual disambiguation as described in Section 3.

Table 2. Number of Queries

Query Terms	Queries	Results	
		Concept Search	Keyword Search
1	2 062	9.25	8.87
2	2 349	4.38	4.20
3	1 653	2.40	2.32
4	1 000	1.44	1.44

Table 3. Precision (%) vs. Query Clauses

Tag Type	Query Clauses			
	1	2	3	4
preprocessed	93.82	97.07	98.98	99.70
raw	93.95	97.48	99.14	99.70

In order to address the specificity gap problem, the concept-based search described above was extended to support searching of more specific terms. In this we followed the approach described in [13]. In short, we introduced a variable *"semantic depth"* parameter that indicated the maximum distance between a query concept and a concept according to the `is-a` hierarchy of concepts in the underlying taxonomy in order for a resource annotated with such a concept to be considered as a query result for this query concept. For example, given the following path in the taxonomy: `transport` → `vehicle` → `car` and the query `transport`, then if the semantic depth parameter is set to 1, then resources annotated with the concept `transport` and/or with the concept `vehicle` will be returned as results; if this parameter is set to 2, then the resources annotated with the concept `car` will also be returned.

Queries with different number of terms and different values for the semantic depth parameter were generated and executed as described above (see Table 2 for details). Given that concepts-based queries, by construction, always yield correct and complete results, their results were taken as the gold standard for the evaluation of the performance of the keywords-based search. The measures of *precision* and *recall* were used for the evaluation.

As can be seen in Table 3, the precision of the keywords-based search with one query term is 93.8%, i.e., 6.2% of results may not be relevant to the user query, while this is a small difference, it is statistically significant (paired t-test, $p < 0.01$). The precision improves for keyword queries with more terms as the combination of more keywords disambiguates implicitly each keyword (e.g. if we search for the two terms "java island", resources about the programming language sense of "java" will rarely be returned as they will not have also been tagged with "island"); indeed, with four query clauses, the precision is of 99.7%. We can see that the precision of the keyword-based search is not dependent of the query depth (see

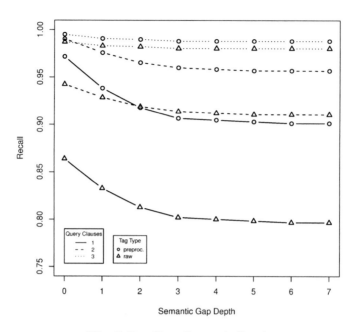

Fig. 6. Recall vs. Semantic Depth

results in Table 3). In fact, the number of true results, generated by the concept-based search will augment with the query depth as explained before, however, the number of results returned by the keyword-based search is constant. The precision of the search, which is computed as the number of true positives returned divided by the total number of results returned, is thus constant as the number of results returned does not change and the number of true positives is also always the same.

The recall of the keywords-based search with one query term and with the semantic depth of zero is about 97%, i.e., about 3% of *correct* results are *not* returned by the query (see Figure 6), again, while it is not a great difference, it is statistically significant (paired t-test, $p < 0.01$). With the increase of the semantic depth the recall decreases; for instance at a semantic depth of three, the recall has already dropped of 6%. This is explained by the fact that concepts-based search is capable of retrieving resources annotated with more specific terms than those used in the query, as discussed above. Therefore, concepts-based search returns more relevant results, whereas the keywords-based search always returns the same results, which leads to a lower recall. Again, as the number of query terms increases, the recall of the keywords-based search improves as the implicit semantic of the keywords is disambiguated by the other keywords.

We can also note that the preprocessing of tags (as discussed in Section 3.3) has a positive effect on recall as shown in Figure 6. Thus, the difference in recall in keyword-based search with and without preprocessing is about 11% for queries with one term (paired t-test, $p < 0.01$) and it diminishes as the number of query clauses grows. The difference in recall is explained by the fact that more correct results can be found if both tags and queries are brought to the same lexical representation (thus, searching with query "blogs" can match tags "blog", "blogging", etc). While preprocessing has a positive effect on recall, it is not predictable that it will have a positive or negative effect on precision as, depending on the dataset, preprocessed queries may yield more or less true positives than unpreprocessed queries. In our particular case, preprocessed and unpreprocessed queries performed equally well (see Table 3 for details).

In practice, in the current evaluation gold standard, the different tags used on resources are very far apart in the taxonomy and thus increasing the semantic depth does not change much the number of results returned by the concept-based search (see Table 2). This is a weak point of our evaluation dataset that is yet not big enough to show a strong *specificity gap* effect. However, we do expect this effect to increase as more concepts in the taxonomy get attached to resources.

One concrete example of a semantic query from the studied dataset is "business" in the meaning of "the activity of providing goods and services involving financial and commercial and industrial aspects". Keywords-based search with "business" as the query returned results in which the word "business" was used also in a different sense: "a commercial or industrial enterprise and the people who constitute it" that led to 27% in precision and to 43% in recall.

As the evaluation results show, the introduction of formal semantics for tags and query terms allows to significantly improve the precision and recall of search in annotation systems such as del.icio.us.

7   Related Work

Library catalogs, such as the Library of Congress [14] and Colon Classification [15], are a well known example of classification schemes where experts annotate resources for future search or navigation. The advantage of this model is that the produced classification is considered to be of good quality, which results in a good organization of the resources. On the other hand, Braun et. al. [16] point out to the cost of having dedicated experts annotating and organizing resources and building controlled vocabularies. This issue is underlined by the observation we made in Section 5.2 as these costly controlled vocabularies are not dynamic enough to follow the vocabulary of the users of the annotation system.

Several studies [3,17,18,19,20] analyse how the collaborative model also provides the system designers with behavioural information about the users' interests through their interaction with other users' annotations and their own annotations. However, as we have discussed in Sections 5.1 and 5.2, the problem of semantic heterogeneity [4,21] can hinder such analysis as matching tags might not be discovered due to homography, synonymy and morphology issues.

Some [22,23,24] have proposed to allow end-users to define their classes. Facetag [25] also follows this direction by incorporating collaborative annotations and collaborative controlled vocabularies in a single system. From the analysis we discussed in Sections 5.2 and 6, such an approach is required to allow the improve the dynamic cataloging of the growing amount of resources available. We believe that the formalisation that we provide in Section 2.2 will help in the storage and reasoning over such complex collaborative annotations.

Word Sense disambiguation (WSD) is known to be a difficult problem [26,27], especially in the domain of short metadata labels such as the categories names of a Web directories [9,28] (e.g. DMOZ[13]). Some work also exists on the disambiguation of tags in the domain of folksonomies; According to the classification presented in a recent survey [1], our approach falls under the *ontology-based* category in which the meaning of tags is an explicit association to an ontology element (such as a class or an instance). In [29], the authors preform WSD by defining the context of a tag as the other tags that co-occur with the given tag when describing a resource, and the senses of these tags are used for the disambiguation of the sense of the tag by using the Wu and Palmer similarity measure between the senses [30]. While we use different measures for the computation of the similarities between senses, we extend them with a POS tagger and the frequency of senses to further refine the selection of the tag sense. The WSD approach presented in [31] uses Wikipedia as the source of possible meanings of a tag. To compute the sense candidate, the WSD uses a vectors distance metric between the tag's context and the frequent terms found in the Wikipedia page; note that their approach does not use relations between senses at all for disambiguation. As was pointed out by the authors of [31,1,6], without having any gold standards and benchmarks, it is difficult to conduct a comparative analysis with the existing approaches. Therefore, for the time being we can only describe relevant approaches pointing to the differences in algorithms with respect to our approach, however, a quantitative evaluation of our algorithm is provided in Section 4.

8   Conclusion

In this article we revisited the classical social annotation model and pointed to some of its shortcomings, which mainly derive from the fact that the model is based on annotations with no formal semantics. We then proposed a model which is based on formal semantics and which can potentially overcome these shortcomings. We then described a process by which the classical model can be converted to the proposed formal model and reported on the results of such a conversion for a subset of a del.icio.us dataset. As our studies showed, the "semantified" dataset allows for a more precise and complete search, which is one of the key functionalities in social annotation systems. We observe that a fully automatic conversion of existing folksonomies to the formal model can hardly be possible; it should be a manual task to a significant extent, where the user can be motivated by the improved quality of services such as searching. We also observe that the use of static vocabularies such as WordNet provides ca. 50% coverage of the meaning of the tags, therefore, more dynamically evolved vocabularies need to be provisioned for semantic annotation systems, either by motivating the users to evolve, manually, the controlled vocabulary or by using automatic methods of sense induction.

---

[13] http://www.dmoz.org

Acknowledgements

This work has been partly supported by the INSEMTIVES project (FP7-231181, see http://www.insemtives.eu). We would also like to thank Sergey Kanshin for his contribution to the development of a system used for the evaluation.

References

1. Garcia-Silva, A., Corcho, O., Alani, H., Gomez-Perez, A.: Review of the state of the art: Discovering and associating semantics to tags in folksonomies. The Knowledge Engineering Review (2010) (to be published)
2. Wal, T.V.: Folksonomy: Coinage and definition, http://www.vanderwal.net/folksonomy.html
3. Mika, P.: Ontologies are us: A unified model of social networks and semantics. In: Web Semantics: Science, Services and Agents on the WWW, vol. 5, pp. 5–15 (2007)
4. Golder, S., Huberman, B.A.: The structure of collaborative tagging systems. Journal of Information Science 32(2), 198–208 (2006)
5. Baader, F., Calvanese, D., McGuinness, D., Nardi, D., Patel-Schneider, P.: The Description Logic Handbook: Theory, Implementation and Applications. Cambridge University Press, Cambridge (2003)
6. Körner, C., Strohmaier, M.: A call for social tagging datasets. SIGWEB Newsl 2:1–2:6 (January 2010)
7. Miller, G.: WordNet: An electronic Lexical Database. MIT Press, Cambridge (1998)
8. Wetzker, R., Zimmermann, C., Bauckhage, C.: Analyzing Social Bookmarking Systems: A del.icio.us Cookbook. In: Proceedings of the ECAI 2008 Mining Social Data Workshop, pp. 26–30. IOS Press, Amsterdam (2008)
9. Zaihrayeu, I., Sun, L., Giunchiglia, F., Pan, W., Ju, Q., Chi, M., Huang, X.: From web directories to ontologies: Natural language processing challenges. In: Aberer, K., Choi, K.-S., Noy, N., Allemang, D., Lee, K.-I., Nixon, L.J.B., Golbeck, J., Mika, P., Maynard, D., Mizoguchi, R., Schreiber, G., Cudré-Mauroux, P. (eds.) ASWC 2007 and ISWC 2007. LNCS, vol. 4825, pp. 623–636. Springer, Heidelberg (2007)
10. Dutta, B., Giunchiglia, F.: Semantics are actually used. In: International Conference on Semantic Web and Digital Libraries, Trento, Italy, pp. 62–78 (2009)
11. Artstein, R., Poesio, M.: Inter-Coder Agreement for Computational Linguistics. Journal of Computational Linguistics 34(4) (2008)
12. Echarte, F., Astrain, J., Cordoba, A., Villadangos, J.: Self-adaptation of ontologies to folksonomies in semantic web. Proc. World Acad. Sci. Eng. Tech. 33, 335–341 (2008)
13. Giunchiglia, F., Kharkevich, U., Zaihrayeu, I.: Concept search. In: Aroyo, L., Traverso, P., Ciravegna, F., Cimiano, P., Heath, T., Hyvönen, E., Mizoguchi, R., Oren, E., Sabou, M., Simperl, E. (eds.) ESWC 2009. LNCS, vol. 5554, pp. 429–444. Springer, Heidelberg (2009)
14. Library of Congress, http://www.loc.gov/index.html (last accessed on February 11, 2011)
15. Ranganathan, S.R.: Colon Classification, 7th edn. Asia Pub. House (1987)
16. Braun, S., Schmidt, A., Walter, A., Nagypal, G., Zacharias, V.: Ontology maturing: a collaborative web 2.0 approach to ontology engineering. In: Proceedings of (CKC 2007) at, WWW 2007 (2007)

17. Schmitz, P.: Inducing ontology from flickr tags. In: Proc. of the Collaborative Web Tagging Workshop, WWW 2006 (May 2006)
18. Golder, S.A., Huberman, B.A.: Usage patterns of collaborative tagging systems. J. Inf. Sci. 32, 198–208 (2006)
19. Marlow, C., Naaman, M., Boyd, D., Davis, M.: Ht06, tagging paper, taxonomy, flickr, academic article, to read. In: Proceedings of the Seventeenth Conference on Hypertext and Hypermedia, HYPERTEXT 2006, pp. 31–40. ACM, NY (2006)
20. Körner, C., Benz, D., Hotho, A., Strohmaier, M., Gerd, S.: Stop thinking, start tagging: tag semantics emerge from collaborative verbosity. In: Proceedings of WWW 2010, pp. 521–530. ACM, NY (2010)
21. Kolbitsch, J.: WordFlickr: a solution to the vocabulary problem in social tagging systems. In: Proceedings of I-MEDIA (2007)
22. Mathes, A.: Folksonomies - cooperative classification and communication through shared metadata. Technical report, Graduate School of Library and Information Science. University of Illinois Urbana-Champaign (December 2004)
23. Gazan, R.: Social annotations in digital library collections. D-Lib 14(11/12) (December 2008)
24. Ronzano, F., Marchetti, A., Tesconi, M.: Tagpedia: a semantic reference to describe and search for web resources. In: SWKM 2008: Intl. Workshop on Social Web and Knowledge Management @ WWW (2008)
25. Quintarelli, M., Resmini, A., Rosati, L.: Facetag: Integrating bottom-up and top-down classification in a social tagging system. In: IASummit, Las Vegas (2007)
26. Yang, C., Hung, J.C.: Word sense determination using wordnet and sense co-occurrence. In: Proceedings of the 20th International Conference on Advanced Information Networking and Applications, vol. 1, pp. 779–784. IEEE, USA (2006)
27. Agirre, E., Rigau, G.: A proposal for word sense disambiguation using conceptual distance. In: The First International Conference on Recent Advances in NLP, Tzigov Chark, Bulgaria (September 1995)
28. Autayeu, A., Giunchiglia, F., Andrews, P.: Lightweight parsing of classifications into lightweight ontologies. In: Lalmas, M., Jose, J., Rauber, A., Sebastiani, F., Frommholz, I. (eds.) ECDL 2010. LNCS, vol. 6273, pp. 327–339. Springer, Heidelberg (2010)
29. Angeletou, S., Sabou, M., Motta, E.: Semantically enriching folksonomies with flor. In: Proc of the 5th ESWC. workshop: Collective Intelligence & the Semantic Web (2008)
30. Wu, Z., Palmer, M.: Verb semantics and lexical selection. In: Proc. of the 32nd annual meeting on Association for Computational Linguistics, pp. 133–138 (1994)
31. Garca-Silva, A., Szomszor, M., Alani, H., Corcho, O.: Preliminary results in tag disambiguation using dbpedia. In: Proc. of the First International Workshop on Collective Knowledge Capturing and Representation (KCAP), USA (2009)

Advances in Deep Parsing of Scholarly Paper Content

Ulrich Schäfer and Bernd Kiefer

Language Technology Lab
German Research Center for Artificial Intelligence (DFKI)
Campus D3 1, 66123 Saarbrücken, Germany
{ulrich.schaefer,kiefer}@dfki.de
http://www.dfki.de/lt

Abstract. We report on advances in deep linguistic parsing of the full textual content of 8200 papers from the ACL Anthology, a collection of electronically available scientific papers in the fields of Computational Linguistics and Language Technology.

We describe how – by incorporating new techniques – we increase both speed and robustness of deep analysis, specifically on long sentences where deep parsing often failed in former approaches. With the current open source HPSG (Head-driven phrase structure grammar) for English (ERG), we obtain deep parses for more than 85% of the sentences in the 1.5 million sentences corpus, while the former approaches achieved only approx. 65% coverage.

The resulting sentence-wise semantic representations are used in the Scientist's Workbench, a platform demonstrating the use and benefit of natural language processing (NLP) to support scientists or other knowledge workers in fast and better access to digital document content. With the generated NLP annotations, we are able to implement important, novel applications such as robust semantic search, citation classification, and (in the future) question answering and definition exploration.

1 Introduction

Scientists in all disciplines are nowadays faced with a flood of new publications every day. In addition, more and more publications from the past become digitally available and thus even increase the amount of data. Therefore, finding relevant information and avoiding redundancy and duplication of work have become urgent issues to be addressed by the scientific community.

The organization and preservation of scientific knowledge in scientific publications, vulgo text documents, thwarts these efforts. From a viewpoint of a computer scientist, scientific papers are just 'unstructured information'.

Automatically precomputed, normalized semantic representations of textual utterances could help to structure the search space and find equivalent or related propositions even if they are expressed differently, e.g. in passive constructions, using synonyms etc. Domain-relevant semantic similarity can be computed automatically and exploited as additional knowledge source to support robust search.

R. Bernardi et al. (Eds.): NLP4DL/AT4DL 2009, LNCS 6699, pp. 135–153, 2011.

To again constrain the so expanded search space, users can ask the system in simply structured subject-predicate-object queries and get all matching, precomputed predicate-argument structures along with the original sentence from the paper. On the other hand, by storing the structure along with the original text in a structured full-text search engine such as Apache Lucene, it can be guaranteed that recall cannot fall behind the baseline of a fulltext search engine.

The basis of our scientific paper corpus is a subset of the ACL Anthology[1], a collection of conference and workshop papers in the field of Computational Linguistics and Language Technology. We concentrate on 8200 papers from the years 2002 through 2009 from which we extracted the textual content using Abbyy PDF Transformer.

Except for named entity recognition which is partly based on instances and concepts of a domain ontology, the processing pipeline we describe below is independent of the science domain.

To make the deep parser robust, it is embedded in a hybrid NLP workflow starting with a tokenizer, a part-of-speech tagger, and a named entity recognizer. These components help to identify and classify open class words such as person names, events (e.g. conferences) or locations. The trigram-based tagger helps to guess part-of-speech tags of words unknown to the deep lexicon. For both unknown words and named entities, generic lexicon entries are generated in the deep parser running the open source broad-coverage grammar ERG [5].

In contrast to shallow parsers, the ERG not only handles detailed syntactic analyses of phrases, compounds, coordination, negation and other linguistic phenomena that are important for extracting semantic relations, but also generates a formal semantic representation of the meaning of the input sentence in the MRS (Minimal Recursion Semantics; [6]) representation format. Ambiguities resulting in multiple readings per input sentence are ranked using a statistical parse ranking model.

In an earlier experiment, we obtained full deep parses for 64.89% of 955,581 sentences and 35.11% of the sentences were parsed by a fall-back shallow parser. Only 0.24% of the sentences could not be parsed at all.

In this chapter, describe the fine-grained mapping of punctuation and other tokenization details by means of a chart mapping technique [1] ensuring that this information is now optimally used by the deep grammar for disambiguation. We also report on progress that we achieved by applying a chart pruning technique [7] that, as already proven on another corpus, helps to considerably increase parsing speed of the deep parser and the number of successfully parsed sentences.

With both techniques applied together, we could not only increase parsing speed considerably, but also the coverage on the ACL Anthology corpus to more than 85%.

This chapter is structured as follows. In section 2, we present the improved parsing approach and results. In Section 3, we describe the semantic search application based on the improved parsing results. Section 4 discusses related work, and we finally conclude and give an outlook to future work in Section 5.

---

[1] http://www.aclweb.org/anthology

2   Deep Parsing of Scholarly Papers

The general idea of the semantics-oriented access to scholarly paper content is to apply NLP analysis to each sentence they contain and distill a structured representation that can be searched for in addition to fulltext. Different levels of analysis such as part-of-speech (PoS) tagging, named entity recognition (NER), chunking, shallow and deep parsing are suitable for different tasks.

While citation sentence classification in scholarly papers, a further application described in [16], is currently based on shallow NLP tasks such as tokenization, PoS tagging and patterns thereof only, the semantic search application is based on the full range of hybrid, robustness-oriented NLP. This includes shallow preprocessing with statistical taggers up to full deep parsing with generation of sentence semantics representations from which basically predicate-argument structure is derived. Thus, both applications share the preprocessing, and in the future, also citation sentence classification could make use of linguistic features extracted by more advanced NLP.

2.1   The Corpus

The basis of our scientific paper corpus is a subset of the ACL Anthology [2], a collection of conference and workshop papers in the field of Computational Linguistics and Language Technology. We concentrate on 8200 papers from the years 2002 through 2009 available in a native PDF format, i.e. not optically scanned at limited quality such as many older papers. Except for named entity recognition which is partly based an a domain ontology, the processing pipeline we describe below is independent of the science domain. However, we expect improvements in the future by modeling domain knowledge, e.g. through automatically extracted domain specific terms and ontology concepts.

2.2   PDF Extraction

The preprocessing step starts extracting clean text from the digital PDF documents. In a first version, we used PDFBox[2] to gain raw text content from the papers. This works well for most (especially recent) papers. However, it is problematic in general because PDFBox relies on the logical, digital content of the page (layout) description language PDF. Its internal structure is very much dependent on the tool that was used to generate the PDF, and there are many tools and of varying quality. Thus, decoding text from it does not work 100% correctly, and imposes severe problems up to complete garbage because of non-standard character encodings or no output on about 10% of the corpus.

To overcome these problems and become independent of the PDF encoder that was used to generate the digital paper, we recently moved to OCR-based PDF extraction with the commercial product Abbyy PDF Transformer[3]. It also reliably resolves hyphenated words using its own language model as well as text

---

[2] http://pdfbox.apache.org
[3] http://www.abbyy.com

(order) in tables. Moreover, and in contrast to PDFBox, it also works on scanned documents, provided that the scan quality is good enough. However, recognition of non-Latin characters such as in mathematical formulae remains a problem. It can be ignored for the time being because the NLP tools used also do not understand mathematics.

After text extraction, a sentence splitter segments into sentence units in order to provide suitable input for subsequent NLP. For each sentence, we record a unique document ID (in case of our corpus the ACL Anthology paper ID, e.g. C02-1023 for a paper from the COLING-2002 proceedings), the page on which it appeared, and the sentence number relative to the whole document. Amongst others, this information is important to highlight a search result or citation sentence within the original PDF paper layout.

2.3 Hybrid Parsing

To make the deep parser robust, it is embedded in a hybrid NLP workflow implemented using the hybrid NLP platform Heart of Gold [15]. Heart of Gold is an XML-based middleware architecture for the integration of multilingual shallow and deep natural language processing components, developed under the umbrella of the DELPH-IN initiative[4].

The employed Heart of Gold configuration instance starts with a tokenizer, the shallow part-of-speech tagger TnT [3] and the named entity recognizer SProUT [8]. These components help to identify and classify open class words such as person names, events (e.g. conferences) or locations.

The (trigram-based) tagger helps to guess part-of-speech tags of words unknown to the deep lexicon. For both unknown words and named entities, generic lexicon entries are generated in the deep parser. By means of the PET input chart XML format FSC [1], the shallow preprocessing results are combined and passed to the high-speed HPSG [12] parser PET [4] running the open source broad-coverage grammar ERG [5] (cf. Fig 2).

2.4 Precise Preprocessing Integration with Chart Mapping

Chart mapping [1] is a novel mechanism for the non-monotonic, rule-based manipulation of chart items that are described by feature structures. There are currently two chart mapping phases in PET during parsing: (1) Token mapping, where input items as delivered by external preprocessors are adapted to the expectations of the grammar. This requires that input items are described by feature structures – the *token feature structures*. (2) Lexical filtering, where lexical items can be filtered by hard constraints after lexical parsing has finished.

Token mapping requires tokens to be described by feature structures. Token feature structures can be arbitrarily complex. This allows users to pass information of various preprocessing modules into the parser. To this end, a new format, the XML-based FSC input format, was developed.

---

[4] http://www.delph-in.net/heartofgold/

Following is an excerpt from the FSC for the sentence "Resnik and Smith (2003) extract bilingual sentences from the Web to create parallel corpora for machine translation." (from anthology document N07-1043) generated by Heart of Gold preprocessing from TnT and SProUT output.

```
<fsc version="1.0">
  <chart id="hog://session1284321397757/collection1/TnT">
    <lattice init="v0" final="v20">
      <edge source="v0" target="v1">
        <fs type="token">
          <f name="+FORM"><str>Resnik</str></f>
          <f name="+FROM"><str>0</str></f>
          <f name="+TO"><str>6</str></f>
          <f name="+TNT">
            <fs type="tnt">
              <f name="+TAGS" org="list"><str>NNP</str></f>
              <f name="+PRBS" org="list"><str>1.000000</str></f>
            </fs>
          </f>
        </fs>
      </edge>
      ... <!-- more token edges from TnT -->
      <edge source="v6" target="v7">
        <fs type="token">
          <f name="+FORM"><str>extract</str></f>
          <f name="+FROM"><str>24</str></f>
          <f name="+TO"><str>31</str></f>
          <f name="+TNT">
            <fs type="tnt">
              <f name="+TAGS" org="list"><str>VB</str></f>
              <f name="+PRBS" org="list"><str>1.000000</str></f>
            </fs>
          </f>
        </fs>
      </edge>
      ... <!-- more token edges from TnT -->
      <!-- this edge comes from the Named Entity Recognizer -->
      <edge source="v0" target="v6">
        <fs type="token">
          <f name="+FORM"><str>Resnik and Smith (2003)</str></f>
          <f name="+FROM"><str>0</str></f>
          <f name="+TO"><str>23</str></f>
          <f name="+TNT"><fs type="null_tnt"/></f>
          <f name="+CLASS"><fs type="proper_ne"/></f>
          <f name="+TRAIT"><fs type="generic_trait"/></f>
        </fs>
      </edge>
    </lattice>
  </chart>
</fsc>
```

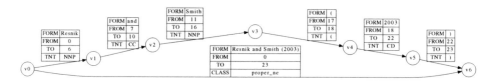

Fig. 1. FSC input to PET with combined information from tokenizer, PoS tagger and concurrent SProUT citation string item for input fragment "Resnik and Smith (2003) extract ..."

Figure 1 shows how tokenized and PoS-tagged input is combined with possibly concurrent information from a named entity recognizer, in the example SProUT delivering hypothetical information on named entities (here a citation string) in a single named entity item spanning over multiple words.

Concerning punctuation, the deep grammar can e.g. make use of information on opening and closing quotation marks. This information is often not explicit in the input text, e.g. when gained through OCR techniques, which make no distinction between ' and ' or " and ". However, a tokenizer can often guess (reconstruct) leftness and rightness correctly. This information, passed to the deep parser via FSC, helps it to disambiguate.

Furthermore, a new way of generic lexical instantiation has been introduced with token feature structures and chart mapping. In this new setup, the parser tries to instantiate all generic lexical entries for each word. Upon lexical instantiation, the token feature is unified into a designated path of the lexical entry. Only if this unification succeeds, the lexical item is instantiated. In order to control the instantiation of generic lexical entries, the token feature structures are appropriatly constrained in the generic lexical entry, for instance by requiring that a generic verbal entry is only applicable for token feature structures where the highest ranked part-of-speech tag is a verb.

2.5   Increased Processing Speed and Coverage through Chart Pruning

The use of statistical models for result selection is well established for parsing with PET and ERG. We use a discriminative maximum entropy model based on WeScience data [9] to compute the best parse results. Recently, [7] described the use of a generative model to increase efficiency by shaping the search space of the parser towards the more likely constituents and pruning very unlikely ones. This method not only results in lower parse times, but also in slightly better coverage, since sentences which could not be parsed due to timeouts now fit into the given time bounds.

The generative model is in fact a probabilistic context-free grammar (PCFG) computed from the same tree banks as the discriminative model. The parser in PET is a straightforward bottom-up chart parser with agenda, which makes it easy to use a model that has only local dependencies, such as PCFG. What is missing is a heuristics to prune unlikely items in a way that has a small

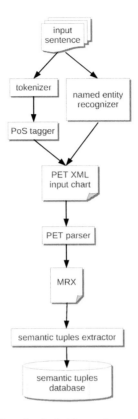

Fig. 2. Heart of Gold workflow for hybrid parsing and semantic tuples extraction

computation overhead and will retain most of the items that are needed for the globally best results.

[11] did a very thorough comparison of different performance optimization strategies, and among those also a local pruning strategy which is similar to the one used by [7]. It restricts the number of items given both their length and start point in the chart. This is easy to implement and avoids the use of complicated heuristics to compensate the bias that shorter items become over longer chart items because of decreasing probability, which leads, without compensation, to a breadth-first strategy for the whole parse. The number of items per chart cell is restricted to a fixed number to hinder the parser from getting lost in local probability maxima.

There is an important difference to the system of [11], namely that their system works on a reduced context-free backbone of the grammar and then reconstructs the full results, while PET uses the full HPSG grammar directly, with subsumption packing and partial unpacking to achieve a similar effect as the packed chart of a context-free parser.

The local chart pruning results in a measurable speed-up with a negligible decrease in parsing accuracy; in fact, an increase in f-measure has been observed

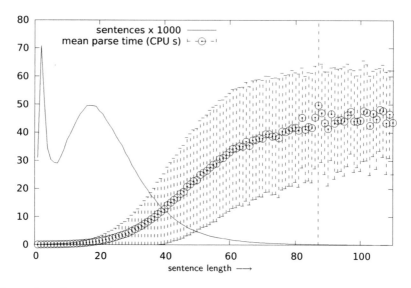

Fig. 3. Distribution of sentence length and mean parse times for mild pruning

because complicated sentences that had originally failed due to resource restrictions could now be parsed.

Processing Results. In total, we parsed 1,537,801 sentences, of which 57,832 (3.8%) could not be parsed because of lexicon errors which are mostly due to OCR artifacts.

Figure 3 displays the average parse time of processing with moderate chart pruning, together with the mean quadratic error. In addition, it contains the distribution of input sentences over sentence length. Obviously, the vast majority of sentences has a length up to 60 words maximum.

Parse time was limited to 60 CPU seconds, and main memory consumption to 4 GB, which was far more than ever needed by the processes. Overall, the parse times only grow mildly due to the many optimization techniques in the original system, and also the new chart pruning method. The sentence length distribution has been integrated into Figure 3 to show that the predominant part of our real-world corpus can be processed using this information-rich method with very modest parse times.

The large amount of short inputs is at first surprising, moreover as most of these inputs can not be parsed, as can be seen in Figure 5. The explanation is easy: most of these inputs are non-sentences such as headings, enumerations, footnotes and such. How we deal with this kind of input will be described in the section about fragmentary input.

All measurements were carried out on an Intel XEON E5430 2.66GHz cluster computer. Except for the parallelization, the used hardware equals a modern standard desktop PC, which again shows the feasibility of the used method.

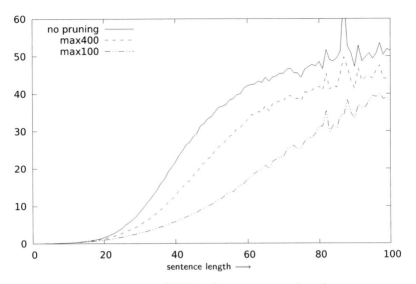

Mean parse time (CPU sec) over sentence length

	No pruning	Max. 400 passive	Max. 100 passive
Avg. Parse Time (CPU sec)	5.90	3.95	2.17
Unparsed Sentences	433104 (28.2%)	392758 (25.5%)	381019 (24.8%)
Recall	71.8%	74.5%	75.2%
Best Parse Lost		5.43%	19.7%

Fig. 4. Comparison of results with different chart pruning settings

Figure 4 shows the effects of the chart pruning approach using moderate as well as more aggressive pruning. The last row displays the amount of parsed sentences which do not get the best results due to pruning. Note that the increase in parsed sentences is only due to the reduced resource needs through pruning, and that the lexical failures are not contained in the unparsed sentences figures.

Figure 5 shows the amount of unparsed sentences, split into two categories. The dots represent the sentences that could not be parsed due to time limitations, the solid lines those that were rejected by the grammar. Not surprisingly, the fraction of sentences hitting the time bound increases noticeably for sentences longer that 60 words, but it should be noted that the percentage that can not be parsed because of grammatical reasons stays almost constant.

For sentences with less than 40 words, aggressive chart pruning loses parses (around 0.8%) that the mild pruning still does successfully, because edges needed for a full parse are pruned from the chart. In toto, the aggressive pruning gets more readings because it greatly improves recall on the longer sentences, but some are lost in the important middle range, which is also why we use the results from the mild pruning for the extraction of the semantics. An advanced

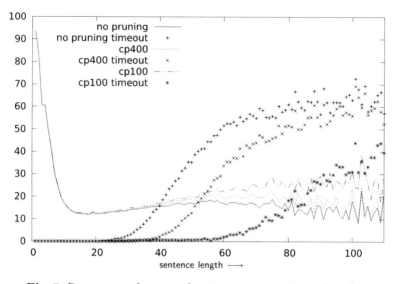

Fig. 5. Percentage of unparsed sentences over sentence length

system could adapt pruning to the input length, or try to come up with better local models that minimize the loss of useful subconstituents.

We also compared the (absolute) scores of the discriminative model for the two variants. While the method without chart pruning always finds the best parse, this is not true for the pruned chart. The result is displayed in the fourth row of the table in Figure 4. Since the scores of the maximum entropy model are not probabilities, we can not give meaningful numbers on the loss of quality, but a rough comparison of the scores suggests that in most cases the penalty is minor.

Fragmentary Input. There are several alternatives to deal with input like headings and footnotes, one to identify and handle them in a preprocessing step, another to use a special root condition in the deep analysis component that is able to combine phrases with well-defined properties for inputs where no spanning result could be found.

We employed the second method, which has the advantage that it handles a larger range of phenomena in a homogeneous way. Figure 6 shows the change in percentage of unparsed and timed out inputs for the mild pruning method with and without the root condition combining fragments.

As Figure 6 shows nicely, this changes the curve for unparsed sentences towards more expected characteristics and removes the uncommonly high percentage of short sentences for which no parse can be found.

Together with the parses for fragmented input, we get a recall (sentences with at least one parse) over the whole corpus of 85.9% (1,321,336 sentences), without a significant change for any of the other numbers.

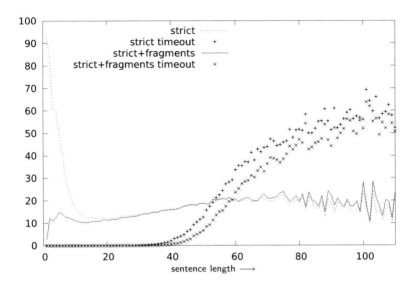

Fig. 6. Unparsed and timed out sentences with and without fragment combination

$\langle\,h_1,$
$\quad h_3\!:\!\text{udef\_q}\big(x_5\{\text{PERS } 3, \text{NUM } sg\},\ h_4,\ h_6\big),$
$\quad h_7\!:\!\text{\_semantic\_a\_1}\big(e_8\{\text{SF } prop, \text{TENSE } untensed, \text{MOOD } indicative\},\ x_5\big),$
$\quad h_7\!:\!\text{\_similarity\_n\_to}\big(x_5,\ i_9\big),$
$\quad h_{10}\!:\!\text{\_measure\_v\_1}\big(e_2\{\text{SF } prop, \text{TENSE } pres, \text{MOOD } indicative, \text{PROG -}, \text{PERF -}\},\ p_{11},\ x_5\big),$
$\quad h_{10}\!:\!\text{parg\_d}\big(e_{12}\{\text{SF } prop\},\ e_2,\ x_5\big),$
$\quad h_{10}\!:\!\text{\_in\_p}\big(e_{13}\{\text{SF } prop, \text{TENSE } untensed, \text{MOOD } indicative\},\ e_2,\ x_{14}\{\text{PERS } 3, \text{NUM } pl, \text{IND } +\}\big),$
$\quad h_{15}\!:\!\text{udef\_q}\big(x_{14},\ h_{16},\ h_{17}\big),$
$\quad h_{18}\!:\!\text{\_term\_n\_of}\big(x_{14},\ x_{19}\{\text{PERS } 3, \text{NUM } pl\}\big),$
$\quad h_{20}\!:\!\text{udef\_q}\big(x_{19},\ h_{21},\ h_{22}\big),$
$\quad h_{23}\!:\!\text{compound}\big(e_{25}\{\text{SF } prop, \text{TENSE } untensed, \text{MOOD } indicative, \text{PROG -}, \text{PERF -}\},\ x_{19},\ x_{24}\big),$
$\quad h_{26}\!:\!\text{udef\_q}\big(x_{24},\ h_{27},\ h_{28}\big),$
$\quad h_{29}\!:\!\text{\_similar\_a\_to}\big(e_{30}\{\text{SF } prop, \text{TENSE } untensed, \text{MOOD } indicative\},\ x_{24}\big),$
$\quad h_{29}\!:\!\text{comp}\big(e_{32}\{\text{SF } prop\},\ e_{30},\ u_{31}\big),$
$\quad h_{29}\!:\!\text{\_word\_n\_of}\big(x_{24},\ i_{33}\big),$!
$\quad h_{23}\!:\!\text{\_context\_n\_1}\big(x_{19}\big)$
$\quad \{\,h_{27} =_q h_{29},\ h_{21} =_q h_{23},\ h_{16} =_q h_{18},\ h_4 =_q h_7\,\}\,\rangle$

Fig. 7. Sample MRS for the sentence "Semantic similarity is measured in terms of similar word contexts"

2.6 Parser Output

In contrast to shallow parsers, the ERG not only handles detailed syntactic analyses of phrases, compounds, coordination, negation and other linguistic phenomena that are important for extracting relations, but also generates a formal semantic representation of the meaning of the input sentence in the MRS representation format (Minimal Recursion Semantics; [6]). It is comparable to a first order logic form. It consists of so-called elementary predications for each token and larger constituents, connected via argument positions and variables/labels, from which the predicate-argument structure can be derived (example in Figure 7).

As in previous work [18] and because of the increased parsing recall, we again opt for precision and only use results from the deep parser instead of extending the hybrid workflow (Figure 2) in such a way that a shallow parser with less detailed analyses is used as fall-back in case deep parsing fails (as done in an intermediate system, [17]).

3 Application: Semantic Search Based on Extracted Predicate-Argument Structure

The idea of the semantic search application is to use the sentence-wise semantic representations generated offline by the deep parser. From its output, a normalized predicate-argument structure is extracted that is stored in a search index. The main motivation is at least partial abstraction from syntactic variants. Thus, the extraction process includes dividing sentences with coordination into independent structures, and using the semantic subject and object in both active and passive sentence construction independently of the syntactic realization.

The user interface for this application is simple. Instead of a single search text input field, the user will see three: one for subject, one for predicate and another one for further objects. This is easy to understand also for non-linguists, and fields may be left emtpy to match anything. In the current version, the search interface supports the use of synsets of predicates only.

3.1 Extracting Predicate-Argument Structure from MRS

The MRS representations resulting from hybrid parsing are relatively close to linguistic structures and contain more detailed information than a user would like to query and search for. Therefore, an additional extraction and abstraction step is necessary before storing the semantic structures in the search index.

The format we devised for this purpose we call *semantic tuples*, a blend of triples and quintuples, as we store quintuples (subject, predicate, direct object, other complements and adjunct), but to ease search term input for the user, only distinguish between a triple of subject, predicate and any other objects in the query structure.

The algorithm to generate the semantic tuples first performs an intermediate transformation into isomorphic, serializable Java objects that can be made persistent. On these objects, efficient graph manipulation resulting in extracted semantic tuples can take place. Handling of coordination has been implemented by generating multiple tuples. Passive constructions are elegantly handled by the grammar itself and lead to identical semantic tuples regardless of active or passive formulation of the same proposition.

Due to semantic ambiguity, the deep parser may return more than one reading per sentence. Currently up to three readings are considered (the most probable ones according to the treebank-trained parse ranking model), and semantic tuples are generated for each reading respectively. Multiple readings may collapse into the same semantic tuple structure, in which case only a single one is stored in the database. Otherwise, a voting mechanism based on rank and number of isomorphic semantic tuples decides for the best selection.

The following sentence includes the semantic tuple structure (in brackets):

"[We]$_{\text{SUBJ}}$ [evaluate]$_{\text{PRED}}$ [the efficiency and performance]$_{\text{DOBJ}}$ [against the corpus]$_{\text{ADJU}}$."

In this example, the conjunction relation connects two noun phrases, both of them being DOBJ; therefore, no new semantic tuple is necessary. However, we decided to distinguish cases where conjunction connects two sentences or verb phrases. In such cases, semantic tuples are generated for each part respectively. The following example shows an *AND* relation. Conjunction relations may also be realized in different lexemes, e.g. *and, but, or, as well as*, etc.

For the sentence *"The system automatically extracts pairs of syntactic units from a text and assigns a semantic relation to each pair."*, two semantic tuples are generated separately with their own PRED, DOBJ and OCMP:

"[The system]$_{\text{SUBJ}}$ [extracts]$_{\text{PRED}}$ [pairs of syntactic units]$_{\text{DOBJ}}$ [from a text]$_{\text{OCMP}}$ [automatically]$_{\text{ADJU}}$."

and

"[The system]$_{\text{SUBJ}}$ [assigns]$_{\text{PRED}}$ [a semantic relation]$_{\text{DOBJ}}$ [to each pair]$_{\text{OCMP}}$ [automatically]$_{\text{ADJU}}$."

In passive sentences, the syntactic subject becomes the semantic object and vice versa:

"[Unseen input]$_{\text{DOBJ}}$ [was classified]$_{\text{PRED}}$ [by trained neural networks with varying error rates depending corpus type]$_{\text{SUBJ}}$."

3.2   Filling the Search Index

For each sentence, the semantic tuple structure together with associated character span information relative to the sentence start is then stored in an Apache Solr[5] search index. It also contains metainformation on page number, sentence number, offset and document ID.

In case a named entity is identified by the named entity recognizer, further information on span and type (such as location, person, time) of the item is stored.

---

[5] http://lucene.apache.org/solr

This named entity type information is used to identify the answer candidate type in an additional question answering interface we will not further describe in this paper. The following snippet from Solr input for a single sentence may give an impression of the underlying index schema.

```
<doc>
  <field name="aclaid">N07-1043</field>
  <field name="page">2</field>
  <field name="sentno">56</field>
  <field name="prefix">N07-1043-s56-p2</field>
  <field name="offset">353</field>
  <field name="qgen">PET</field>
  <field name="sentence">Sahami et al., (2006) measure semantic
     similarity between two queries using the snippets returned
     for those queries by a search engine.</field>
  <field name="subj">Sahami 2006 et al.</field>
  <field name="subj_start">0</field>
  <field name="subj_end">12</field>
  <field name="pred">measure</field>
  <field name="pred_start">22</field>
  <field name="pred_end">28</field>
  <field name="dobj">semantic similarity</field>
  <field name="dobj_start">30</field>
  <field name="dobj_end">48</field>
  <field name="ocmp">between two queries using the snippets
     returned for those queries by a search engine</field>
  <field name="ocmp_start">0</field>
  <field name="ocmp_end">133</field>
  <field name="ner_types">citation ne-term ne-term </field>
  <field name="ner_cstart">0 30 121 </field>
  <field name="ner_cend">20 48 133 </field>
  <field name="ner_surface">"Sahami et al., (2006)"
                            "semantic similarity"
                            "search engine" </field>
</doc>
```

To sum up the overall offline analysis for search index generation, Figure 8 depicts the offline NLP and semantic tuple extraction workflow.

3.3   Query Interface

As depicted in Figure 9, the user interface for semantic paper search contains three text fields where the user can input subject, predicate and all remaining structures (rest). The latter is combined to ease input (otherwise users would become worried about what to put in OCMP or ADJU) and will be expanded to a disjunctive Solr/Lucene query expression.

To give an example, a semantic tuple search expression with input to field subject=*, input to field predicate='measure', and input to field rest='semantic similarity' is translated into an Apache Solr query

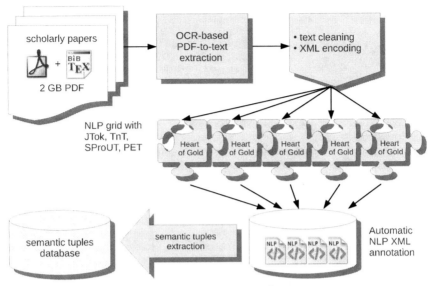

Fig. 8. Grid-based hybrid parsing of the scientific paper corpus

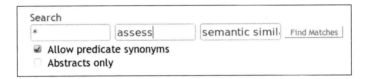

Fig. 9. Simple query interface

```
pred:measure +(dobj:"semantic similarity"
          OR ocmp:"semantic similarity"
          OR adju:"semantic similarity")
```

In case WordNet synset [10] expansion is enabled, `measure` is replaced by
(`measure OR evaluate OR quantify OR value OR assess OR valuate`).

It is planned to also allow for synonym search in the SUBJ and REST field.
Here, domain ontology information as well as automatically identified similar
(multi-word) terms could be used to expand the query.

The result is then a list of sentence snippets (Figure 10). By clicking on a
hyperlink underlying the snippet text, the original PDF is opened. By using
the information on page and sentence text/offset in the Apache Solr answer,
the result sentence is highlighted as shown in Figure 11. This helps to quickly
identify relevance of the answer by looking at context in the original layout.

Search Results for * "measure" "semantic similarity"

- N07-1043: Sahami et al., (2006) [measure]$_{PRED}$ [semantic similarity]$_{DOBJ}$ between two queries using the snippets returned for those queries by a search engine.
- W04-0106: [Semantic similarity]$_{DOBJ}$ [is measured]$_{PRED}$ in terms of similar word contexts.
- N07-1044: [The semantic similarity]$_{DOBJ}$ between neighbors and senses [is measured]$_{PRED}$ using a manually crafted taxonomy such as WordNet (see Budanitsky and Hirst 2001 for an overview of WordNet-based similarity measures).
- P08-1028: We [assessed]$_{PRED}$ [a wide range of semantic similarity measures]$_{DOBJ}$ using the WordNet similarity package (Pedersen et al., 2004).
- W06-3802: Using WordNet, we [can measure]$_{PRED}$ [the semantic similarity]$_{DOBJ}$ or relatedness between a pair of concepts (or word senses), and by extension, between a pair of sentences.
- W06-1659: Using WordNet, we [can measure]$_{PRED}$ [the semantic similarity]$_{DOBJ}$ or relatedness between a pair of concepts (or word senses), and by extension, between a pair of sentences.
- W05-1203: For entailment identification, since this is a directional relation, we [only measure]$_{PRED}$ [the semantic similarity]$_{DOBJ}$ with respect to the hypothesis (the text that is entailed).
- W06-1104: We [measured]$_{PRED}$ [semantic relat-edness instead of semantic similarity]$_{DOBJ}$.
- P06-1112: 3. [The semantic similarity SemSim(h , h)]$_{DOBJ}$ [is measured]$_{PRED}$ using Word-Net and eXtended WordNet.

. . .

Fig. 10. The first matching sentences in the ACL Anthology subset 2002-2008 with recognized variation in predicate synsets (assess, measure, evaluate) and passive constructions

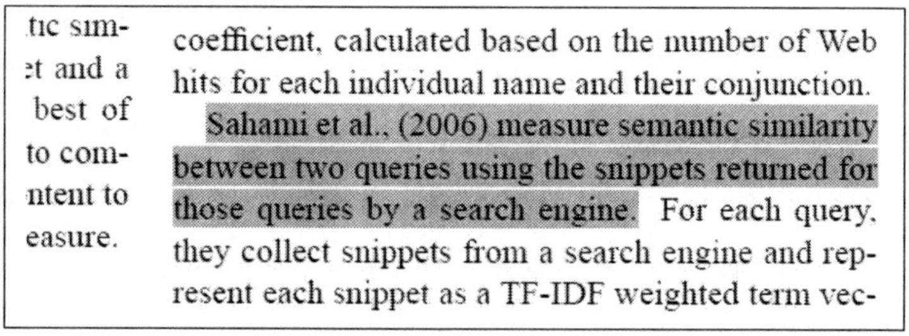

Fig. 11. First result sentence (from N07-1043) highlighted in original PDF

4 Related Work

Using HPSG combined with shallow domain-specific modeling for high-precision analysis of scientific texts is an emerging research area. Another ERG-based approach to relation and information extraction from scientific texts is SciBorg [13]. SciBorg mainly deals with chemistry research papers and handles domain-specific phenomena with a specialized named entity recognizer. It relies on a shallow parser as robustness fall-back for MRS generation.

Other groups use less elaborated and fine-grained HPSG grammars than ERG. [11] report on large-scale parsing of MEDLINE articles (1.4 billion words) with such a simplified grammar.

[14] use shallow dependency structure and results from HPSG parsing for extracting protein-protein interactions (PPI) from research papers. The same group has also worked on medical texts: MEDIE[6] is a semantic search engine to retrieve biomedical correlations from MEDLINE articles.

What distinguishes our approach from those, besides concentration on a different scientific area, is the focus on and use of ontology information as integrated part of linguistic analysis, use of the most comprehensive and elaborated HPSG grammar for English (ERG), and the interactive user interface (Scientist's Workbench application; [17]) and editor [18].

5   Conclusion and Future Work

We have presented our recent advances in full, robust parsing of scientific papers texts. By careful preprocessing and novel approaches to efficient parsing of long sentences, we could improve coverage from 65 to more than 85%.

The semantic search application built on the semantic representations generated by the deep grammar is a useful extension to cope with synonyms and syntactic variation when querying full scientific publication content. The search space, initially expanded by adding synonymns, can be again constrained by imposing semantic subject-predicate-object structure in the query.

Further research goals are improving robustness of the NLP tool chain. We are also working on generic techniques to automatically extract and use science domain information from the underlying paper corpus to improve targeted search. Three main tasks in our focus are coreference resolution, term extraction and ontology extraction viz. population. The idea is that these techniques, in a first step gained independently from the text corpus or partially from NLP analyses of it, will benefit from each other and can be used to build more reliable and precise resources and tools in a bootstrapping process.

Handling of negation, modal constructions, subclauses etc. also fall into the category deep NLP can handle, but this will be addressed in the future as it also requires lexico-semantic information of verbs etc. in the extraction process. It will definitely be an important extension helping to improve precision in search.

The semantic search application is part of the Scientist's workbench and is complemented by a visualization and navigation tool TeeCeeGeeNav [16] that supports scientists in quickly getting an overview of a (new) research field by browsing through a typed citation graph computed from the scientific paper corpus. The citation classification with categories such as use or refutation of

---

[6] http://www-tsujii.is.s.u-tokyo.ac.jp/medie/

results of the cited paper currently builds on shallow NLP (such as PoS tagging) only. In the future, deep semantics could help too further improve this difficult classification task.

Acknowledgments

The authors would like to thank Peter Adolphs, Dan Flickinger and Stephan Oepen for their support and numerous fruitful discussions. We would also like to thank Yi Zhang and Bart Cramer for the implementation of chart pruning in PET and their support to put it into use. The work described in this paper has been carried out in the context of the project TAKE (Technologies for Advanced Knowledge Extraction), funded under contract 01IW08003 by the German Federal Ministry of Education and Research, and in the context of the world-wide DELPH-IN collaboration[7].

References

1. Adolphs, P., Oepen, S., Callmeier, U., Crysmann, B., Flickinger, D., Kiefer, B.: Some fine points of hybrid natural language parsing. In: Proc. of LREC, Marrakesh, Morocco, pp. 1380–1387 (2008)
2. Bird, S., Dale, R., Dorr, B., Gibson, B., Joseph, M., Kan, M.Y., Lee, D., Powley, B., Radev, D., Tan, Y.F.: The ACL anthology reference corpus: A reference dataset for bibliographic research. In: Proc. of LREC, Marrakesh, Morocco, pp. 1755–1759 (2008)
3. Brants, T.: TnT – A Statistical Part-of-Speech Tagger. In: Proc. of ANLP 2000, Seattle, WA, pp. 224–231 (2000)
4. Callmeier, U.: PET – A platform for experimentation with efficient HPSG processing techniques. Natural Language Engineering 6(1), 99–108 (2000)
5. Copestake, A., Flickinger, D.: An open-source grammar development environment and broad-coverage English grammar using HPSG. In: Proc. of LREC, Athens, Greece, pp. 591–598 (2000)
6. Copestake, A., Flickinger, D., Sag, I.A., Pollard, C.: Minimal recursion semantics: an introduction. Research on Language and Computation 3(2-3), 281–332 (2005)
7. Cramer, B., Zhang, Y.: Constraining robust constructions for broad-coverage parsing with precision grammars. In: Proc. of COLING, Beijing, China, pp. 223–231 (2010)
8. Drożdżyński, W., Krieger, H.U., Piskorski, J., Schäfer, U., Xu, F.: Shallow processing with unification and typed feature structures – foundations and applications. Künstliche Intelligenz 1, 17–23 (2004)
9. Flickinger, D., Oepen, S., Ytrestøl, G.: WikiWoods: Syntacto-semantic annotation for English Wikipedia. In: Proc. of LREC, Valletta, Malta, pp. 1665–1671 (2010)
10. Miller, G.A., Beckwith, R., Fellbaum, C., Gross, D., Miller, K.J.: Five papers on WordNet. Tech. rep., Cognitive Science Laboratory, Princeton University (1993)
11. Ninomiya, T., Tsuruoka, Y., Miyao, Y., Taura, K., Tsujii, J.: Fast and scalable HPSG parsing. Traitement automatique des langues (TAL) 46(2) (2006)

---

[7] DEep Linguistic Processing with Hpsg INitiative; http://www.delph-in.net

12. Pollard, C., Sag, I.A.: Head-Driven Phrase Structure Grammar. Studies in Contemporary Linguistics. University of Chicago Press, Chicago (1994)
13. Rupp, C., Copestake, A., Corbett, P., Waldron, B.: Integrating general-purpose and domain-specific components in the analysis of scientific text. In: Proc. of the UK e-Science Programme All Hands Meeting 2007, Nottingham, UK (2007)
14. Sætre, R., Kenji, S., Tsujii, J.: Syntactic features for protein-protein interaction extraction. In: Baker, C.J., Jian, S. (eds.) Short Paper Proc. of the 2nd Int. Symp. on Languages in Biology and Medicine (LBM 2007), Singapore, pp. 6.1–6.14 (2008)
15. Schäfer, U.: Middleware for creating and combining multi-dimensional NLP markup. In: Proc. of the EACL-2006 Workshop on Multi-dimensional Markup in Natural Language Processing, Trento, Italy, pp. 81–84 (2006)
16. Schäfer, U., Kasterka, U.: Scientific authoring support: A tool to navigate in typed citation graphs. In: Proc. of the NAACL-HLT 2010 Workshop on Computational Linguistics and Writing, Los Angeles, CA, pp. 7–14 (2010)
17. Schäfer, U., Spurk, C.: TAKE Scientist's Workbench: Semantic search and citation-based visual navigation in scholar papers. In: Proc. of the 4th IEEE Int. Conference on Semantic Computing (ICSC 2010), Pittsburgh, PA, pp. 317–324 (2010)
18. Schäfer, U., Uszkoreit, H., Federmann, C., Marek, T., Zhang, Y.J.: Extracting and querying relations in scientific papers. In: Dengel, A.R., Berns, K., Breuel, T.M., Bomarius, F., Roth-Berghofer, T.R. (eds.) KI 2008. LNCS (LNAI), vol. 5243, pp. 127–134. Springer, Heidelberg (2008)

Robust Argumentative Zoning for Sensemaking in Scholarly Documents

Simone Teufel[1] and Min-Yen Kan[2]

[1] University of Cambridge Computer Laboratory
sht25@cl.cam.ac.uk
[2] Department of Computer Science, National University of Singapore
kanmy@comp.nus.edu.sg

Abstract. We present an automated approach to classify sentences of scholarly work with respect to their rhetorical function. While previous work that achieves this task of *argumentative zoning* requires richly annotated input, our approach is robust to noise and can process raw text. Even in cases where the input has noise (as it is obtained from optical character recognition or text extraction from PDF files), our robust classifier is largely accurate. We perform an in-depth study of our system both with clean and noisy inputs. We also give preliminary results from *in situ* acceptability testing when the classifier is embedded within a digital library reading environment.

1 Introduction

Even as early as 1984, Cleverdon estimated an annual output of 400,000 papers from the most important journals covering the natural sciences and technology [1]. Today's scholars, even if focusing on a small slice of science that is to become their thesis, need to keep abreast of a large, growing number of scientific developments.

In particular, in the current trend towards interdisciplinarity, researchers will increasingly need to gain an overview of a new field. We call this task *sensemaking*, which is a task that we want to contribute towards. To achieve this goal through the digital library, we need to first generalize some of the needs that researchers must meet. Shum [2] states that what is most interesting to researchers in such a situation is what the main problems and approaches field are. Another question of particular interest is which researchers and groups are connected with which scientific concepts. Knowledge that a scientist acquires over years is a complex network [3]; a system that simply returns an individual publication belies this fact.

Contextual knowledge is needed in order to place and understand the work within the confines of the already existing literature, in all stages of information gathering, *e.g.*, relevance assessment, exploration, reading and utilizing. There is no immediate mechanism in today's digital libraries that addresses this. While most modern digital libraries have keyword search, this ability does little to

R. Bernardi et al. (Eds.): NLP4DL/AT4DL 2009, LNCS 6699, pp. 154–170, 2011.

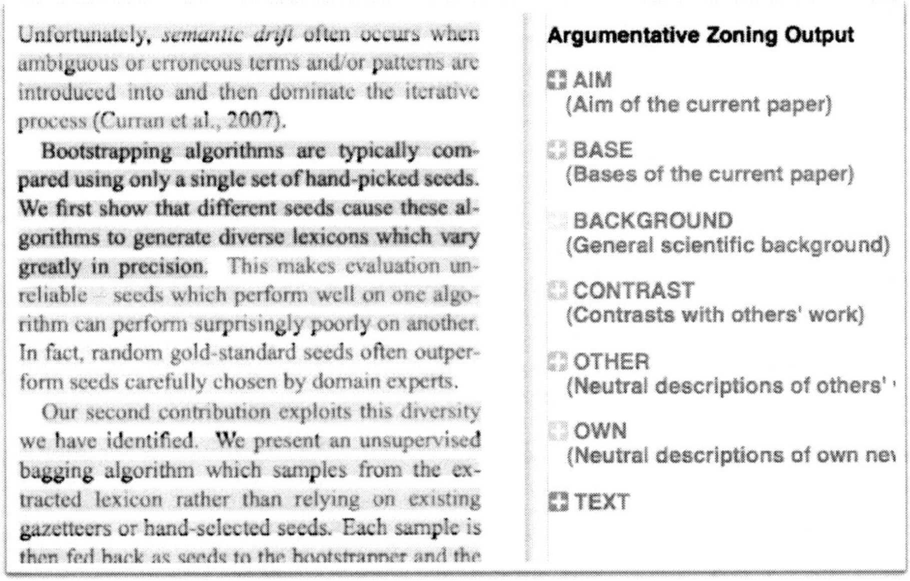

Unfortunately, *semantic drift* often occurs when ambiguous or erroneous terms and/or patterns are introduced into and then dominate the iterative process (Curran et al., 2007).

Bootstrapping algorithms are typically compared using only a single set of hand-picked seeds. We first show that different seeds cause these algorithms to generate diverse lexicons which vary greatly in precision. This makes evaluation unreliable — seeds which perform well on one algorithm can perform surprisingly poorly on another. In fact, random gold-standard seeds often outperform seeds carefully chosen by domain experts.

Our second contribution exploits this diversity we have identified. We present an unsupervised bagging algorithm which samples from the extracted lexicon rather than relying on existing gazetteers or hand-selected seeds. Each sample is then fed back as seeds to the bootstrapper and the

Argumentative Zoning Output

▣ **AIM**
  (Aim of the current paper)

▣ **BASE**
  (Bases of the current paper)

  BACKGROUND
  (General scientific background)

▣ **CONTRAST**
  (Contrasts with others' work)

▣ **OTHER**
  (Neutral descriptions of others' ·

▣ **OWN**
  (Neutral descriptions of own ne\

▣ **TEXT**

Fig. 1. Argumentative zoning overlaid on a page image from a scholarly article (detail). The sidebar explains the color highlighting of the annotation.

address our challenges [4,5]. What is needed is the provision of assistance so that readers can understand the text.

While as varied as other types of text, scientific discourse is a coherent genre with fixed rhetorical expectations, and with a clear argumentative function. Research articles are biased reports of problem-solving, oriented towards the author's own viewpoint [6]. This fact facilitates the automated analysis of document structure, which largely follows canonical scientific argumentation. Roughly speaking, aims and hypothesis are given first, and are followed by the proof in empirical terms, *e.g.*, the description of an experiment to satisfy the critical and skeptical reader. Particularly important is the embedding of the new work in the research niche, *i.e.*, in relation to already published work. A step towards this sensemaking could be implemented as shown in Figure 1, where a scholarly work is annotated to show which of its sentences discuss the relationship between the work and its contextual literature.

Teufel and Moens [7] introduced *Argumentative Zoning* (AZ), a sentence-based classification of scientific text according to rhetorical status. The AZ classification was designed to be domain-independent and easy for subjects to annotate reliably. In particular, proper AZ annotation highlights how the current work relates to the context of other referenced work in the article.

Given its advantages, it would seem useful to show argumentative zoning alongside an article in a digital library reading environment. However there are substantial barriers that have thus far prevented the practical, widespread use of AZ. As manual annotation is prohibitively expensive, only an automated system could be considered. However, thus far, automated AZ has only been tried with articles that take rich semantic markup, such as SciXML [8]. Furthermore, to our knowledge, no existing digital library system has fielded a production version of AZ nor shown whether such markup is effective.

Our work in this paper is to address these weaknesses. Specifically, we have created a Robust AZ (RAZ) system that functions over raw English input. We benchmark this system against the original work done previously in Teufel's thesis, which required richly annotated semantic markup, using both clean plain text (extracted from the original richly annotated text) as well as noisy text (extracted directly from the PDF). We have also fielded our classifier within a production digital library system and report preliminary results on the usefulness of such annotation.

2 Argumentative Zoning

Argumentative Zoning (AZ) [7] is an analysis of document structure based on the idea that there are distinct rhetorical moves in scientific papers which together form a scientific argument. An example of a rhetorical move is a goal statement or the criticism of some existing piece of work. The analysis also assumes that rhetorically neutral pieces of text should be classified according to the ownership of the ideas described in the text: are they new contributions (*i.e.*, just being contributed by the authors), statements that nobody in particular lays claim to (*e.g.*, because they are too commonplace), or are they somebody else's (citable) ideas? Another important aspect of the scheme is sentiment, in particular the authors' sentiment towards cited work, as addressed in Nanba and Okumura's work [9].

The categories in the scheme are based on similar rhetorical moves in the literature, *e.g.*, Liddy's Empirical Summary Components [10], Shum's conceptual categories [2], Swales' argumentative moves [6], and Kando's rhetorical categories for information retrieval [11].

AZ is defined as a sentence-based classification according to the following categories (example sentences given in italics; three letter abbreviations in parentheses):

- **Aim** (AIM): Sentences that describe the specific research aims, contributions and conclusions of the current work. *We describe and experimentally evaluate a method for automatically clustering words according to their distribution in particular syntactic contexts.*
- **Basis** (BAS): Other work that describes tools, theory or findings that the current work uses as a foundation for argument. *The corpus used in our first experiment was derived from newswire text automatically parsed by Hindle's parser Fidditch (Hindle, 1993).*

- **Background** (BKG): Knowledge that the author feels is generally accepted, not needing argumentative proof or citation. *Methods for automatically classifying words according to their contexts of use have both scientific and practial interest.*
- **Contrast** (CTR): Statements of contrast, comparison, weaknesses of other solutions. These can help identify contradictions or suprising results that differ from established thought. *His notion of similarity seems to agree with our intuitions in many cases, but it is not clear how it can be used directly to construct classes and corresponding models of association.*
- **Other** (OTH): Other work that is specifically mentioned or cited. Includes work done by the author previously, outside of the current work. *In Hindle's proposal, words are similar if we have strong statistical evidence that they tend to participate in the same events.*
- **Own** (OWN): Sentences that describe the author's own work, method, results, discussion and future work. These sentences comprise the majority of a scholarly document. *More specifically, we model senses as probabilistic concepts or clusters c with corresponding cluster membership probabilities $p(c|w)$ for each word w.*
- **Text** (TXT): Sentences that describe the text's internal structure. *We then describe our experimental results in Section 4.*

Teufel *et al.* [12] showed that trained humans are able to produce consistent AZ annotation with acceptable Kappa (κ) [13] of 0.71[1]. Teufel and Moens [7] describe a Naïve Bayes implementation of AZ which is based on 16 sentential features. This model achieves an agreement of $\kappa = 0.45$, whereas Siddharthan and Teufel report $\kappa = 0.48$ for the same data set [14].

3   Related Work

Hachey and Grover [15] present an AZ-based model for the rhetorical classification of legal texts. Their main improvement over Teufel is to use a maximum entropy model, which allows them to use unigrams and bigrams over words as a feature. This improves results considerably. Merity *et al.* [16] use a similar Maximum Entropy approach to AZ which uses unigrams, bigrams and Viterbi search over the category history as its main features. They evalute directly on Teufel and Moens' dataset, and although the evalutation metric used in the paper is not comparable to earlier results (they report weighted accuracy), their classification is more accurate than the earlier results from Teufel and Moens.

A much simpler task than AZ is that of re-introducing rhetorical headlines into structured abstracts in the medical and biological domain [17,18,19]. These typically use structured abstracts to learn a statistical model of what kind of information follows what kinds in abstracts. The models can then be applied to unstructured abstracts in their collection (*e.g.*, only 9% of MEDLINE abstracts are structured).

---

[1] Kappa values range from 1 (perfect agreement) to -1 (perfect disagreement). A score of 0 indicates no correlation.

4   Method

To accomplish the classification for RAZ, we also turn to maximum entropy (ME) modeling. Like other forms of supervised classification, a ME classifier casts each problem instance as a set of features associated with an appropriate class label. Two key characteristics that differentiate it from other approaches are that the features only take on binary values, and that problem instances are typically chracterized by hundreds of thousands of features. In natural language tasks where word forms are often used as features, the latter characteristic is of utmost importance. Vocabulary sizes in typical English discourse often take a range in the tens of thousands of wordforms.

Each training instance thus can be represented as an n-dimensional feature vector. Even with thousands of training examples, each acting as a constraint on the model, there exist many models that fit the data, as the problem is underconstrained. To select an appropriate model from the multitude possible, the ME classifier seeks out the model where the distribution is most uniform; *i.e.* the model with the maximum entropy.

Finding the unique exact maximum entropy model is usually not possible analytically, but when the feature functions take on an exponential form as in Equation 1, iterative scaling can be used to find a model within an arbitrary ϵ-bound of the exact solution, $\hat{p}$.

$$\hat{p}(y|x) = \frac{1}{Z(x)} exp(\sum_i \lambda_i f_i(x,y)) \tag{1}$$

where $Z(x)$ is the partition function $\sum_y exp(\sum_i \lambda_i f_i(x,y))$, that ensures the $p(\cdot|\cdot)$ values are normalized to actual probabilities. A key consideration of ME is that features for such classifiers do not have to be independent of each other. ME can be implemented to perform feature selection implicitly, so the practitioner is free to introduce a large set of features without much concern with respect to their relevance to the classification task.

During both training and testing, we transform each instance into its vector form: a set of binary valued $f(x,y)$ features. Each feature combines a class label y and a predicate x, as in Equation 2:

$$f(x,y) = \begin{cases} 1 & \text{if } y = other \text{ and } x \text{ is the predicate that} \\ & \text{the current sentence contains the word "they",} \\ 0 & \text{otherwise.} \end{cases} \tag{2}$$

To describe the features for our particular classification task of argumentative zoning, we must describe the classes and predicates. The class labels Y correspond to the set of Teufel's full argumentative zone scheme: {AIM, BKG, BAS, CTR, OTH, OWN, TXT}. The predicates X fall into different categories of information that we compute from each sentence.

As discussed previously, RAZ takes as input an entire text in plain text (ASCII, UTF-8), processes it to delimit sentences [20] and adds part-of-speech annotation with part-of-speech tagger [21]. These sentence are fed into the feature computation process, which generates the feature vectors for each sentences. We list these categories below, along with their motivation.

- **Raw tokens:** Individual words in a sentence can be indicative of certain argumentative zone classes. For example, "we" often occurs in a sentence where the authors are describing their own work (OWN). We register each alphanumeric word of the sentence as an individual feature. In addition to the form present in the sentence, we register both lowercased and (English) stemmed forms as different features. Stemming is provided by an implementation of Porter's stemmer [22]. We also capture the word's part-of-speech, to differentiate between different senses of individual words (*e.g.*, "direct" as a adjective or verb). Equation 2 gives an example of a specific word feature.
- **Bigram and Trigram tokens:** Individual words can be ambiguous, and certain word combinations have different meanings and can be strongly indicative of certain classes. For example, "in contrast" strongly signals a contrastive sentence (CTR). We capture contiguous bigram and trigrams from the sentence, and use these as features as well. We create separate bigram and trigram sequences from the raw tokens, as well as from their stemmed form.
- **Cue Words and Phrases:** We look for whether the word contained within a list of 881 known English keywords and 157 cue phrases that may signal a rhetorical move, as defined in Teufel's thesis [23]. She categorized these words and phrases manually in her study of computational linguistics literature. This feature partially overlaps with the previous two classes – "in contrast" and "we" are both listed in these lists – but provide an extra weighting mechanism for the ME classifier to weight the presence of these key terms and phrases more heavily. Some of these cue phrases (about 10%) are actually lexical regular expressions containing part-of-speech constraints which we currently do not handle.
- **Position:** Certain classes of argumentative zones are more prevalent at certain points in the scientific discourse than others. For example, BKG knowledge generally comes in the introduction and surveys of related work. We register the sentence's position in the document, in both absolute and relative terms. We count the number of sentences from the beginning for absolute features, and normalize these versus the number of sentences in the entire document for relative features. Both types of sentence position features are binned at a coarse and fine grained resolution to alleviate problems with data sparsity.
- **Citation Presence:** Citations also strongly indicate certain argumentative classes, such as other work (OTH). Previous studies have differentiated between self-citation (often the basis for the current work; BAS) and citation to others. In RAZ, we built a simple citation presence detector using regular expressions to find standard citation marker patterns. These include numbers in square brackets, tokens that are followed by the suffix "et al." and potential year numbers in parentheses ("[1]", "Wong et al.", "Brown (1988)",

Table 1. Features generated from an example sentence

Sentence (with POS Tagging)	The_DT back-off_JJ model_NN of_IN Katz_NNP (1987)_NNP provides_VBZ a_DT clear_JJ separation_NN between_IN frequent_JJ events,_NN for_IN ...
Tokens	The back off model of katz 1987 provides a clear separation ... STEMSthe STEMSback-off STEMSmodel STEMSof STEMSkatz STEMS(1987 ...
Bigrams / Trigrams	The_DT_back-off_JJ back-off_JJ_model_NN model_NN_of_IN of_IN_Katz_NNP ... The_DT_back-off_JJ_model_NN back-off_JJ_model_NN_of_IN ...
Cue Phrases	CPWORK CPPOS
Sentence Position	REL_POSITION2 ABS_POSITION1 REL_POSITION2_1 ABS_POSITION25
Citation Presence	CITEyear CITEcount1
Sentence Length	SENTLENGTH3
Title Overlap	(N/A)
Agent	AGENTmodel_nn
Verb tense	VERBprovides_vbz VERBTENSEvbz

respectively). Our citation detector is quite simple, aiming for a balance of precision and recall while maintaining efficiency.

– **Sentence Length:** Longer sentences can correlate to detailed discussion and data analysis. We measure the length of a sentence in ten word units as a feature.
– **Title Overlap:** If a sentence's words overlap with the title, there is a higher probability that it elaborates on the theme of the article (*e.g.*, OWN). We treat the first 100 words of the article as a "title" and identify which words in a candidate sentence overlap with these title words. We use this span because in the raw input text, we have no explicit way to capture the title, so we use this approximation.
– **Agent:** Syntactic information can further discriminate the role of certain words. The token "we" can be the agent of a sentence (*e.g.*, "We performed...") or can be the patient receiving an action ("...is different from what we measure"). Given the part-of-speech input, we use a set of simple heuristics to locate the agent of the sentence, and encode this as an individual feature.
– **Verb tense:** Similarly, verb identity and tense can also signal particular argumentative classes. Sentences in past tense can disclose past work (OTH), for example. We use the part-of-speech information to locate the main verb in the sentence, using a set of heuristics, and create features for its identity and tense.

Finally we feed the feature vectors to the maximum entropy software[2]) to generate models in training, or to label new unseen sentences in testing.

Table 1 illustrates a concrete example of the different features that are computed, given a sample sentence.

5   Evaluation

Our formal evaluation tests our RAZ system in with both perfect input (with correct splitting of sentences) as well as realistic, noisy input (using automatic

---

[2] We use Le Zhang's toolkit, available at:
  http://homepages.inf.ed.ac.uk/lzhang10/maxent_toolkit.html

sentence splitting and part of speech tagging done programatically). We benchmark RAZ against the original AZ system devised by Teufel [23], which used richly annotated SciXML as input.

In contrast, our RAZ system handles impoverished input of plain text that has been extracted from PDF files. It is well known to the community that extracting text from PDF files (especially legacy PDF files) can be problematic, due to accents, ligatures (*e.g.*, "fi" combined into a single glyph) and font substitutions.

In our formal evaluation, we wish to answer the following questions to better understand RAZ.

Question A. How much does argumentative zoning recognition decrease if we use clean text instead of the "perfect" semantically rich markup provided by SciXML?

Question B. How much does argumentative zoning recognition decrease if we use noisy text instead of clean text?

Question C. What performance is achieved in using the different sets of features? How important is each feature class towards achieving the maximum classification accuracy?

Question D. What types of errors commonly occur in the best performing classifier?

5.1   Corpus

We obtained the 74 gold standard files from [23], which represent open-access computational linguistics research articles contributed to the arXiV digital library from a period of 1994 to 1996. These have "perfect" XML structure and "perfect" human AZ annotation; we call this set "Dataset P". The SciXML markup used in Dataset-P provides annotations of correct paragraph and sentence boundaries, topic changes, hierarchical logical structure (including headers), equations, citations (differentiating self-citations from others), and citation function.

We then further stripped Dataset-P of the rich markup XML, to reveal "clean" text, which is however not perfect because it lacks the important structural markup. We call this set of "Dataset C" (for "clean").

Finally, we located the original corresponding 74 source .PDF files from arXiv. By programmatically extracting the text from the PDF files, we obtained a final

Table 2. Dataset descriptions

	Perfect (Dataset P)	Clean (Dataset C)	Noisy (Dataset N)
Text obtained via	Manual Entry	Manual Entry	Automatic Extraction from PDF
Structural markup (XML)	Hand-annotated	Absent	Absent
Paragraph and Sentence Boundaries	Hand-corrected	Hand-corrected	Automatic
POS Tags	Hand-corrected	Hand-corrected	Automatic

"noisy" dataset, complete with all imperfections that come with such a method – incorrectly extracted words, hypenation, font substitutions and occasional column flow problems. We call this set of papers "Dataset N" (for "noisy").

The performance of Dataset N against the gold standard Dataset P measures the system's errors. Dataset C measures the portion of system errors that are attributable to differences in modeling (Q1). The difference between Datasets C and N, however, quantifies the system's robustness (Q2); i.e., how much decrease in performance is due to the textual noise in the PDF texts, as opposed to the loss of structure information. The perfect AZ data set has both clean text and structure information, but the implementation of all AZ features is only possible with structural information.

5.2   Noisy Evaluation – Questions A and B

A heuristic alignment of sentences in Dataset P with Datasets N and C is necessary, as the automatic creation of Dataset N from the PDF incurs errors in detecting sentence boundaries, in detecting non-running text (such as titles, authors, headers, footnotes, etc), and might incorporate non-running text partially into "sentences". Our implementation uses edit-distance, by calculating the ratio of the longest common substring shared between two potentially aligned sentences, to their average length [24]. Matches are accepted if a threshold (currently 0.65) is exceeded; heuristic search attempts to maintain relative sentence ordering, but can jump over up to 30 sentences, as the PDF conversion is often unable to exclude non-running text which occurs as tables or figures.

The alignment reveals a precision and recall of aligning Dataset P with Dataset N of 9.71% and 15.88%, which is very low. This number might underestimate the real precision and recall, which we believe to be in the range of 70%, but latest measurements were not possible due to time limits. The numbers are also lowered by the fact that Dataset P has an idiosyncratic marking of sentences containing equations. This results in Dataset C, although the text is entirely clean, also does not reach 100% precision and recall on alignment: Precision of aligning Dataset P with Dataset C is 0.97, and recall is 0.99.

Once sentences are aligned, normal agreement figures can be reported for both Dataset N and C. We use 2-fold cross-validation.

Results and Discussion. Table 3 shows the results of the comparison to the 74 gold standard files. Agreement is measured using κ, which corrects for chance agreement [25,26,27]. We also report accuracy $P(A)$, chance agreement $P(E)$, number of items (N) and 95% confidence interval for κ.[3]

Table 3 answers Questions A and B. On first inspection, RAZ in both its clean and noisy incarnations, fares significantly worse than the previously reported AZ system that uses "perfect" data. However, one should note that the ceiling we compare against (AZ with 16 features as reported in [14]) is not directly comparable, as 6 additional files are used in their case.

---

[3] Reporting *kappa* with a confidence interval is one of the recommendations brought forward in [28].

Table 3. Agreement with gold standard for RAZ with Noisy and Clean input data, in comparison to AZ with Perfect input from [14]

Proc.	Dataset; # Files	X-val Folds	κ	N	$P(A)$	$P(E)$
RAZ	N (74)	2	0.23 ± 0.016	8,494	0.63	0.53
RAZ	C (74)	2	0.28 ± 0.014	11,732	0.68	0.56
AZ	P (80)	10	0.48 ± 0.014	12,464	0.76	0.54

The good news is that RAZ fares respectably on Dataset N when compared to Dataset C, answering Question B, and validating our claim of robustness. When interpreting this gap, one also needs to consider that on Dataset N, performance can only be evaluated on *aligned* sentences, whereas RAZ on Dataset C is evaluated on practically all sentences (alignment is trivial, as the RAZ pipeline was given texts from original gold standard corpus[4]. Thus, Dataset N has far fewer sentences than Dataset C and would be perceived by a human user as obviously inferior, due to this fact.

The RAZ results at $\kappa = 0.23$ (Dataset N) and $\kappa = 0.28$ (Dataset C) are respectable considering how little information the classifier has at its disposal, in comparison to full AZ, where structural information, syntactic information, and full regular expressions for meta-discourse can be exploited. One should also take into consideration that RAZ classification is immediately and practically usable, in contrast to any other AZ implementation we know of: it is robust, can be performed on practically any scientific text available on the web and it produces its classification in real-time (about 10 milliseconds per sentence on a standard desktop PC; equivalent to 3-5 seconds per conference paper).

5.3   Clean Evaluation – Questions C and D

In our clean evaluation, we examine the performance over Dataset C, the dataset used to train the final, deployed RAZ classifier. Here, we wish to assess the usefulness of individual feature classes towards overall classification performance. We used 10-fold stratified cross validation to assess our ME classification model performance with the differing feature classes introduced previously. Table 4 gives the raw accuracy, macro averaged precision, recall and F_1 performance levels for these different combinations.

In addition to this macro-level analysis, we also wish to assess the performance of individual AZ categories. As such, we carried out a more detailed error analysis. Table 5 gives the full confusion matrix among the classifier's decision using the full model that utilizes all features.

Results and Discussion. Question C of our evaluation is answered by the data in Table 4. Surprisingly, performance peaks (when measured by macro F_1) when we use all of the features except the bigrams and trigrams. We believe this is caused by the sparsity of data that comes from this feature, causing minority AZ classes to suffer. As there is some redundancy between the word (unigram)

---

[4] Of course the system was never tested on any text it was trained on.

Table 4. Feature ablation test performance, averaged over stratified 10-fold cross valiation. Precision, Recall and F_1 are macro averaged over all 7 AZ categories.

Feature Classes	Accuracy	Precision	Recall	F_1
All	66.8%	47.8%	37.6%	.4142
All features except one				
All − Words	67.4%	45.5%	33.4%	.3739
All − 2,3 grams	66.4%	46.8%	40.9%	.4339
All − Title	66.7%	47.1%	38.0%	.4151
All − Sent Position	65.3%	45.6%	35.5%	.3908
All − Cue Phrases	66.6%	47.2%	36.2%	.4019
All − Cite	67.1%	49.3%	36.9%	.4121
All − Sent Length	66.8%	46.7%	37.8%	.4116
All − Agent	66.6%	47.1%	37.4%	.4102
All − Verb	67.4%	48.7%	37.3%	.4133
Single features				
Words	59.7%	36.9%	34.4%	.3553
2,3 grams	59.0%	34.9%	31.2%	.3268
Title	−	−	−	−
Sent Position	66.9%	18.2%	20.6%	.1810
Cue Phrases	22.4%	23.8%	8.8%	.1229
Cite	68.3%	16.1%	17.2%	.1604
Sent Length	66.8%	9.5%	14.2%	.1145
Agent	52.5%	38.0%	22.7%	.2686
Verb	37.9%	23.0%	10.7%	.1332

Table 5. Confusion matrix for the RAZ classifier using all feature classes for our clean evaluation. Gold standard answers in rows, RAZ automatic classification in columns. Bolded figures are correct classification instances. The *Undefined* (Un.) class is used for text that is not body text (*e.g.*, section headers, page numbers).

n=12898	AIM	BAS	BKG	CTR	OTH	OWN	TXT	Un.	# of instances	Precision	Recall	F_1
AIM	**138**	5	14	10	7	50	4	1	229 (1.77%)	60%	44%	51%
BAS	10	**45**	5	10	39	45	1		155 (1.20%)	29%	18%	22%
BKG	10	4	**157**	46	105	167	2	2	493 (3.82%)	32%	20%	24%
CTR	3	6	40	**86**	52	111	4		302 (2.34%)	28%	14%	19%
OTH	16	60	148	102	**559**	695	14	4	1598 (12.38%)	35%	28%	31%
OWN	131	119	419	342	1253	**7526**	85	14	9889 (76.67%)	76%	87%	81%
TXT	5	3	2	1	4	26	**117**		158 (1.22%)	74%	52%	61%
Un.			4	4	1		3	**62**	74 (0.5%)	−	−	−

and the bi-/tri-gram features, omitting either one does not cause much change in the model.

It is more obvious which features are most significant to the ME models when only a single feature class was used. All single feature models underperform the combined classifiers significantly. While some simple models (*e.g.*, Sentence Position, Citation, Sentence Length) are as accurate as the combined classifiers on a per-instance basis, their F_1 scores are dismal (∴11–.18), showing that they mostly just classify all sentences as OWN, the majority class. Our tests show that the battery of features is robust on its own (from our All – single feature tests), and that no single feature performs well outright (from our single feature tests).

To answer Question D, we turn to the detailed analysis of the confusion matrix of the full classifier (Table 5). Focusing first on the number of instances of each class, we notice right away the problem of skewed input in the dataset – almost 90% of the ground truth belongs to just two classes: OTH and OWN. This skewed input certainly makes the recognition of the minority classes difficult, as only a modicum of training data is available for these classes.

Among the remaining 5 minority classes, textual structure (TXT) and aims (AIM) are relative easy to identify, likely due to the presence of key words (*e.g.*, "propose", "Section") and common positions (following other TXT, or at the beginning of the paper). Background, Basis and Other are also commonly mistaken for each other, due to their similarity in wording. This is also a common mistake for people to make as well – in some sense, all three of these classes describe contextual information needed to understand the author's own claims, but differ in the nuances of attribution. We believe being able to attribute personal names and citations to either the paper's authors (self-citation) or to others would help to improve these classes' recognition. Finally, the contrast class CTR is the most difficult to classify, with a meagre .19 F_1. Contrasts are sometimes built over multiple sentences and are not always signaled explicitly by discourse cues, contributing to false negatives. On the other hand, some strong lexical cues for contrast are also used in other ways (*e.g.*, "We were able to detect the objects however small they appear in the video dataset"), leading to false positives.

6   Deployment

We believe that argumentative zoning is useful in obtaining an overview of a document's purpose, structure of argumentative and relationship to other documents. To test this theory, we must integrate the AZ classifer within a digital library reading interface, where the reader can view AZ annotations directly on the document. For this purpose, we retrained the RAZ classifier over the full training dataset, and incorporated it into ForeCite [29], a digital library that has a web-based reading environment that can display arbitrary, word-span based annotations, as shown in earlier in Figure 1 (which is actually a detail of the screenshot of the system), and in Figure 2.

The interface overlays a transparent colored layer over each sentence in the document, where the color is determined by the RAZ classifier. The interface allows the reader to see the AZ annotation of a sentence in the context of other sentences (in the reader window, left panel), as well as jump to other parts of the document, grouped by AZ classes (right panel). The AZ panel features a collapsable hierarchical interface that allows quick access to the text and location of sentences of a particular AZ class.

The careful reader will note that RAZ annotation is omitted from the bullet points and headers in 2. The ForeCite framework automatically determines (with

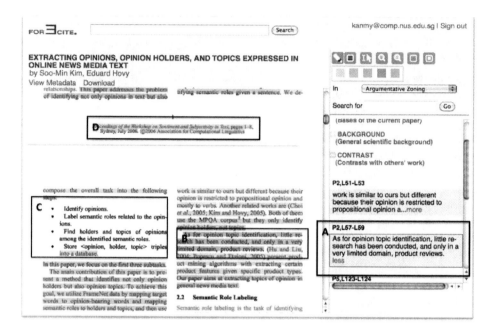

Fig. 2. RAZ annotations in the ForeCiteReader environment. The reader has clicked on a particular Contrast sentence in the sidebar (Inset A), which has been automatically highlighted in the reader (Inset B, slightly darker green than other CTR sentences). Some lines have been misidentified by the environment as non-body text and vice versa (Insets C and D).

some noise) which text in the document is body text, where sentences start and end, and passes only these body text sentences to the RAZ classifier.

6.1   In Situ Usability

To assess whether RAZ does help in sensemaking, we have carried out a preliminary indicative study with the ForeCite reading interface. The task in the experiment was to answer four central questions about the paper, and then to critique the interface and annotation shown.

Four graduate research students in information systems were asked to skim two computational linguistics 8-page conference papers (not from the training data), for which they had little previous background. However, they had general background in reading conference papers. They were shown one document in the ForeCiteReader plain reading interface, and one displaying RAZ annotation. Each subject experienced a different ordering of the papers and of the interfaces, to mitigate order and learning effects.

The students were given a copy of the task instructions, while the interviewer verbally went over the instructions. Before answering the questions and providing feedback, the students were to first skim the documents. The entire interview

took about 30 minutes per subject. The four questions that were given are repli-
cated below, paraphrased for length considerations:

Q1: Please name the central contribution(s) of the work.
Q2: Name two related works in this paper and describe their relationship to
this paper.
Q3: Identify any datasets that were used in evaluation and its origin.
Q4: (*one variant shown*) Let's suppose that another paper cites this paper as:
"*[This paper] describes the first approach to apply co-training in a bilingual
setting, that is with a pair of languages.*" Can you identify whether this
citation claim is a valid or not?

The students were informed that they would be timed, but that a longer or
shorter time to task completion would not affect them in any way. In designing
the questionnaire, we hypothesized that Q1 and Q2 could be addressed by using
the AZ markup, specifically by the AIM for Q1 and OTH, CTR and BAS classes,
for Q2. Q3 was inserted as a control, as AZ does not specifically indicate sentences that describe datasets (as the AZ scheme is general and does not presume
experimental validation). Q4 was tailored to each of the two articles, and asks
whether a claim in another (hypothetical) paper citing the target paper could
be validated.

   We emphasize that our study is indicative and not designed to be summative
or statistically accurate, since the sample size is small. With this in mind, we
discuss salient observations from the survey with respect to AZ.

Time to Task Completion. AZ did not have a measureable effect on task
   time completion. Using AZ required the subject to experiment with the
   interface and also required subjects to shift attention (the left vs. right of the
   interface) and to change task (reading vs. focused navigation). The sentence
   previews in the AZ sidebar alleviated this somewhat, but when context was
   needed to interpret the sentence, subjects had to return to the reading panel
   to verify evidence.
AZ Effectiveness. In both subjective opinion and interviewer observation, AZ
   had a positive effect in locating answers to Q2 when used by the subjects.
   For Q1, it did not help as both papers indicated the goal within the abstract
   or introduction, and most of the subjects started off reading. However, one
   subjects did use the AIM class to read off the contributions of the paper as
   listed throughout different sections of the paper.
Annotation Noise. While our current AZ classifier performs only at a mediocre
   level (.41 macro F_1), differentiating the minority classes (*i.e.*, AIM, BAS, CTR,
   OTH) from the OWN majority helped to identify candidate sentences that
   might contain answers. Subject commented that the annotations were largely
   correct for key sentences and that errors in the automatic segmentation of the
   body text and sentence delimitation were larger barriers than the AZ classification itself (as seen in Figure 2).
Interaction with Reading. Subjects universally complained that the AZ
   coloring detracted from their reading experience, as it decreased the contrast

of the text. Subjects suggested that the interface should be loaded plain but that spans could be colored on demand from the right hand side AZ sidebar.

Unknown Terminology. While unknown terminology kept subjects from deep understanding of the goal, they were generally able to recognize sentences that describe answers to the questions. Two subjects stated that an extension of AZ could help identify definitions.

Other Extensions of AZ. Two of the four subjects suggested that AZ be extended to work to extract key facts, such as the identity of datasets and specific tools or methodologies used. They also mentioned that contributions (rather than aims) and experimental results could be part of the AZ schema.

The pilot evaluation hints that RAZ can be a useful part of a holistic sense-making interface. Our current RAZ system certainly assists the reader, along with the authors' own careful text structuring, in interpreting the major points in a work as well as its contextual place among referenced documents. While the reading interface should place reading functionality first, AZ (and possibly other) annotations should be called on demand and displayed in an unobtrusive manner.

We are currently revising the integrated system to account for the feedback. Our current work can be categorized along two fronts. The first front is in improving the interface, such that reading ease is maximized. Standard, digital reading affordances (locating a section, page, or finding instances of individual words) need to be supported. Parallel work within the ForeCite digital library project has achieved this goal of the re-discovery of logical sections from scientific documents (both modern ones born digitally as well as legacy documents that are only represented by scanned images) [30].

Second, as our subjects have commented, AZ highlighting should be done on demand by the user and only for a particular AZ class. We have modified the display framework to account for this feedback. OWN sentences in particular are not helpful to identify (as this is the majority of the paper), so are now omitted from the interface entirely. The second front is to extend information extraction and classification further into the document content. Our longer term plans are to extract definitions of terms, identify the semantic categories of pertinent keyphrases as methods, systems, tools, or other domain-specific constructs. These may further aid the understanding of the document.

7   Conclusion

Abstracts have been acknowledged as the author's view of the importance of their own work. Recently, the community has acknowledged that sentences that cite a paper describe the community's view of the importance of a paper [31,32]. We claim that the document itself has its own voice about what is important. The discourse and argumentative structure in a well-written paper also direct a reader to its important aspects within the reading context.

We have captured this notion of argumentative zoning (AZ) in an implemented classifier and described the textual features it uses to render its judgment.

To our knowledge, we describe the first robust AZ system (RAZ) that is able to perform such classification on noisy inputs that come from PDF text extraction, as well as the relatively clean output of optical character recognition.

Our work also represents the first system that has been integrated into a production digital library system, ForeCite. Our preliminary *in situ* study indicates that robust AZ can be a helpful source of evidence in sensemaking for understanding the contributions and context of the individual scholarly paper.

Acknowledgments

The second author would like to acknowledge the help of the graduate student volunteers at UC Irvine for their help in evaluating the RAZ interface.

References

1. Cleverdon, C.W.: Optimizing convenient online access to bibliographic databases. Information Services and Use 4, 37–47 (1984)
2. Shum, S.B.: Evolving the web for scientific knowledge: First steps towards an "HCI knowledge web". Interfaces, British HCI Group Magazine 39, 16–21 (1998)
3. Bazerman, C.: Physicists reading physics, schema-laden purposes and purpose-laden schema. Written Communication 2(1), 3–23 (1985)
4. Kircz, J.G.: The rhetorical structure of scientific articles: The case for argumentational analysis in information retrieval. Journal of Documentation 47(4), 354–372 (1991)
5. Ingwersen, P.: Cognitive perspectives of information retrieval interaction: Elements of a cognitive ir theory. Journal of Documentation 52, 3–50 (1996)
6. Swales, J.: Research articles in English. In: Genre Analysis: English in Academic and Research Settings, ch. 7, pp. 110–176. Cambridge University Press, Cambridge (1990)
7. Teufel, S., Moens, M.: Summarising scientific articles — experiments with relevance and rhetorical status. Computational Linguistics 28(4), 409–446 (2002)
8. Copestake, A., Corbett, P.T., Murray-Rust, P., Rupp, C.J., Siddharthan, A., Teufel, S., Waldron, B.: An architecture for language technology for processing scientific texts. In: UK e-Science All Hands Meeting (2006)
9. Nanba, H., Okumura, M.: Towards multi-paper summarization using reference information. In: Proceedings of IJCAI 1999, pp. 926–931 (1999)
10. Liddy, E.D.: The discourse-level structure of empirical abstracts: An exploratory study. Information Processing and Management 27(1), 55–81 (1991)
11. Kando, N.: Text-level structure of research papers: Implications for text-based information processing systems. In: Proceedings of BCS-IRSG Colloquium, pp. 68–81 (1997)
12. Teufel, S., Carletta, J., Moens, M.: An annotation scheme for discourse-level argumentation in research articles. In: Proceedings of European ACL (EACL 1999), Bergen, Norway, pp. 110–117 (1999)
13. Siegel, S., Castellan, N.J.J.: Nonparametric Statistics for the Behavioral Sciences, 2nd edn. McGraw-Hill, Berkeley (1988)

14. Siddharthan, A., Teufel, S.: Whose idea was this, and why does it matter? attributing scientific work to citations. In: Proceedings of the North American chapter of the Association of Computational Linguistics, NAACL 2007 (2007)
15. Hachey, B., Grover, C.: Extractive summarisation of legal texts. Artificial Intelligence and Law: Special Issue on E-government 14(4), 305–345 (2006)
16. Merity, S., Murphy, T., Curran, J.R.: Accurate argumentative zoning with maximum entropy models. In: Proceedings of ACL-IJCNLP 2009 Workshop on text and citation analysis for scholarly digital libraries (NLPIR4DL), Singapore, pp. 19–26 (2009)
17. McKnight, L., Arinivasan, P.: Categorization of sentence types in medical abstracts. In: AMIA 2003 Symposium Proceedings, pp. 440–444 (2003)
18. Lin, J., Karakos, D., Demner-Fushman, D., Khudanpur, S.: Generative content models for structural analysis of medical abstracts. In: Proceedings of the HLT/NAACL 2006 Workshop on Biomedical Natural Language Processing (BIONLP 2006), New York City, USA, pp. 65–72 (2006)
19. Hirohata, K., Okazaki, N., Ananiadou, S., Ishizuka, M.: Identifying sections in scientific abstracts using conditional random fields. In: Proceedings of the Third International Joint Conference on Natural Language Processing (IJCNLP 2008), Hyderabad, India, pp. 381–388 (2008) ACL Anthology Ref. I08-1050
20. Reynar, J.C., Ratnaparkhi, A.: A maximum entropy approach to identifying sentence boundaries. In: Proceedings of the Firth Conference on Applied Natural Language Processing, pp. 803–806 (1997)
21. Ratnaparkhi, A.: A maximum entropy model for part-of-speech tagging. In: Empirical Methods for Natural Language Processing. Association for Computational Linguistics, New Jersey (1996)
22. Porter, M.F.: An algorithm for suffix stripping. Program (3), 130–137 (1980)
23. Teufel, S.: Argumentative Zoning: Information Extraction from Scientific Text. PhD thesis, School of Cognitive Science, University of Edinburgh, Edinburgh, UK (2000)
24. Hirschberg, D.S.: A linear space algorithm for computing maximal common subsequences. Communications of the ACM 18(6), 341–343 (1975)
25. Fleiss, J.L.: Measuring nominal scale agreement among many raters. Psychological Bulletin 76, 378–381 (1971)
26. Carletta, J.: Assessing agreement on classification tasks: The kappa statistic. Computational Linguistics 22(2), 249–254 (1996)
27. Krippendorff, K.: Content Analysis: An Introduction to its Methodology, 2nd edn. Sage Publications, Beverly Hills (2004)
28. Krenn, B., Evert, S., Zinsmeister, H.: Determining intercoder agreement for a collocation identification task. In: Proceedings of Konvens 2004 (2004)
29. Nguyen, T.D., Kan, M.Y., Dang, D.T., Hänse, M., Hong, C.H.A., Luong, M.T., Gozali, J.P., Sugiyama, K., Tan, Y.F.: ForeCite: towards a reader-centric scholarly digital library. Under Review (2010)
30. Luong, M.T., Nguyen, T.D., Kan, M.Y.: Logical structure recovery in scholarly articles with rich document features. International Journal of Digital Library Systems (2011)
31. Nakov, P., Schwarz, A., Hearst, M.: Citances: Citation sentences for semantic analysis of bioscience text. In: SIGIR 2004 Workshop on Search and Discovery in Bioinformatics (2004)
32. Qazvinian, V., Radev, D.R.: Scientific paper summarization using citation summary networks. In: Proceedings of COLING 2008, Manchester, UK (2008)

Author Index